Introduction to
GROUP WORK PRACTICE

Custom Edition for New York University

RONALD W. TOSELAND
ROBERT F. RIVAS

Taken from:

An Introduction to Group Work Practice, Fifth Edition
by Ronald W. Toseland and Robert F. Rivas

PEARSON
Custom
Publishing

Taken from:

An Introduction to Group Work Practice, Fifth Edition
by Ronald W. Toseland and Robert F. Rivas
Copyright © 2005, 2001, 1998, 1995, 1984 by Pearson Education, Inc.
Published by Allyn and Bacon
Boston, Massachusetts 02116

This special edition published in cooperation with Pearson Custom Publishing.

Printed in the United States of America

10 9 8 7 6 5 4 3 2 1

ISBN 0-536-86238-9

2004500122

CS

Please visit our web site at *www.pearsoncustom.com*

PEARSON CUSTOM PUBLISHING
75 Arlington Street, Suite 300, Boston, MA 02116
A Pearson Education Company

Contents

Taken from:
An Introduction to Group Work Practice, Fifth Edition,
by Ronald W. Toseland and Robert F. Rivas

part **I**

The Knowledge Base of Group Work Practice

chapter 4

Leadership

Leadership is the process of guiding the development of the group and its members. The goal of effective leadership is twofold: (1) to help the group and its members to achieve goals that are consistent with the value base of social work practice, and (2) to meet the socio-emotional needs of members.

Although the leadership role is most often associated with the designated leader—that is, the worker—it is important to distinguish between the worker as the designated leader and the indigenous leadership that emerges among members as the group develops. Leadership is rarely exercised solely by the worker. As the group unfolds, members take on leadership roles.

Workers should do as much as possible to stimulate and support indigenous leadership. Encouraging indigenous leadership helps to empower members. Members begin to feel that they have some influence, control, and stake in the group situation. Exercising leadership skills in the group increases members' self-esteem and the likelihood that they will advocate for themselves and for others outside of the group context.

Encouraging indigenous leadership also helps members to exercise their own skills and abilities. This, in turn, promotes autonomous functioning and ensures that members' existing skills do not atrophy. Thus, this chapter emphasizes both the importance of the worker as group leader and the importance of members' sharing in leadership functions as the group develops.

There is an increasing amount of evidence that gender roles play an important role in emerging leadership. In studies of emerging leaders, males are generally viewed more positively than females (Kolb, 1997). Also, the same leadership behaviors are often viewed more positively when attributed to males than to females (Shimanoff & Jenkins, 1991). Group leaders who are aware of this evidence will be better prepared to provide females with opportunities to assert their leadership abilities, and to guard against male dominance of leadership roles within task and treatment groups.

LEADERSHIP AND POWER

Workers who are new to the leadership role are sometimes uncomfortable with their power and influence and react by denying their power or by trying to take too much control. These strategies are rarely effective. Especially in early group meetings, members look to the leader for guidance about how to proceed. Experienced leaders are comfortable with their power and influence. They use it to empower members, which gradually enables members to take increasing responsibility for the group as it develops.

Workers use their influence as leaders within and outside the group to facilitate group and individual efforts to achieve desired goals. Within the group, the worker intervenes by guiding the dynamics of the group as a whole or by helping individual members change. In exercising leadership outside the group, the worker intervenes to influence the environment in which the group and its members function. For example, the worker might try to change organizational policies that influence the group or obtain additional resources from a sponsor so the group can complete its work. In exerting leadership inside or outside the group, the worker is responsible for the group's processes, actions, and task accomplishments.

In considering a worker's power, it is helpful to distinguish between attributed power and actual power. *Attributed power* comes from the perception among group members or others outside the group of the worker's ability to lead. Workers who take on the responsibilities inherent in leading a group are rewarded by having attributed to them the power to influence and the ability to lead. Such power is attributed by group members, peers, superiors, the sponsoring agency, and the larger social system.

The attributed power of the worker comes from a variety of sources. Among these sources are professional status, education, organizational position, experience, defined boundaries between worker and group members' roles, fees for service, and the commonly held view that a group's success or failure is the result of its leadership. Workers should recognize that attributed leadership ability is as important as actual power in facilitating the development of the group and its members.

Workers can increase the power attributed to them by group members. Studies have shown that members' expectations about the group and its leader influence the group's performance (Bednar & Kaul, 1994; Karakowsky & McBey, 2001; Piper, 1994). Preparing members with films, brochures, or personal interviews that offer information about the group, its leader, and the success of previous groups has been shown to be effective in increasing the change-oriented expectations of members and in helping individuals and groups accomplish their goals (Bednar & Kaul, 1994; Karakowsky & McBey, 2001; Kaul & Bednar, 1994). When formal preparation is impossible, informal preparation by word of mouth or reputation can be used.

As their attributed power increases, workers are more likely to be regarded with esteem by group members and to be looked to as models of effective coping skills whose behaviors are emulated and whose guidance is followed. Workers should not, however, attempt to gain power for its own sake or unilaterally impose their own values, standards, and rules concerning conduct inside or outside the group.

Actual power refers to the worker's resources for changing conditions inside and outside the group. Actual power depends on the sources of a worker's influence. The power bases first described by French and Raven (1959) follow.

Power Bases

- Connection power—being able to call on and use influential people or resources
- Expert power—having the knowledge or skill to facilitate the work of the group
- Information power—possessing information that is valuable to and needed by others
- Legitimate power—holding a position of authority and the rights that accrue to that position in the organization or larger social system
- Reference power—being liked and admired; the group members want to be identified with the worker
- Reward power—being able to offer social or tangible rewards
- Coercive power—being able to sanction, punish, or deny access to resources and privileges

Use of power can have both negative and positive consequences. For example, coercive power is sometimes used to compel clients to receive treatment. However, coercion can have negative effects such as hostility, anger, rebellion, and absence from group meetings. Therefore, the worker should exercise power judiciously, in a manner consistent with personal, professional, and societal values.

At the same time, the worker's power as leader cannot, and should not, be denied, which sometimes occurs when suggestions are made that members should take total responsibility for leading the group. Groups need leaders to avoid disorganization and chaos; leadership and power are inseparable (Etzioni, 1961).

Anyone who has attended the first meeting of a new group recognizes the power the worker has as the designated leader. This power can be illustrated most vividly by examining members' behaviors and feelings during the initial portion of the first group meeting. Members direct most of their communications to the worker or communicate through the worker to other group members. Members are often anxious and inquisitive, wondering what they can expect from the group and its leader. They comply readily with requests made by the worker. Although members may wonder about the worker's ability to help them and the group as a whole, they usually give the worker latitude in choosing methods and procedures to help the group achieve its objectives.

Beginning with the first group meeting, it is essential that workers move as rapidly as possible to share their power with members and the group as a whole. This encourages members to begin to take responsibility for the group and makes the group more potent. Some methods for sharing power are presented here.

Methods for Sharing Power with the Group

- Encourage member-to-member rather than member-to-leader communications
- Ask for members' input into the agenda for the meeting and the direction the group should take in future meetings

- Support indigenous leadership when members make their first, tentative attempts at exerting their own influence in the group
- Encourage attempts at mutual sharing and mutual aid among members
- Model and teach members selected leadership skills early in the life of the group
- Use naturally occurring events in the life of the group to "process" information about leadership skills and style

Theories of Group Leadership

Early theories about the best method to use in leading a group focused primarily on leadership style. Leadership was considered a trait rather than a cluster of behaviors that could be learned (Halpin, 1961). Three positions on a continuum of leadership behavior—laissez-faire, democratic, and autocratic—were the subject of early investigations (Lewin & Lippitt, 1938; Lewin et al., 1939). The continuum can be seen in Figure 4.1. Findings from these studies indicated that there were more aggression, hostility, and scapegoating in autocratic groups than in democratic groups. There were no differences in the tasks completed by the groups, although there was some indication that the products of democratic groups were qualitatively superior to those of groups that used autocratic or laissez-faire styles of leadership.

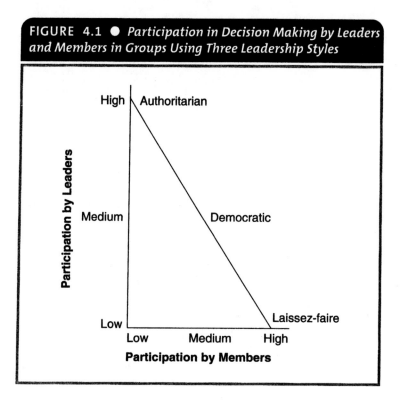

FIGURE 4.1 ● *Participation in Decision Making by Leaders and Members in Groups Using Three Leadership Styles*

Group members also preferred the democratic group's process—that is, they liked the leader better and felt freer and more willing to make suggestions. These early findings seemed to suggest that allowing members to participate in the group's decision-making process was the preferred leadership style.

Factors Influencing Group Leadership

The early theories that focused on leadership styles were found to be too simplistic to explain leadership in most situations (Chemers, 2000). Gradually, contingency theories became more popular. These theories emphasized that situational factors helped to determine what skills and leadership style are most appropriate and effective for a particular group. For example, Nixon (1979) has suggested that at least seven factors must be assessed before predicting what leadership styles or behaviors are most effective.

Influences on Leadership

- The leadership expectations held by group members
- The way leadership has been attained
- Whether there is competition between designated leaders and the leaders that emerge as groups develop
- The needs, tasks, and goals of the group as a whole
- The task and socioemotional skills of members
- The nature of authority within and outside of the group
- The environmental demands placed on the group and its leadership

The growing recognition that group leadership is affected by a variety of interacting factors has resulted from empirical findings in social psychology, sociology, and business administration (Fiedler, 1967; Gibb, 1969; Hersey & Blanchard, 1977; Luft, 1984; McClane, 1991; McGrath, 1984, 1992; Nixon, 1979; Vroom & Yetton, 1973). These investigators found that to understand the dynamics of leadership in diverse treatment and task groups, several factors in addition to the personality and leadership style of the worker must be considered. For example, in analyzing leadership in task groups, a number of investigators have shown that leaders develop different relationships with different members of a group (Dienesch & Liden, 1986; Graen & Schiemann, 1978; McClane, 1991). For example, an "individualized consideration" of each member is one of the central components of Bass's (1985, 1998) transformational leadership theory.

Several group work practitioners have also suggested that leadership must be seen as a process within the context of the group and its environment. For example, Garvin (1997) emphasizes the role of the agency in influencing the work of treatment groups.

When studying group leadership, Heap (1979) observed that the degree of activity of a worker is directly related to the social health of the group's members. Thus, a worker should be more active in groups in which members are "out of touch with reality" or "withdrawn or very aggressive" (p. 50). For example, a worker might need to be directive and structured in a remedial group for severely mentally ill inpatients of a state hospital. The worker, as "expert," may work with each member in turn for 5 or 10 minutes. Other members may be asked to offer opinions or provide feedback, but the primary focus is on helping an individual achieve particular treatment goals.

Similarly, Toseland (1995) notes that group workers have to be active when working with the frail elderly in groups. The energy level of these group members is often low, and they are often preoccupied with their own physical functioning. Also, frail, older group members tend to relate to the group leader rather than to each other. Being energetic and working hard to establish connections among members can counteract these tendencies.

In contrast, when working with interested, eager, competent members, the worker should take on a less active, enabler role. For example, a group-centered leadership approach is usually more effective in support, growth, and socialization groups in which members are eager, competent, and not severely impaired. In using a group-centered method, the worker facilitates communication, interaction, understanding, and mutual aid and encourages members to help one another rather than to look to the worker as an expert who can solve their concerns or problems.

Overall, one conclusion that can be drawn from social science findings and from data accumulated from group work practice is that one method of leadership is not effective in all situations. The worker's leadership skills and intervention strategies should vary depending on the degree to which the group as a whole and its individual members can function autonomously. The less autonomous the group, the more the worker must play a central role in leading the group. Conversely, the more autonomous the group, the more the worker can facilitate the members' own self-direction and indigenous leadership abilities.

Effective Leadership

Although research on contingency theories of leadership has continued, research on "transformational" leadership has taken preeminence in recent years. A major contribution to leadership theory was made by Burns in 1978 when he distinguished between transactional (contingency-based leadership) and transformational leadership. Transformational leaders are those who (1) display high levels of competency and trustworthiness, (2) inspire and motivate members with their vision, (3) stimulate independent and creative thinking among members, and (4) individualize members by understanding their personal needs and goals (Bass, 1985, 1998; Bass & Avolio, 1990a, 1990b, 1993). Transformational leadership models suggest that the leader should be a charismatic role model with vision who helps members to align their own goals with group and organizational goals (Alimo-Metcalfe & Alban-Metcalfe, 2001; Bass & Avolio, 1994). Transformational leaders empower members by affirming and reinforcing their autonomy and individuality as they pursue individual, group, and organizational goals. Members are encouraged to question assumptions and to approach problems in new ways so that they are creative and innovative problem solvers (Alimo-Metcalfe & Alban-Metcalfe, 2001). Thus, transformational leaders use the power bases available to them, but the focus is on inspiring and empowering members rather than inducing compliance (Sosik & Jung, 2002). Transformations occur as members embrace group and organizational goals, and view their own personal goals as a part of these larger goals.

In an attempt to unify contingency theories and transformational theories of leadership, Chemers (2000) suggests that effective leaders first have to establish the legitimacy of their leadership by being competent and trustworthy. He refers to this as "image management." Thus, effective leaders are highly respected individuals who have a vision. They promote safe, welcoming environments that avoid the extremes of aggressive confrontation of members or passive abdication of leadership to members who attempt to dominate groups (Kivlighan & Tarrant, 2001; Smokowski, Rose, & Bacallao, 2001). Next, leaders have to understand the abilities, values, and personalities of members. They use this understanding to encourage and guide members as they contribute to group goal attainment, while at the same time helping members to satisfy their own needs and achieve their own personal goals. Effective leaders must also skillfully deploy the resources they have at their disposal. This includes empowering members and reinforcing feelings of confidence and individual and group efficacy (Bandura, 1995, 1997b). It also includes making sure that the group engages in good information processing and decision making, so that when resources are deployed, the environmental demands on members and the group are carefully considered (Chemers, 2000).

AN INTERACTIONAL MODEL OF LEADERSHIP

Unlike contingency and transactional leadership theories that focus exclusively on the leader, the model of leadership presented in this book focuses on the group, the worker as designated leader, the members, and the environment in which the group functions. This "interactional model" is presented in Figure 4.2. Because this model views leadership as being derived from the interactions of the group, its members, the designated leader, and the environment, the model is closely related to the ecological systems perspective of social casework proposed by Germain and Gitterman (1996) and Siporin (1980) as well as the interactional perspective presented by Gitterman and Shulman (1994) and Maluccio (1979).

The interactional model represents leadership as a shared function that is not lodged solely in the designated group leader. In addition to the worker's role as designated leader, the model in Figure 4.2 clearly shows that leadership emerges from a variety of interacting factors as the group develops. These factors are (1) the purposes of the group, (2) the type of problem the group is working on, (3) the environment in which the group works, (4) the group as a whole, (5) the members of the group, and (6) the leader of the group.

Purposes of the Group

When one considers how leadership emerges in a group, it is essential to consider the purposes of the group. According to Browning (1977), a group may be formed (1) to perform tasks that require more than one or two people, (2) to meet individual needs, (3) to bring people together who are involved in the same or similar problems, (4) to represent a larger collection of people, (5) to form the largest collection of people that can be man-

FIGURE 4.2 ● *An Interactional Model of Group Leadership*

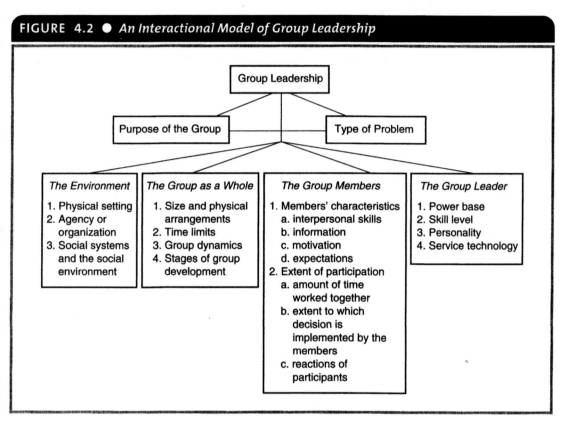

aged together, (6) to help maintain an organization more economically than individuals, (7) to increase motivation, or (8) as a result of physical factors such as working together in the same office. To this list can be added the purpose of using the group to change conditions or situations outside the group in an organization, a service delivery system, or an entire social system.

A group may have a single purpose or several purposes. The worker should consider how a group's purposes are interpreted by all systems that interact with it. The worker should ensure that the purpose of the group and the type of problem to be worked on are consistent. For example, if the purpose of a group is to meet the needs of socially isolated individuals, the types of problems on which the group works should be related to group members' needs for increased social interaction; that is, the group should not be working on problems of housing or finances unless they are linked to the primary purpose of decreasing isolation.

The purpose of a group helps determine how workers guide group processes. For example, in a group whose purpose is solely to complete a task or solve a problem, a worker might choose to encourage members to structure and focus the interactions more than in a group whose purpose is to have members share common concerns and ideas about an issue.

Type of Problem

The type of problem or task a group works on also has important implications for leadership. It has been found that groups do better than individuals on certain types of tasks, but individuals working alone do better on others (Hare et al., 1995). Generally, groups do better when the task is additive, such as collecting information. Thus, it would be better to form a treatment conference group to collect information about a client from all the professionals working with the client rather than to get the information from each professional separately. Groups are also more effective when they are choosing between clearly delineated alternatives. For example, Toseland, Rivas, and Chapman (1984) found that groups were more effective than individuals working alone when making decisions about funding priorities for medically underserved counties.

Groups also do better on tasks requiring a wide range of responses (Thorndike, 1938). For example, it is preferable to have group members and the leader generate alternative solutions with a woman who is having trouble expressing her anger rather than to have the woman generate the alternatives with one worker. For these kinds of tasks, the worker should promote interaction, input, and feedback from all group members so that a wide range of responses is generated and evaluated.

Individuals working alone solve some problems or accomplish some tasks faster and better than they would working in a group. Individuals working alone more readily solve complex problems requiring many variables to be synthesized into a whole. In these cases, the group's product is no better than the best performance of a member of the group (Thorndike, 1938).

● **CASE EXAMPLE** *Individual and Group Problem Solving*

In preparing a countywide plan for distributing emergency allocation funds to communities affected by a recent tornado, a worker decided to use a nominal group procedure that encouraged members to work alone before sharing their ideas with the group. In addition, the worker formed subgroups to work on specific ideas generated by the individual before they were considered in formal group discussion. By using both individual work and group interaction, the worker helped the group deal with a complex problem more efficiently.

Several other aspects of problems should be considered when leading a group. One is whether the problem is of concern to the group as a whole, to a subgroup, or to an individual. All members of the group might not be affected to the same extent by a particular problem or task being considered by a group. For example, when leading a group to teach parenting skills to foster parents, the worker should try to get all members involved in discussing parenting problems that are of interest to everyone in the group. When a member raises a problem unique to his or her particular situation, the worker should try to develop from this information generalized principles of child rearing of interest to all group members. This technique is often called *universalizing*.

When considering the type of problem confronting a group, workers should also be aware of where their legitimate influence ends. It may not be appropriate for the worker to encourage discussion of certain topics. For example, a worker leading a task group planning for an emergency housing shelter should not encourage a group member to talk about personal family life. In other situations, however, workers may want to encourage discussion of taboo areas. For example, when the problem being discussed is child abuse, it might be helpful for the worker to encourage all members to talk about how they were disciplined during their early childhood.

The Environment

The environment in which the group conducts its work has a profound effect on how leadership emerges in the group. Environmental influences come primarily from three interrelated sources: (1) the immediate physical setting, (2) the agency or organization in which the group functions, and (3) other social systems and the social environment.

The Setting

The worker should ensure that the setting facilitates the group's work. The decor and comfort of the waiting room and meeting area and the availability of equipment and supplies such as tables, blackboard, or newsprint all influence the group's leadership. It is important for the worker to match group members' needs and preferences to a setting that facilitates the group's work. For example, sitting around a table may facilitate the work of a task group because members can spread out papers and write more easily. In contrast, a table may interfere with the observation of nonverbal communication in a therapy group, and it may also hamper role playing and engagement in other program activities.

The Agency Context

In addition to the physical environment, the agency influences the group and its leader in several ways. The worker, for example, must be aware of agency policies, rules, and regulations that govern the group's behavior, its process, and its product. The worker is given legitimate authority by the agency or organization to help the group perform its tasks. The agency's delegation of this authority to the worker often assumes the worker will use the method of service delivery that currently exists in the agency. For example, two group workers trying to help pregnant women stop abusing alcohol may use quite different means, depending on the type of program sponsored by each agency. One group leader may use a reality-therapy group approach; the other may use a group format based on cognitive-behavioral self-control procedures.

A worker's position within an agency or organization can also affect the form leadership takes in a group. For example, a worker with a high-level administrative position may elicit different reactions from group members than would a worker with a lower-level position. Similarly, the leader's position in an organization often signifies the importance placed on the work of the group.

Other Social Systems

The third way the environment influences group leadership is through large social systems, such as the community in which the group operates. The worker's behavior is influenced by norms established by society. For example, in a group for abusive parents, the worker intervenes to help members comply with societal norms and values concerning appropriate parenting behaviors. Smaller social systems can also affect a group's work. For example, an agency committee might hesitate to become involved in a search for additional emergency housing if a delegate council formed by a community planning agency is already looking at ways to develop additional emergency housing resources.

The Group as a Whole

At least four properties of the group as a whole influence how leadership emerges. These are (1) the size of the group, (2) the time limit in which the group is expected to accomplish its goals, (3) group dynamics, and (4) the stage of a group's development.

Group Size

As the size of a group increases, the opportunity for member participation decreases. The number of rules may increase as workers use them to maintain order and control in the group. Subgroups are more likely to form. The leader is more likely to be in the front of a large group, and leader-to-member and member-to-leader interactions are more likely than member-to-member interactions to occur.

Time Limits

Time limits may be voluntary or mandatory. A treatment group, for example, might decide to use a time-limited method such as a behavioral group approach or a task-centered group approach. A task group, such as a delegate council, might feel responsible for making a speedy decision on an issue for an upcoming statewide meeting. In either case, time limits affect leadership behavior. Generally, time limits are associated with greater structuring of interactions, an increase in task-focused behavior, and fewer opportunities for indigenous leadership to emerge.

Group Dynamics

The third property that can influence leadership is the dynamics that operate in a group. As discussed in Chapter 3, these include communication and interaction patterns, cohesion, social control, and group culture. Workers should use their skills to foster the development of group dynamics that help the group accomplish its tasks and contribute to members' satisfaction. Interventions to change the dynamics of the group as a whole are discussed in Chapter 10.

Stage of Development

The stage of a group's development is the fourth group-as-a-whole factor that can affect leadership behavior. If the group is to develop successfully, the worker must be aware of the developmental tasks that face the group during each stage. A large portion of this text focuses on the specific skills and methods that workers can use during each stage of a group's development.

The Group Members

Group members influence how leadership emerges in three important ways: (1) through the unique characteristics and life experiences they bring to the group, (2) by the extent that they participate in the group, and (3) by the extent that they share in leading the group.

Member Characteristics

Several characteristics of members affect members' ability to influence the group. These include members' interpersonal skills, access to information, perceived responsibility for the work of the group, motivations, and expectations about the process and outcome of the group. The importance of these characteristics should not be overlooked when considering how leadership develops in a group. It has been shown, for example, that members' expectations influence outcomes in both treatment (Piper, 1994) and task groups (Gibb, 1969) and that interpersonal skill level and knowledge about a particular problem also help determine how well a group functions (Browning, 1977; Hersey, Blanchard, & Natemeyer, 1979).

Because members' attributes differ, one member who is knowledgeable about a particular topic may become the task leader while that topic is being discussed. Another member may serve as the group's socioemotional leader by expressing feelings and responding to other members' feelings. This suggests that the worker should remain aware of each member's leadership potential as the group progresses and help members to take on appropriate leadership roles that match their interests and skills.

Extent of Participation

The extent of members' participation also influences how a worker leads a group. Some members' lack of interpersonal skills or motivation may prevent them from participating fully. In other cases, the worker may purposefully prevent a group member from making verbal communications. For example, a worker leading a delegate council may decide to limit discussion and thereby effectively stop some members from speaking about an issue.

The worker should anticipate members' reactions when they are encouraged or discouraged from active participation in a group. Generally, discouraging or limiting a member's participation in a group leads to the member's dissatisfaction with the group. In some situations, however, members may be more interested in hearing what the worker or a guest speaker has to say than in what other members have to say, and they may readily accept limits on their participation. This response is particularly true in educational groups where members' participation may be limited to a discussion period after a presentation by the worker. In task groups, some members may not have an interest in or a knowledge of certain issues, and the worker may want to encourage more knowledgeable or interested members to express their views. In other cases, the worker may want to limit discussion so the group can come to a speedy decision.

Sharing Leadership

Members' willingness to share leadership responsibilities is determined by their feelings of competency, their previous leadership experiences, and their perceptions of the openness of the designated leader to sharing leadership functions. It is also affected, in part, by the amount of time the member has been a part of the group. A new group member often has difficulty exerting leadership in a group in which the relationship among members has been established. Similarly, a member of a street gang that has been together for several years has more influence with the gang than a worker who is just beginning to interact with the gang.

The Group Leader

When one examines how leadership emerges in a group, the power base, skill level, personality, and choice of service technology of the designated leader all play important roles. As indicated earlier, seven types of power bases can be used to influence a group: connection, expert, information, legitimate, referent, reward, and coercive. Most workers draw on a variety of power bases; workers should realize the power bases at their disposal when they are considering leading a group. For example, a worker planning to lead a group of alcoholics who have been referred because of a driving-while-intoxicated offense may influence members by refusing to certify that they are fit to have their licenses returned until they have successfully completed a group treatment program.

The level of skill that workers possess also influences their ability to lead. Experience and training of workers have been correlated with effectiveness in working with individuals and groups (Dies, 1994). Even when workers have a number of strong power bases they can use to influence group members, unskillful application of their power often results in members' becoming angry and uncooperative or submissive and passive. Through the appropriate use of leadership skills, the worker can more readily achieve objectives and satisfy group members. Leadership skills are described in greater depth in the next section of this chapter.

A worker's personality, interpersonal style, and preferences for how to lead all influence how leadership emerges in a group. For example, a worker who is shy and sensitive about others' feelings is less likely to use confrontation as a technique when leading a group. Workers should be aware of how their interpersonal style affects their attempts to objectively analyze what the group needs and their attempts to intervene in the group's processes. Some methods for becoming more aware of one's leadership style and how to modify it are described later in this chapter.

The service technology that workers use also affects how they conduct their groups. *Service technology* refers to particular theories or methods of intervention used by a worker. Three leaders of groups for alcoholics, for example, may intervene in quite different ways—by using transactional analysis or behavior therapy or, perhaps, reality therapy. Workers' choice of service technologies may be influenced by their personal preferences, their training, or the ideology of the agency in which they work.

A worker's technological and ideological stance often helps in organizing interventions. Workers may wish to receive specialized instruction in a particular service technology, such as behavior modification; however, it is essential that they become familiar with basic practice principles of leading groups before they receive specialized training.

GROUP LEADERSHIP SKILLS

Group leadership skills are behaviors or activities that help the group achieve its purpose and accomplish its tasks and help members achieve their personal goals. Both workers and members use leadership skills, although the worker ordinarily uses them more than any other member of the group. Leadership skills are combined when conducting group meetings. For example, in using a problem-solving method, a worker calls on numerous leadership skills to help a committee arrive at a decision concerning personnel practices in a family service agency. Similarly, in an aftercare treatment group for recovering drug addicts, a worker relies on many different skills to help members remain drug free.

There has been long-standing interest in the "skillful use of self" in social work practice (Goldstein, 1983). Most evidence concerning the effect of skill level on desired outcomes has been gathered from the evaluation of work with individuals rather than from work with groups (Dies, 1994). Reviews of the literature suggest that skills can be learned and that skill level makes a difference in performance (Dies, 1994). There is some evidence that specific skills such as attending intently and responding empathically are directly connected to positive outcomes (Shulman, 1978; Toseland, Rossiter, Peak, & Hill, 1990). Results are tentative, however, because it is difficult to design studies to assess the independent effect of one particular skill.

Group leadership skills are somewhat different from skills used in working with an individual. Both members and the worker have greater choice regarding the level and focus of their interaction. For example, they may choose to be active or passive, and they may decide to interact with some members more than others. There is also a greater possibility of shared leadership and the delegation of various leadership responsibilities.

Some of the basic skills necessary for group leadership are categorized in Table 4.1. Skills are listed in three categories: (1) facilitating group processes, (2) data gathering and assessment, and (3) action. Skills are classified on the basis of their most likely function within the group. Skills listed under one category may, however, be used in another category, particularly if they are combined with other skills. For example, responding is classified as a skill in facilitating group processes. Although responding to another group member's actions or words facilitates communication, responding may also lead to additional data gathering, assessment, or action.

Facilitating Group Processes

Table 4.1 lists several different skills in the category of facilitating group processes. All these skills can be used by workers differentially, depending on their intentions when attempting to influence various group processes. In general, however, skills in facilitating group

TABLE 4.1 ● *A Functional Classification of Group Leadership Skills*

Facilitating Group Processes	Data Gathering and Assessment	Action
1. Involving group members	1. Identifying and describing thoughts, feelings, and behaviors	1. Supporting
2. Attending to others		2. Reframing and redefining
3. Expressing self	2. Requesting information, questioning, and probing	3. Linking members' communications
4. Responding to others		
5. Focusing group communication	3. Summarizing and partializing information	4. Directing
		5. Giving advice, suggestions, or instructions
6. Making group processes explicit	4. Synthesizing thoughts, feelings, and actions	6. Providing resources
7. Clarifying content	5. Analyzing information	7. Modeling, role playing, rehearsing, and coaching
8. Guiding group interactions		8. Confronting
		9. Resolving conflicts

processes contribute to positive group outcome when they improve understanding among group members, build open communication channels, and encourage the development of trust so that all members are willing to contribute as much as they can to the problem on which the group is working.

Involving Group Members

Ideally, all members should be involved and interested in what is being discussed in the group. Yalom (1995) has called this universalizing a group member's experience. Involving members who have been silent helps identify commonalities and differences in their life experiences. As members become involved they realize how particular problems affect them and how a solution to one member's problem can directly or indirectly help them. Involving others is also essential for building group cohesiveness, developing a sense of mutual aid, and encouraging shared decision making.

Involving group members also means helping them take on leadership roles within the group. The worker should be cautious about doing too much for members and thereby stifling individual initiative. Instead of jealously guarding the leadership role, workers should encourage members to contribute to the content of group meetings and help shape group dynamic processes. This can be done by providing members with opportunities for leadership roles during program activities, by praising members for their leadership efforts, and by inviting and encouraging members' participation and initiative during group interaction. For example, the worker might say "Mary, I know that you are knowledgeable about that;

do you have anything to add to what Tom has said?" Similarly, the worker might say, "Tom, you did such an excellent job in the role play last week. Would you be willing to play the part of the angry storekeeper?"

Attending Skills

Attending skills are nonverbal behaviors, such as eye contact and body position, and verbal behavior that convey empathy, respect, warmth, trust, genuineness, and honesty. Attending skills are useful in establishing rapport as well as a climate of acceptance and cohesiveness among group members. Egan (2002) suggests that, in addition to body position and eye contact, skills that indicate that a worker has heard and understood a member are part of effective attending. Research has shown that effective attending skills are an important characteristic of successful leaders (Johnson & Bechler, 1998). Effective attending skills include repeating or paraphrasing what a member says and responding empathically and enthusiastically to the meaning behind members' communications. They also include what Middleman (1978) has referred to as "scanning" skills. When scanning the group, the worker makes eye contact with all group members, which lets them know that the worker is concerned about them as individuals. Scanning also helps reduce the tendency of workers to focus on one or two group members.

Expressive Skills

Expressive skills are also important for facilitating group processes. Workers should be able to help participants express thoughts and feelings about important problems, tasks, or issues facing the group and to reiterate and summarize them when necessary. Members should also be helped to express their thoughts and feelings as freely as possible in an appropriate and goal-oriented manner. Members of task and treatment groups can often benefit from an open discussion of formerly taboo areas that affect the group or its members. Self-disclosure is an expressive skill that can be used effectively for this purpose. Although self-disclosures should be made judiciously, according to their appropriateness for particular situations, they can often be useful in helping the worker promote open communication about difficult subjects. For example, a worker might say, "I just lost my mother, who also had been ill for a long time. I know what you mean, Bea, when you say that watching a loved one slowly decline right before your eyes is so hard. Your situation is different than mine, because it's your husband, but I can just imagine how terribly difficult it is for you. Do you want to share with us how you have been coping?"

Responding Skills

Skillful responses help the group as a whole and individual members accomplish tasks. The worker might, for example, amplify subtle messages or soften overpowering messages (Middleman & Wood, 1990). The worker can also redirect messages that may be more appropriate for a particular member or the group as a whole.

Workers can use responding skills selectively to elicit specific reactions that will affect future group processes. For example, if a worker's response supports a group member's efforts, the member is more likely to continue to work on a task or a concern. If the worker disagrees with a member's statement or action, the member is likely to react either by responding to the worker's statement or by remaining silent. The member is not likely to continue to pursue the original statement. Thus, by responding selectively to particular communications, the worker can exert influence over subsequent communication patterns.

Focusing Skills

The worker can facilitate group processes by focusing them in a particular direction. This can be done by clarifying, asking a member to elaborate, repeating a particular communication or sequence of communications, or suggesting that group members limit their discussion to a particular topic. Helping the group maintain its focus can promote efficient work by reducing irrelevant communications and by encouraging a full exploration of issues and problems.

Making Group Processes Explicit

The skill of making group processes explicit helps members to become aware of how they are interacting. For example, a worker may point out implicit group norms, particular member roles, or specific interaction patterns. The worker may ask members whether they observed a particular pattern or type of interaction, whether they are comfortable with the interaction, and whether they would like to see changes in the ways members interact. Middleman and Wood (1990) point out that it is important for the worker to verbalize therapeutic group norms and to encourage the development of traditions and rituals. For example, pointing out that at the beginning of each group meeting members seem to take turns "telling their story" and receiving feedback about how they handled a particular situation encourages members to consider whether they want to continue this pattern of interaction.

Pointing out the here-and-now of group interaction is an underused skill. Sometimes, workers get so caught up in the content of interaction that they forget to pay attention to group processes. Other workers are reluctant to make their observations public. Workers who have difficulty directing the group's attention to group processes should consider practicing this skill by setting aside a few minutes at the beginning or end of each meeting for a discussion of group processes or by making a conscious effort to point out group processes in brief summary statements at intervals during meetings. Clinical and supervisory experience suggests that the process of pointing out here-and-now group interaction becomes easier with practice. A brief example of how to point out here-and-now interactions during group meetings follows.

● **CASE EXAMPLE** *Pointing Out Group Dynamics*

In order to help members understand how their interactions affected the group-as-a-whole, the leader of a support group for recovering alcoholics often took time out from discussion of members' issues to bring up group dynamics and processes. He noted that members sometimes ignored nonverbal reactions of other members and often asked members to observe what was going on with the group-as-a-whole. Eventually, members became more skilled at observing this and other communication dynamics within the group. The leader frequently asked members to evaluate the leadership behavior of other members, using this "processing" time to discuss both member and group strengths. As the group progressed, the leader and members structured these discussions into the final few minutes of the session, giving them time each week to discuss group processes.

Clarifying Content

Just as it can be beneficial to make group processes explicit, it can also be beneficial to point out the content of members' interactions. The worker's purpose in clarifying content is to help members communicate effectively. The skill of clarifying content includes checking that a particular message was understood by members of the group and helping members express themselves more clearly. It also includes pointing out when group interaction has become unfocused or has been sidetracked by an irrelevant issue.

The skill of clarifying content can also be used to point out the possible avoidance of taboo subjects. For example, in a support group for caregivers of the frail elderly, the worker might point out that the subject of nursing home placement has not arisen.

Guiding Group Interactions

To help a group accomplish the goals it has set for itself, the worker will often find it helpful to guide the group's interaction in a particular direction. By limiting or blocking a group member's communications, by encouraging another member to speak, or by linking one group member's communication to those of other group members, the worker can guide the group's interaction patterns. This method has been referred to as selecting communications patterns purposely (Middleman & Wood, 1990).

The skill of guiding group interactions has many uses. For example, the worker may want to correct a dysfunctional aspect of the group's process, such as the development of a subgroup that disrupts other members. A worker who can skillfully guide group interaction patterns can limit the communication between subgroup members and increase their communication with other group members. The worker may also want to use guiding skills to explore a particular problem or help members sustain their efforts in solving a problem or completing a task. At other times, the worker may want to encourage open communication. For example, by redirecting a communication, the worker can help members speak to one another. The worker might say, "John, your message is really intended for Jill. Why don't you share your message directly with her rather than through me?"

Data Gathering and Assessment

Data-gathering and assessment skills are useful in developing a plan for influencing communication patterns as well as in deciding on the action skills to use to accomplish the group's purposes. These skills provide a bridge between the process-oriented approach of facilitating group processes and the task-oriented approach of using action skills to achieve goals and satisfy members' needs. Without effective data-gathering and assessment skills, workers' interventions are not grounded in a complete understanding of the situation. This can result in the use of premature, oversimplified, or previously attempted solutions that have not been carefully analyzed and weighed.

Identifying and Describing Skills

Perhaps the most basic data-gathering skill is helping members identify and describe a particular situation. This skill allows elaboration of pertinent factors influencing a problem or task facing the group. In using this skill, workers should attempt to elicit descriptions that specify the problem attributes as clearly and concretely as possible. To understand the problem, it is often useful for the worker to identify or describe historical as well as current aspects of the problem. It may also be helpful to share alternative ways of viewing the situation to obtain diverse frames of reference, alternative interpretations of events, and potential solutions to a problem. For example, the worker might say, "You have given us a pretty complete description of what happened, Amy, but I wonder, what do you think Jim would say if I asked him to give an account of the same situation? How do you think he would view this?"

Requesting Information, Questioning, and Probing

The skills of identifying and describing a situation are essential to workers' attempts to gather data by requesting information, questioning, and probing. Using these skills, workers can clarify the problem or concern and broaden the scope of the group's work by obtaining additional information that may be useful to all members. The worker should be careful to ask questions that are clear and answerable. Double questions or value-laden questions may be met with resistance, passivity, anger, or misunderstanding. For some issues and for some group members, questioning or probing may be seen as a confrontation or a challenge to what has already been stated, particularly in areas in which the member is reluctant to give additional information, because the information is perceived as emotionally charged or potentially damaging to the member's status in the group. The worker should be particularly sensitive to these concerns when seeking additional information from a member. Helping the member explore fears or concerns about the potentially damaging effect of a disclosure can be a helpful intervention. Another is having the member ask for feedback from other members about the realistic basis of personal fears.

Summarizing and Partializing

When information has been discussed about the problems or concerns facing the group, a worker can use summarizing or partializing skills. Summarizing skills enable a worker to present the core of what has been said in the group and provide members an opportunity to reflect on the problem. Summarizing skills give members and the worker an opportunity to consider the next steps in solving the problem and allow members to compare with the worker's summary their perceptions about what has gone on in the group. Partializing skills are useful for breaking down a complex problem or issue into manageable bits. Partializing is also helpful in determining group members' motivation to work on various aspects of the problem. For example, the worker might say, "John, I heard you talk a lot about your frustration with the group's not sticking to its purpose here. Would you tell us briefly what you would like to see the group do that we aren't doing right now? . . . Okay, so you are suggesting that we could take three steps to stay on track better during future discussions. . . . Am I paraphrasing you correctly? Are these the three things you think would keep us on track?"

Synthesizing

Another useful data-gathering and assessment skill is synthesizing verbal and nonverbal communications. Examples of synthesizing skills include making connections among the meanings behind a member's actions or words, expressing hidden agendas, making implicit feelings or thoughts explicit, and making connections between communications to point out themes and trends in members' actions or words.

Synthesizing skills can be useful in providing feedback to members about how they are perceived by others. Because these skills often involve a considerable amount of judgment and conjecture about the facts available to the worker, they should be used cautiously, and all members should have the opportunity for input into the synthesis. Ideally, when the worker synthesizes a number of interactions or points out similarities in group problem solving or in group communication patterns, all members should be able to give feedback about their perceptions of the situation. For example, during a weekly staff meeting of an adolescent unit in a state mental hospital, a worker might mention the patterns of interactions that have developed among team members. In describing these patterns, the worker would ask members for feedback on how they perceived the group's interaction.

Analyzing Skills

Once the data have been gathered and organized, the worker can use analyzing skills to synthesize the information and assess how to proceed. Analyzing skills include pointing out patterns in the data, identifying gaps in the data, and establishing mechanisms or plans for obtaining data to complete an assessment. For example, in a treatment conference at a group home for adolescents, the worker can use analyzing skills to point out patterns used by staff members in previous work with a particular youngster. The group can then explore new methods and techniques for future efforts to work with the youngster. In an educational treatment group for potentially abusive parents, the worker can use analyzing skills to link parents' behavior patterns to the onset of physical abuse of their children.

Action Skills

Supporting Group Members

Action skills are most often used by the worker to help the group accomplish its tasks. Perhaps the most basic skill in this area is supporting group members in their efforts to help themselves and each other. Skills to support group members will not be effective unless members perceive the group to be a safe place in which their thoughts and feelings will be accepted. Thus, it is essential to begin by helping the group develop a culture in which all members' experiences and opinions are valued. The worker supports members by encouraging them to express their thoughts and feelings on topics relevant to the group, by providing them the opportunity to ventilate their concerns, by soliciting their opinions, and by responding to their requests and comments.

Support also means helping members respond empathically to each other and validate and affirm shared experiences. Skills in supporting members often involve pointing out their strengths and indicating how their participation in the group can help to resolve their problems. It also means providing hope for continued progress or success.

Ventilation and support are the primary goals of some groups. For example, support groups are sometimes formed for the staff of neonatal intensive care units and burn units of regional hospitals. Such groups give staff a chance to talk about and reflect on the emotionally draining situations they frequently face. Medical social workers who form and facilitate these groups encourage staff to ventilate pent-up emotions and provide peer support for one another. Similarly, the therapeutic elements of a treatment group for recently widowed people include the ventilation of feelings about the loss of a loved one, the affirmation of similar feelings and experiences, and the encouragement to cope effectively with the transition despite feelings of grief.

Reframing and Redefining

Often, one of the greatest obstacles to the work of a group or an individual is failure to view a problem from different perspectives to find a creative solution (Clark, 1998). Redefining and reframing the problem can help members examine the problem from a new perspective. Thus, a worker may want to reframe or redefine an issue or concern facing the group. For example, in a group in which one member is being made a scapegoat, the worker might help members redefine their relationship to that member. Redefining can be done by having members talk about how they relate to the person who is being scapegoated and how they might improve their relationship with that person. In this case, reframing the problem from one that focuses on the scapegoated member to one that is shared by all members is a useful way to change members' interactions with this particular member. As the problem is redefined and group members change their relationship with the member being scapegoated, the problem often diminishes or disappears. Reframing is described in greater detail in Chapter 9.

Linking Members' Communications

The skill of linking members' communications involves asking members to share their reactions to the messages communicated by others in the group. Middleman and Wood (1990) refer to this skill as reaching for a feeling link or an information link. Members have a tendency to communicate with the worker rather than with other members, especially in early group meetings. The worker can prevent this from becoming a pattern by asking members about their reactions to a particular communication. For example, in a group in a psychiatric inpatient setting designed to prepare the members for independent living, the worker might say, "Mary, how do you feel about what Joe just said? I recall that during our last meeting, you expressed feeling anxious about living on your own." Alternatively, the worker might say, "Have any of you had the same feeling?" When members of the group validate and affirm each other's experiences and feelings, they develop a sense of belonging. Members no longer feel isolated or alone with their concerns. They stop questioning and doubting their own interpretations of a situation and their own reactions to it.

The skill of linking members' communications also involves asking members to respond to requests for help by other members. Helping members respond to each other fosters information sharing, mutual aid, and the building of a consensus about how to approach a particular problem. For example, in response to a query from a group member about whether the worker knows of a resource for helping her take care of her frail father while she is at work, the worker might ask whether any other members have used adult day care or respite care. Workers find that members are often more receptive to using a service or a resource when they hear positive reports about it from other members of the group.

Particularly when working with mandated and reluctant clients, workers who suggest use of a particular resource may be viewed with skepticism. Members sometimes believe that the worker has a vested interest in getting them to use a particular service. In contrast, the testimonials of one or more group members about the benefits of a particular service are often viewed with less skepticism. Workers should also be aware that once they provide a response, other members are less likely to provide their own perspective. Thus, although a direct response to a member's communication is often warranted, it is often a good practice for workers to turn to other members of the group for their input before jumping in with their own responses.

Directing

Whether the worker is clarifying the group's goal, helping members participate in a particular program activity, leading a discussion, sharing new information, or making an assessment of a particular problem, the worker is directing the group's action. Directing skills are most effective when coupled with efforts to increase members' participation and input (Stogdill, 1974). The worker should not use directing skills without obtaining members' approval or without involving them in decisions about the direction the group should take to accomplish its goals. The worker should be aware of how each member reacts to being directed in a new component of the group's work. For example, when directing a role play in a remedial group designed to help teenagers learn how to handle angry feelings more effectively, the worker should be aware of how the action will affect each member. Depending on the way they express their anger, some group members may benefit more than others from playing certain roles.

Advice, Suggestions, and Instructions

Workers give advice, suggestions, and instructions to help group members acquire new behaviors, understand problems, or change problematic situations. There is some evidence, however, that giving advice, suggestions, or instructions is rarely done. Studies have revealed, for example, that advice, suggestions, and instructions constitute 1 percent to 5 percent of all communications made by practitioners (Boatman, 1975; Mullen, 1969; Pinkus, 1968; Smith, Tobin, & Toseland, 1992).

Nonetheless, advice is expected and wanted by many clients, especially those of lower socioeconomic status (Aronson & Overall, 1966; Davis, 1975; Mayer & Timms, 1970).

Further, these skills appear to have some beneficial effect in helping clients formulate new ideas and approaches to resolving problems (Davis, 1975; Ewalt & Kutz, 1976; Fortune, 1979; Reid & Shapiro, 1969; Smith et al., 1992). For example, in a review of studies of various therapeutic mechanisms of change, Emrick, Lassen, and Edwards (1977) reported that advice giving was strongly associated with positive changes in clients. Effective ways to give advice, suggestions, and instructions follow.

Giving Advice, Suggestions, and Instructions

- Should be appropriately timed
- Should be clear and geared to comprehension level of members
- Should be sensitive to the language and culture of members
- Should encourage members to share in the process
- Should facilitate helping networks among members

Advice, suggestions, and instructions should be timed appropriately so that group members are ready to accept them. They must be clear and geared to the comprehension level of the members for whom they are intended. For example, they should be written at a level that will be readily understood by group members. A group of teenage parents who have not completed high school requires a presentation of ideas, advice, suggestions, and instructions quite different from a presentation to a group of highly educated women who have delayed child rearing until their early thirties.

Workers should also be sensitive to the language and culture of the members of their groups. Certain words in English might not translate appropriately or with the same meaning in another language. Further, the cultural heritage of a population may influence how such individuals receive and decode messages sent from the worker.

The worker should not act alone in giving advice, suggestions, and instructions. This sets the worker off as an expert who may be seen as too directive. The worker should encourage members to share information, advice, and instructions with each other. Middleman (1978) and Shulman (1999) refer to this as the worker's reaching for feelings and information that members may be hesitant to disclose.

To encourage members to share information and advice with each other, the worker should facilitate the development of helping networks where members feel free to share their life experiences, information, and resources, as well as their opinions and views. One of the distinct advantages of group work over individual work is the ability of group members to rely on one another for help in solving problems and accomplishing goals. Experience suggests that well-established helping networks often continue outside the group long after the group experience has ended. For example, a worker who formed a support and parenting skills education group for single parents in an inner city area later helped the group members form a child-care cooperative that flourished for years after the 12-week parenting skills group ended. Similarly, the members of a support group for family members of patients recently discharged from inpatient settings in the inner city were helped by a worker to form a local chapter of a national welfare rights organization.

Providing Resources

Organizations that sponsor groups have access to a wide variety of resources such as medical treatment, home health care, financial assistance, job and rehabilitation counseling, family planning, and financial management consultation, which the worker can make available to members. Making skillful use of these resources through accurate assessment and referral can be helpful to members. The worker can also encourage members to talk about the resources and services they have found to be effective. In this way, the cumulative knowledge of all group members can be used for mutual aid. Members who talk enthusiastically about a resource or service can be more convincing than a worker providing the very same information.

In task groups, workers can also provide a variety of resources for members. They can influence the environment in which a group works, either directly or indirectly, to make it easier for the group to accomplish its tasks. Workers may have access to important people or action groups that can give the group's work proper consideration. In addition, because task groups are often composed of members with a variety of skills and resources, members can also help one another achieve the group's goals.

Modeling, Role Playing, Rehearsing, and Coaching

The action skills of modeling, role playing, and rehearsing situations in the group can be helpful in both task and treatment groups. *Modeling* refers to the worker or a member demonstrating behaviors in a particular situation so that others in the group can observe what to do and how to do it. For example, the worker in an assertion training group might demonstrate how to respond to a spouse who has become quite angry. In another group, the worker might model caring and concern by going over to a group member who has begun to cry and placing an arm around the member's shoulder.

Role playing refers to having group members act out a situation with each other's help. The two primary purposes of role playing are to assess members' skill in responding to an interpersonal situation and to help members improve particular responses. Responses can be improved through feedback, rehearsal of a new response, or coaching (Etcheverry, Siporin, & Toseland, 1987).

Role playing can be a very useful tool when trying to help members improve responses to stressful situations. For example, in a group for couples trying to improve their relationships, the worker might ask each couple to role play an argument they had during the past week. During the role play, the worker asks each couple to switch roles so that each partner could experience how the other felt, thought, and acted in the situation. Role play can help members understand their partner's behavior and how their own behavior influenced their partner. The couples can use the feedback they received to experiment with new and better ways to communicate during an argument. In this way, the couples learn new communication skills and begin to use improved ways of responding to each other during disagreements.

Rehearsing refers to practicing a new behavior or response based on the feedback received after a role play. Because it is difficult to learn new behaviors or to diminish less adaptive but habituated behavior patterns, a member may have to practice a new response several times.

Coaching is the use of verbal and physical instructions to help members reproduce a particular response. For example, members of a group for the mentally retarded might practice expressing their feelings during interpersonal interactions. As members practice, the worker coaches them by giving instructions and demonstrating how to improve their responses. Additional information about different role-playing techniques is presented in Chapter 9.

Confrontation Skills

Confrontation is a useful action skill for overcoming resistance and motivating members. Confrontation is the ability to clarify, examine, and challenge behaviors to help members overcome distortions and discrepancies among behaviors, thoughts, and feelings (Egan, 2002; Toseland & Spielberg, 1982). Confrontation skills should be used only when the worker has carefully assessed the situation and decided that what is said will not be rejected by a member. If a member is not ready to examine thoughts, behaviors, or feelings, the member may react negatively to a confrontation by becoming passive, angry, or hostile.

Because confrontations are potent and emotionally charged, workers should be prepared for strong reactions. In certain circumstances, workers may want to make gentle or tentative confrontations to explore a member's reactions before making direct, full-scale confrontation. Although confrontations are often associated with pointing out a member's flaws or weaknesses, they can be used to help members recognize strengths and assets. For example, in a remedial group for psychiatric inpatients, a depressed group member who is self-deprecating might be confronted and challenged to begin to recognize his strengths and assets. Similarly, a member of a growth group might be confronted by pointing out how her words differ from her actions.

Resolving Conflicts

One of the most important action skills is helping resolve conflicts among the members of the group and with individuals and social systems outside the group. Group members may conflict with one another for a variety of reasons. For example, in a delegate council, members may represent constituencies that have quite different concerns, interests, and goals. In a treatment team, group members' responsibilities for different work functions and tasks may cause conflict or competition, particularly if resources for accomplishing a task are limited.

Many of the models of group development described in the previous chapter indicate that conflict may arise among members as the group develops. The worker should help the group view conflict as a healthy process that can clarify the purposes and goals of the group and the way members can work together.

Although conflicts inevitably arise, skillful group facilitation can help avoid unnecessary conflicts and resolve disagreements before they turn into hostile disputes. To help avoid unnecessary conflicts, workers can suggest that the group develop and maintain rules for participation. These rules are frequently expressed in early contractual discussions with members. Sometimes these rules, which should be developed with the participation of all group members, are stated in a written agreement that all members sign at the beginning of a new group. An example of such a written agreement is shown in Figure 4.3. Having agreed-on rules clearly written and displayed on a blackboard or flip chart is particularly helpful in

---

FIGURE 4.3 ● *Rules for Group Participation*

I, the undersigned, agree to:

1. Attend each group session or call one day before the group meeting to explain my absence.

2. Not talk about anything that occurs in the group to anyone outside the group, unless it applies only to myself and no other group member.

3. Carry out all assignments agreed to in the group between group sessions.

4. Speak in turn so that everyone gets a chance to talk.

5. Give the group two weeks' notice before terminating my participation.

Name	Date

---

children's groups. Children enjoy setting rules for their group, and, with the guidance of a leader, they can help each other follow rules they have made.

When conflicts arise among members, the worker may also use moderating, negotiating, mediating, or arbitrating skills to resolve disagreements before they turn into hostile disputes. Moderating skills help workers keep meetings within specified bounds so that conflict is avoided. Negotiating skills are used to help members come to an agreement or an understanding when initial opinions differ. Mediating skills are used when two or more members are in conflict and action is necessary to help them reach an agreement and resolve the dispute. Arbitration skills involve having an authoritative third person meet with the group. This person listens to the dispute and binds the members to a settlement. Arbitration is sometimes used in task groups that have reached an impasse when working on a labor contract. Specific methods that workers can use to help resolve conflicts in groups are described more fully in Chapter 11.

Members may also come into conflict with forces outside the group. The members of therapy groups, for example, often expect workers to provide guidance about how to resolve conflicts with spouses, other family members, friends, fellow workers, and acquaintances. In attempting to be more assertive, a member of a therapy group might receive hostile, angry, or aggressive responses from family members or friends. In such a case, the worker might attempt to reduce the conflict by intervening directly in the situation or by helping the member develop the skills necessary to overcome the conflict alone. When the conflict is an inevitable by-product of a change the member wishes to make outside the group, the worker can help the member feel comfortable with the conflict until a new state of equilibrium is achieved.

Sometimes it is helpful for the worker to meet with people outside the group to resolve a member's conflict. For example, a worker might meet with the parents of an adolescent group member to discuss how the parents set limits and rules for their child. In other cases, workers can prepare members for the reactions they may encounter outside the group. For example, a worker can help members learn how to respond to potential rejection or hostility when they are more assertive than usual with a particular person. Preparing members for what to expect in a wide range of situations and settings also helps ensure their success when they are using newly learned behaviors in unfamiliar settings or situations.

Workers may also need to resolve conflicts between the group as a whole and the larger society. For example, workers may help resolve conflicts between tenants' associations and housing authorities, welfare rights groups and county departments of social services, or support groups for individuals with chronic illnesses and health-care providers. Moderating, negotiating, mediating, and arbitrating skills can often be used successfully in these situations. However, in some situations, mobilization and social action skills (described in Chapter 11) may have to be used to resolve a conflict.

Learning Group Leadership Skills

Persons who are training to become group workers should begin by becoming thoroughly familiar with the theoretical knowledge about groups as a whole and the way members and leaders function in groups. However, to integrate theoretical knowledge about group dynamics with practical experience, trainees should (1) participate in exercises and role plays illustrating how group dynamics operate, (2) observe others leading and being members of groups, (3) examine their participation as members of natural or formed groups, and (4) lead or colead a group in a supervised field practicum.

In the classroom, trainees can learn to lead groups under a variety of conditions and circumstances by combining didactic and experiential methods of learning. Didactic material should expose trainees to the array of groups they may be called on to lead. Therefore, lectures, discussions, and examples should include groups in several settings with different purposes and clientele. Lecture material can be supplemented with films and videotapes of different social work groups in action. A list of available films is presented in Appendix B.

Cognitive knowledge is, by itself, insufficient for effective group work practice. Training should include exercises and role plays to illustrate and demonstrate the material presented during lectures. Often laboratory groups can be formed to help trainees practice the material that has been presented. Lab groups give trainees a sense of what it is like to be a member of a group. Also, leadership can be rotated in a lab group so that all members are responsible for leading a group at least once. Exercises to illustrate the concepts in each chapter of this book can be found in a manual entitled *Student Workbook: An Introduction to Group Work Practice* that accompanies this book (Furman, 2005), and other interactive group exercises can be found in Barlow, Blythe, and Edmonds (1999).

Laboratory group experiences can be enhanced by the use of video and audio equipment. These devices give trainees feedback about their verbal and nonverbal behavior as they participate in or lead a meeting. Tapes made during labs can be reviewed by trainees and the lab leader during supervisory sessions to help members develop their leadership skills.

Trainees can also learn how to lead a group by observing a group or by becoming a member of an existing group in the community. The trainee learns vicariously by observing the leader's behavior. The leader acts as a model of leadership skills for the member.

Learning also occurs through critiques of the group's process. Critiquing the group helps ensure that trainees do not accept all the activities of the group's leader without question. It gives trainees an opportunity to examine the development of a group over time and to observe the effects of leadership skills in action. It is relatively easy to structure lab groups so that part of the group's time is spent analyzing the group process, but trainees may not have this opportunity in community groups. Therefore, to achieve maximum benefit from participation in a community group, trainees should have an opportunity to discuss their experiences in supervisory sessions or in the classroom.

When trainees become familiar with basic skills in leading a group through these experiences, they are ready for a field practicum. The field practicum may include leading several sessions of a group, coleading a group, or leading an entire group while receiving supervision. For purposes of learning about group leadership skills, group supervision is preferable to individual supervision because the supervisor models group leadership skills while reviewing a trainee's work with a group. Rivas and Toseland (1981) have found that a training group is an effective way to provide supervision. Methods for conducting group supervision are discussed by Rose (1989). If not enough practicum sites are available, trainees can form their own task or treatment groups by providing group services to students or community residents (Rivas & Toseland, 1981).

Before leading a group, it is helpful for trainees to discuss their concerns about the first meeting. Lonergan (1989) reports that these concerns can include (1) unmanageable resistance exhibited by members, such as not talking; (2) losing control of the group because of members' excessive hostility or acting out; (3) inability to deal with specific behaviors such as a member dropping out of the group capriciously, members dating each other, or individuals making sexual advances within the group or between group meetings; (4) overwhelming dependency demands by members; and (5) lack of attendance and the disintegration of the group. Because trainees react differently to their first group experience, supervisors should explore each individual's concerns and help them deal with their anxiety by discussing likely group reactions and reviewing what could be done in the unlikely event that a trainee's worst concern is realized. For additional information about effective methods for learning group leadership skills, see Berger (1996) or Barlow and others (1999).

Leadership Style

It is important to recognize that, although leadership skills can be learned, they are not applied in a mechanical, objective fashion. Group work is a subjective encounter among the members of the group, all of whom have distinct personalities, viewpoints, and methods of relating to objective reality. Workers and members bring expectations, preferences, and styles of relating to the group. Although these may be modified during the course of interaction, they continuously color and shape the evolving interaction and the skills that workers use to facilitate the group. As Goldstein (1988) states, "As people enter into a group and take part in shaping its purpose and goals, the underlying premises that they bring to the encounter and their ways of perceiving, thinking and interpreting will inexorably determine how the process unfolds" (p. 25).

The degree to which styles of relating influence what occurs in the group depends on the nature of the group. The more a group is structured and the more it is focused on impersonal issues that the members have little stake in, the less likely group processes are to be affected by the personalities of the individuals. For example, in a delegate council using parliamentary procedure, the individual personalities of agency representatives are likely to have relatively little influence on group decisions. In contrast, Reid (1997) aptly points out that in therapy groups, "each [person] brings to the [group] experience a history of relating to others, sometimes with success and at other times without. In this therapeutic alliance group members may react to the therapist as if he or she were a significant figure from their own family. Similarly, the leader may react in exactly the same way, projecting onto others his or her own unresolved feelings and conflicts" (pp. 105–106).

In the psychoanalytic tradition, projection of feelings by members onto the leader is called *transference*. Projection of feelings onto members by the leader is called *countertransference*.

To become an effective group leader it is not sufficient, therefore, to learn group leadership skills without paying attention to how they are applied. It is essential for leaders to become self-reflective practitioners who consider carefully the meaning of their interactions with all members of the group. One of the hallmarks of an effective leader is the ability and willingness to examine the effect of personal beliefs, expectations, preferences, personality, style of relating, and subjective experience of reality on a particular group. Effective leaders are not afraid to explore with members, supervisors, or colleagues the possible ramifications of their behavior in a group. They observe carefully and think deeply about the meaning of members' reactions to particular interactions.

The first step in helping leaders become more aware of the effect of their style of interaction is for them to do a self-assessment of their strengths and weaknesses as a leader. In the workshops that we conduct, we often begin by asking participants to complete the Leadership Comfort Scale (LCS) shown in Figure 4.4. The LCS allows participants to rate their degree of comfort with 10 situations that group leaders frequently experience. Participants are also asked to write down their responses to a series of open-ended questions, such as:

- Describe what you perceive to be your major strengths and weaknesses as a leader.
- What types of group members make you feel uncomfortable?
- What situations or events during group meetings do you find particularly difficult to deal with?
- What feedback have you received from others about your leadership skills?
- What steps have you taken to improve your leadership skills? What steps have you considered but not yet taken?

Participants' anonymous answers to the LCS are tabulated and the aggregate answers are presented on a flip chart or blackboard. Volunteers who are willing are asked to share their answers to the open-ended questions, which inevitably leads to a lively discussion of difficult leadership situations and participants' strengths and weaknesses in dealing with them. The discussion also helps point out the diversity of responses to challenging leadership situations.

FIGURE 4.4 ● *Leadership Comfort Scale*

Indicate your feelings when the following situations arise in the group. Circle the appropriate feeling.

1. Dealing with silence	Comfortable	Uncomfortable
2. Dealing with negative feelings from members	Comfortable	Uncomfortable
3. Having little structure in a group	Comfortable	Uncomfortable
4. Dealing with ambiguity of purpose	Comfortable	Uncomfortable
5. Having to self-disclose your feelings to the group	Comfortable	Uncomfortable
6. Experiencing high self-disclosure among members	Comfortable	Uncomfortable
7. Dealing with conflict in the group	Comfortable	Uncomfortable
8. Having your leadership authority questioned	Comfortable	Uncomfortable
9. Being evaluated by group members	Comfortable	Uncomfortable
10. Allowing members to take responsibility for the group	Comfortable	Uncomfortable

---

Completing the Beliefs About Structure Scale (BASS), shown in Figure 4.5, can further the process of self-assessment. When completing the BASS, workshop participants sometimes state that their answers depend on the purpose of the group, the types of group members, and so forth. Leadership is interactive, but individuals have preferences about the degree of structure they are most comfortable with. Participants should be asked to respond to the inventory in a way that best describes their natural tendencies and preferences.

After completing the BASS, participants can be asked to total the number of items they circled in column A and column B and to form two groups—one for those who had higher column A scores favoring a higher level of structure, and one for those who had higher column B scores favoring a lower level of structure. Participants in each group are asked to discuss why they preferred a higher or lower level of structure. They may also be asked to prepare for a debate with members of the other group about the benefits of their approach to structuring the work of the group.

Workshop participants are also asked to complete the How Members Achieve Change Scale, which is presented in Figure 4.6. Once this scale is completed, different approaches to helping members change are discussed. For example, the importance of insight in psychoanalytic group psychotherapy is contrasted with the importance of identifying here-and-now feelings in gestalt therapy. Similarly, the importance of cognition in cognitive therapy is contrasted with the importance of action in behavior therapy. Participants can also be asked to provide examples of the methods they use to help members change. For example, participants who prefer to help group members change through action strategies might describe role-playing or psychodrama procedures that they have found to be particularly effective.

FIGURE 4.5 ● *Beliefs About Structure Scale (BASS)*

Circle the statement in Column A or B that best describes your preference when running a group.

Column A	Column B
Time-limited group	Open-ended group
High structure/rules	Low structure/rules
Formal contract	Informal contract
Leader sets group purpose	Members decide purpose
Focus on member goals	Focus on group process
Leader-centered authority	Shared authority
Closed membership	Open membership
Homogeneous membership	Heterogeneous membership
Use of program activities	Use of open discussion
Focus on member behavior	Focus on meaning of communication
Directive leadership	Nondirective leadership

Summarize what you have learned about your style from the above choices. What are the major themes that emerge about your preferences for a particular level of structure within a group?

Workshop participants also discuss preferences for process-oriented or outcome-oriented leadership styles and preferences for member-centered or leader-centered leadership styles. Discussion is not intended to promote a particular style of leadership or even to help leaders identify what style of leadership they are most comfortable with. Rather, the aim is to encourage leaders to become more self-reflective, to consider their natural tendencies and preferences, and to gain greater insight into how their natural tendencies and preferences affect their interaction with group members.

COLEADERSHIP

Coleadership presents a dilemma for the practicing group worker (Kolodny, 1980). Do the benefits of coleadership exceed its potential disadvantages? An entire issue of the journal *Social Work with Groups* has been devoted to this topic.[1] Although there is little empirical evidence to suggest that two leaders are better than one (Yalom, 1995), there are many clinical reports of the benefits of having two leaders (Cooper, 1976; Davis & Lohr, 1971; Levine, 1980; MacLennon, 1965; McGee & Schuman, 1970; Roller & Nelson, 1991; Schlenoff & Busa, 1981; Starak, 1981).

---

[1]*Social Work with Groups* (1980), 3 (4).

FIGURE 4.6 ● *How Members Achieve Change Scale*

Group leadership style is partly a function of how one believes members achieve change in their lives and how one believes the group should take responsibility for helping members change. Answer the following questions about these dynamics. Avoid using the term *it all depends*. Instead, choose the answer that best expresses your natural preference or inclination.

1. Do people achieve change best through insight or action?
2. Do people achieve change best by focusing on their affect (feelings) or their cognition (thoughts)?
3. When helping a member to achieve change, would you concentrate on changing the member's behavior or the member's thoughts?
4. When evaluating whether a member was making progress in the change efforts, would you assess whether the member did what the member wanted, what you wanted, or what society wanted?
5. Is it more important to give your attention to group content or group process?
6. Do you think the responsibility for the functioning of the group rests with the leader or the members?

Choose the statement that best characterizes your opinion. (circle one)

7. The purpose for group work is:
   a. Raising social consciousness, social responsibility, informed citizenship, and social and political action.
   b. Restoring and rehabilitating group members who are behaving dysfunctionally.
   c. Forming a mutual aid system among members to achieve maximum adaptation and socialization.
8. The role of the worker is to be a:
   a. Role model and enabler for responsible citizenship.
   b. Change agent, problem solving with members to meet their goals.
   c. Mediator between the needs of the members and the needs of the group and larger society.
9. Which methods would you tend to use in the group?
   a. Discussion, participation, consensus, group task
   b. Structured exercises, direct influence in and out of group
   c. Shared authority, support, building a positive group culture

Based on your responses to the previous nine questions, summarize your preferences for how to help members change.

Some of the most frequently cited benefits of having a coleader follow.

Benefits of Coleadership

- Leaders have a source of support.
- Leaders have a source of feedback and an opportunity for professional development.

- A leader's objectivity is increased through alternative frames of references.
- Inexperienced leaders can receive training.
- Group members are provided with models for appropriate communication, interaction, and resolution of disputes.
- Leaders have assistance during therapeutic interventions, particularly during role plays, simulations, and program activities.
- Leaders have help setting limits and structuring the group experience.

This list suggests several ways in which coleadership can be helpful. For the novice worker, probably the greatest benefit of coleadership is having a supportive partner who understands how difficult it is to be an effective leader. As Galinsky and Schopler (1980) point out, "The support of a compatible co-leader lessens the strains of dealing with difficult and often complicated group interactions" (p. 54). During group meetings, coleaders help each other facilitate the work of the group. Between group meetings, they share their feelings about the group and their roles in it. In addition to supporting each other's efforts at group leadership, coleaders can share feedback with each other about their mutual strengths and weaknesses and thereby foster each other's professional growth and development.

Coleadership can also be helpful because it allows workers to share alternative frames of reference regarding the interaction that has taken place in the group. This helps fill in gaps in each worker's memory of events and helps each view the interaction from a different perspective. This process, in turn, may lead to a more complete and accurate assessment as well as to more adequate planning when the coleaders prepare for future group meetings.

Coleadership provides a group with the benefit of having two experts who can help with problem solving. It provides two models of behavior for members to identify with and helps in role plays, simulation, and program activities engaged in by the group. Coleaders can increase workers' abilities to establish and enforce limits as long as they share common goals (Davis & Lohr, 1971). Coleaders also have the opportunity to structure their roles to meet the needs of members. For example, one worker can focus on members' socioemotional needs and the other worker can focus on members' task needs. In its most refined form, coleadership can be used strategically to promote therapeutic goals in a powerful and effective fashion. For example, when describing the benefits of male and female coleadership of spouse abuse groups, Nosko and Wallace (1997) point out that male and female coleaders who are perceived as different but equal can be effective at structuring their leadership and interaction to promote the resolution of faulty gender socialization among members. Effective coleaders use their relationship with each other to model effective interpersonal interactions that members can emulate both within and outside of the group.

Despite the benefits, coleadership has some potential disadvantages.

Disadvantages of Coleadership

- Can be more expensive than solo leadership
- Need to coordinate planning between meetings

- If leaders do not function well together they may not serve as role models for members
- Training new leaders by placing them in groups with experienced leaders may create conflict and tension
- Conflict between leaders can negatively affect group outcomes

Because it requires the time of two leaders, coleadership is expensive. Leaders must coordinate their actions in planning for the group. Between group sessions, communication can be a problem if workers do not make a concerted effort to find the time to discuss their work together (Herzog, 1980). If leaders do not function well together, they may not serve as therapeutic role models for members (Davis & Lohr, 1971). Yalom (1995) recommends that coleaders have equal status and experience. He suggests that the apprenticeship format— that is, training new group leaders by placing them in groups with experienced leaders— may create conflict and tension.

Conflict between coleaders can have detrimental effects on the outcome of a group (Cooper, 1976; Edelwich & Brodsky, 1992; Yalom, 1995). Members may be able to side with one leader against the other or avoid working on difficult issues. When coleaders experience conflict with one another, it can be helpful to resolve the conflict in the group. This lets members know that the leaders are comfortable with conflict and are able to work together to resolve it. It also enables the coleaders to act as models by demonstrating appropriate conflict-resolution strategies.

Galinsky and Schopler (1980) caution that, in some situations, it may not be helpful to resolve a conflict between coleaders in the group. For example, when conflicts are deep-seated and when there is little hope of a successful resolution, they may be better handled in supervisory sessions. There is also a danger that conflict resolution can go awry, such as when members are pulled into the conflict and asked to take sides. It is also not a good idea to express conflict in early group meetings because this may add to the anxious tension that members are already experiencing (Yalom, 1995).

The decision about whether to resolve a conflict in a group should depend on its potential effect on members. Because members are usually aware of conflicts between coleaders, it is generally preferable to resolve them within the group, especially if the resolution process is amicable and not too distressing for members. When conflict is resolved outside the group, some members may not be aware that resolution has occurred. Also, resolving a conflict outside the group does not enhance members' conflict-resolution skills. Additional information about conflict-resolution skills is provided in Chapter 11.

Because of the lack of empirical evidence about its effectiveness, the benefits and drawbacks of coleadership should be carefully considered before two leaders are used in a group. In an article about coleadership, Wright (2002) points out that the decision to have co-facilitators should be based on the needs of the group rather than on worker preferences for solo or coleadership. In situations in which it is especially important to have models who represent different points of view, it may be important to have coleaders. For example, in a group of couples, it can be useful to have both male and female leaders. In other situations, however, the expense of coleadership or the incompatibility of potential coleaders may negate any potential benefits.

When the decision is reached to colead a group, it is essential that coleaders meet together regularly to plan for the group and to discuss group process issues that arise as the group develops (Davis & Lohr, 1971). To avoid coleaders' becoming too busy to meet together, it is helpful if they schedule a specific time to meet after each group meeting. During these meetings, coleaders should review what they did well in working together, what difficulties they experienced, how they plan to work together during the next meeting, and how members and the group as a whole are progressing. Coleaders should be particularly aware of any attempts to divide their effort that could result in working toward different purposes or on behalf of different group factions. Coleaders should schedule their review meeting soon after a group meeting because they are more likely to remember what has occurred, and they have more time to prepare for the next meeting.

To avoid the difficulties that may be associated with coleadership, it is recommended that coleaders feel at ease with one another's leadership style (Yalom, 1995). According to Davis and Lohr (1971), coleaders should be selected for their complementary characteristics rather than for their similarity. This will help broaden the perspective used to assess the group and its members, provide an additional model of ways to handle problematic behaviors, and widen the scope of intervention strategies that may be used in the group.

Experience has shown that it is worse to have a coleader with whom one does not agree than to lead a group alone. Therefore, group workers should be cautious in choosing a coleader. Difficulties may arise when workers agree to colead a group without carefully considering whether they can work together effectively. Potential coleaders may want to examine each other's styles while leading a group or during team meetings before agreeing to colead a group. Figure 4.7 presents some issues to discuss before deciding to colead a group.

SUMMARY

This chapter focuses on leading task and treatment groups effectively. Although leadership is sometimes viewed as a function executed exclusively by the worker, leadership functions should be shared with group members. In this regard, the text distinguishes between the worker's role as the designated leader of the group and the leadership roles of group members that emerge as the group develops.

Leadership has been defined as the process of guiding the development of the group and its members to achieve goals that are consistent with the value base of social work practice. A worker's ability to guide group members depends on the power attributed to the worker by group members, by the supporting agency or organization, and by the larger society that sanctions the work of the group.

The power bases that can be used to guide the development of the group and its members include (1) connection power, (2) expert power, (3) information power, (4) legitimate power, (5) referent power, (6) reward power, and (7) coercive power. Leaders vary in the degree to which they have access to each power base and the extent to which they use the power bases to guide the group.

FIGURE 4.7 ● *Issues to Talk Over with a Potential Coleader*

1. Describe your leadership style. Discuss whether your style is characteristically nurturing or confrontational, whether you tend to be a high-profile or a low-profile leader, and to what extent you are comfortable with spontaneity as contrasted with sticking with a planned agenda.

2. Describe your strengths and weaknesses as a leader. What makes you feel uncomfortable when leading a group?

3. Describe your beliefs about how people change and grow, and how you will intervene in the group. For example, discuss your favorite interventions, and whether you typically intervene quickly or slowly, waiting for members of the group to engage in mutual aid.

4. Share your expectations for group accomplishments.

5. Discuss your respective roles in the group. Discuss specifically (1) where you will sit, (2) starting and ending group meetings, (3) how you will divide responsibility for any content you will be presenting, (4) what you will do about talkative and silent members, (5) scapegoating and gatekeeping, and (6) what you will do about lateness and absenteeism.

6. Discuss where, when, and how you will deal with conflict between you, and between either of you and the members of the group.

7. Discuss how you will deal with strong expressions of emotion such as crying and anger.

8. Is there anything that is nonnegotiable regarding your coleadership of a group?

Leadership is affected by a variety of situational factors that act in combination. Thus, there is no one correct way to lead all groups. Rather, leadership methods should vary according to the particular group a worker is leading. This chapter reviews the remedial, social goals, and reciprocal models of group leadership and examines several variables that affect group leadership. To help workers examine situational variables, the text describes an interactional model of group leadership. The model includes (1) the purpose of the group, (2) the type of problem the group is working on, (3) the environment in which the group is working, (4) the group as a whole, (5) the members of the group, and (6) the leader of the group.

It is essential that workers be familiar with a range of leadership skills that can be applied in many different types of groups and in many different settings. Skills include (1) facilitating group processes, (2) data gathering and assessment, and (3) action. Together, these skills constitute the core skills needed for effective leadership of task and treatment groups.

It is also essential that workers be aware of their leadership styles. A number of exercises are presented to help workers identify their preference for a particular leadership style and understand how their preferences influence their practice with treatment and task groups.

The chapter ends with an examination of coleadership. The benefits, drawbacks, and pitfalls of coleadership are described.

chapter 5

Leadership and Diversity

Group leaders often work with people from a wide range of backgrounds. Diversity within the group can be based on a variety of characteristics such as race, ethnicity, culture, national origin, religion, social class, gender, sexual orientation, and disability. When differences exist among members or between the leader and members, leadership can be particularly challenging.

APPROACHES TO MULTICULTURAL GROUP WORK

It is helpful for leaders to develop a perspective on how to work with people whose backgrounds are different from their own. Such a perspective has been referred to as anti-oppressive group work (Brown & Mistry, 1997), ethnic-sensitive practice (Devore & Schlesinger, 1999), minority practice (Lum, 2003), a cross-cultural approach (Green, 1999; Pinderhughes, 1979; Sue & Sue, 1999), and cultural/multicultural competence (Diller, 1999; Vasquez & Han, 1995). According to Pinderhughes (1995), cultural competence includes (1) the ability to perceive others through their own cultural lens, (2) knowledge of specific beliefs and values in the client's community, (3) personal comfort with differences, (4) a willingness to change previous ideas and stereotypes, (5) the ability to be flexible and adapt one's thinking and behavior in novel settings, and (6) the skill to sort through diverse information about a community to understand how it might apply to particular individuals. Green (1999) points out that cultural competence can be learned. An empirically based approach for learning about issues of race, gender, and class in groups is presented by Davis and Proctor (1989). More recently, Davis, Galinsky, and Schopler (1995) developed a comprehensive framework for leadership of multiracial groups that highlights areas of potential difficulty for group workers and suggests practice guidelines for selecting appropriate intervention techniques. Important aspects of their framework, recognize, anticipate, problem-solve (RAP), follow.

Leadership of Multiracial Groups

- Engage in ongoing self-assessment and assessment of the group, its members, and their environment
- Anticipate potential sources of tension in composing the group, in formulating the purpose, and in structuring the group's work together
- Intervene at the individual, group, and environmental levels to promote harmony and understanding; to resolve racial, ethnic, and cultural issues; and to involve members in confronting and resolving problems within and outside the group

Understanding the dynamics of race, ethnicity, and culture is essential for effective group work practice, but people also differ from each other in gender, social class, geographic background, educational and disability level, language, level of acculturation and assimilation, and age. Thus, in addition to learning practice principles for use with particular groups such as Native Americans (Marsiglia, Cross, & Mitchell-Enos, 1998; Weaver, 1999) and African Americans (Aponte, Rivers, & Wohl, 2000; McRoy, 2003), leaders can benefit from using a broader conceptual framework about diversity within groups, which includes:

- Developing cultural sensitivity
- Assessing cultural influences on group behavior
- Intervening with sensitivity to diversity

Developing Cultural Sensitivity

The terms *identity* and *culture* are often used to refer to the many ways people can differ. To develop a perspective on effective work with people of diverse cultural backgrounds, the group leader should engage in a process of self-exploration. Green (1999) describes this process as developing "cultural competence" (pp. 88–108) and suggests that workers who are culturally competent have an awareness of their own cultural limitations, are open to cultural differences, and acknowledge the integrity of other cultures. It is difficult to develop cultural competence in multiple cultures, and some argue that this is impossible. There are, however, some steps that can be taken to improve ability to practice in a culturally sensitive manner. Steps in the process of developing cultural sensitivity follow.

Developing Cultural Sensitivity in Groups

- Explore your own cultural identity
- Learn how members define and identify themselves culturally
- Frame discussions of differences by emphasizing the strengths of various cultures
- Provide members with opportunities to describe how they experience their cultural backgrounds and identities
- Become familiar with the backgrounds of client groups with whom you frequently work

- Gain knowledge about particular cultural communities
- Become immersed in a particular culture
- Model acceptance and a nonjudgmental attitude about the values, lifestyles, beliefs, and behaviors of others by recognizing the value of diversity
- Acknowledge the effect of societal attitudes on members of diverse groups
- Honestly explore members' prejudices, biases, and stereotypical assumptions about working with people from diverse backgrounds

Workers can become more culturally sensitive by exploring their feelings about their own identity. Sometimes leaders fail to take into account how they experience their identity and how this might affect their interactions with members from other backgrounds. Among both leaders and members, there may be little acknowledgment of identity issues and how these issues affect values, beliefs, and skills, perhaps because of discomfort with the subject of identity or because leaders fear that raising identity issues may reduce cohesion within the group. However, to ignore differences within the group denies the background and self-identity of each member. Davis, Galinsky, and Schopler (1995) note, for example, that "whenever people of different races come together in groups, leaders can assume that race is an issue, but not necessarily a problem" (p. 155).

Leaders can also benefit from knowledge about how members define and identify themselves. Because the manifestation of racial, cultural, ethnic, and other identity variables is the prerogative of the member rather than of the leader, the leader should provide opportunities for members to discuss their identities. For example, the leader can ask, "How do our cultural backgrounds affect how assertive we are in our daily lives?" or "How can we use our differing ethnic backgrounds to brainstorm some innovative solutions to the problem we are discussing here?"

Level of acculturation and assimilation are also important factors to consider. The theory of assimilation views minority status as temporary with everyone living in the United States, regardless of ethnicity or race, gradually acquiring the cultural values of the mainstream culture. Although the assumption that everyone eventually assimilates is deeply rooted in U.S. society, it is clear that some minority groups continue to practice traditional, culturally bound norms for generations. Therefore, cultural pluralism theory may provide a better theoretical framework for culturally competent workers (Pillari, 2002). Cultural pluralism's main premise is that different ethnic and racial groups can interact in the larger society while maintaining their cultural distinctiveness and integrity (Parrillo, 2000). The cultural pluralism framework encourages workers and members to view differences in attitudes, norms, structures, and values positively as distinctive and defining elements of a person's identity.

It is often helpful for the worker to frame the discussion of differences in ways that help members to see the strengths in their backgrounds. Diversity should be viewed as an asset to the group. After reviewing the empirical evidence about the performance of homogeneous versus heterogeneous groups, Forsyth (1999) points out that "the value of diversity has been verified in a wide range of performance settings" (p. 279). McLeod, Lobel, and Cox (1996), for example, found that groups that included Asian Americans, African Americans, Latinos, and whites outperformed groups that included only whites. Similarly, Watson, Johnson, and Merritt (1998) found that diverse teams performed better than nondiverse teams. A heterogeneity of member characteristics is associated with a variety of perspectives, and a variety of perspectives is associated with high-quality idea production. It is important to keep in mind, however, that "diverse teams that actually utilized the variety of perspectives . . . outperformed the homogeneous teams, whereas diverse teams that did not utilize their diversity performed worse than the homogeneous teams" (McLeod et al., 1996, p. 261). Superior performance by groups utilizing the perspectives of a culturally and racially diverse membership clearly suggests that group leaders should promote diversity in group composition. The findings also suggest that workers should develop skills in helping members to understand and work with members with different perspectives and experiences.

Members may have a variety of self-identity issues that affect their participation in the group (Vasquez & Han, 1995). Some members may have clear self-identification with one race, ethnicity, or background or may identify with more than one. Others may have little knowledge about their racial, ethnic, or cultural heritage. It can be helpful if the leader provides members with opportunities to describe how they experience their cultural background and whether they experience any identity conflicts. The case example illustrates this point.

● CASE EXAMPLE *Cultural Sensitivity*

The group worker was concerned about a member's participation in a support group for women preparing to return to the workforce. The member often showed up for the meetings late and appeared tired. Although the worker suspected that the member was stressed by family responsibilities, she sensed there were other factors involved in her situation. During a group meeting, the leader asked members to discuss how their cultural backgrounds influenced their return to work. The member explained that her family duties posed considerable time constraints on her ability to look for work, and she was unsure how her family would react to her holding a full-time job. She explained that as a Latina, there were specific expectations placed on her by her cultural upbringing. These included putting her family first in all of her activities and adhering to specific role expectations about what women should do within and outside the home. The member's disclosure to the group of this aspect of her self-identity and the subsequent discussion facilitated by the worker helped other members to explore their own cultural identities and its impact on their job seeking behavior. The discussion also provided new insights for members about how their background and development affected their job readiness.

Self-identity issues are also important in group work with gay, lesbian, bisexual, and transgendered group members. Groups can provide an important support network and can be helpful in problem solving regarding issues of isolation, prejudice, stereotyping, and coming out. Groups can also be helpful in addressing interpersonal issues that arise with initiation and integration into gay organizations and communities. Getzel (1998); Peters (1997); and Walters, Longres, Han, and Icard (2003) present useful information for working with gay, lesbian, bisexual, and transgendered individuals in groups.

Although it is not possible for a group leader to know all the complexities of diverse cultures and backgrounds, it is helpful for leaders to become familiar with the backgrounds of client groups with whom they frequently work. Green (1999) suggests that knowledge can be gained through several methods. For example, the leader can research literature and other information to develop a personal knowledge base about people from different cultures. When working with a group composed of members from a particular culture, the leader can visit that cultural community, interview leaders and key informants, and become a participant observer.

The leader can also gain knowledge about a particular cultural community through the process of *social mapping,* in which formal and informal relationships among members of a community are systematically observed and analyzed. For example, a leader assigned to conduct an afterschool group that included several Hispanic members visited the local parish priest serving the Hispanic community and interviewed several members of the parish to gain a better understanding of the needs of young people in the community. In addition, the leader attended several social functions sponsored by the church and met with parents and other community members who provided the worker with new insights into the needs of Hispanic youth.

When a leader has little knowledge about a particular culture or background, it is helpful to become immersed in that culture. Living or spending a concentrated period of time in a cultural community can help the leader better understand the common values, norms of behavior, and worldviews held by members of that culture. Immersion also assists the leader in establishing credibility among members of the community, in developing relationships important for connecting members to resources outside the group, and in understanding the importance of natural helping networks.

Leaders should be open to the differences exhibited by diverse cultures. It is particularly important for leaders to be accepting and nonjudgmental about the values, lifestyles, beliefs, and behaviors of others and to recognize the value of difference and diversity (Diller, 1999). Leaders who suspend judgment can learn a great deal about other cultures simply by asking members to describe their own backgrounds. Members are in the best position to describe how they experience their own self-identity. By asking members, leaders express their interest in members and their desire to get to know them individually. Because members are in the best position to describe how they experience their self-identity, the leader can learn much about other cultures by asking members for information about their backgrounds.

It is also important to acknowledge the effect of societal attitudes on members of diverse groups. Leaders should keep in mind that members of minority groups continually experience prejudice, stereotyping, and overt and institutional discrimination. The reality of ethnic and racial superiority themes in our society, as well as classism, sexism, and the history of depriving certain groups of rights and resources, should all be considered when attempting to develop a perspective on diversity. This case example illustrates how one worker attempted to help a group discuss discrimination and to develop a perspective on diversity.

● **CASE EXAMPLE** *Discrimination and Diversity*

During an educational group for parents of children with developmental disabilities, the worker asked members to discuss the effects on themselves and their children of societal attitudes toward children with disabilities. Members were very willing to discuss examples of prejudice and incidents of discrimination. The worker used these discussions to help members share experiences about other forms of discrimination based on race, ethnicity, culture, and sexual orientation. These discussions helped the group understand the universality of such experiences in the group and the dynamics behind prejudice and discrimination. The worker used this discussion to help members confront stereotypes and challenge discrimination when they encountered it outside of the group. The worker also helped the group to examine the strengths in their backgrounds and how these negative experiences had helped them to grow strong and cope more effectively.

It can be helpful for leaders to honestly explore their prejudices, biases, and stereotypical assumptions in working with people from diverse backgrounds. Williams (1992) suggests leaders themselves may go through stages of ethnocultural development in which they experience cultural resistance and "color blindness" before acknowledging the importance of cultural influences and achieving cultural sensitivity. Leaders should acknowledge such thoughts and feelings and work on correcting them. Attending workshops on cultural sensitivity, doing self-inventories, researching one's own cultural heritage, attending specific cultural activities in the community, and joining cultural associations and organizations can help the leader achieve a fuller sense of cultural self-awareness. These activities can also help leaders gain a sense of their strengths and weaknesses in dealing with diversity. Mc-Grath and Axelson (1999) and Hogan-Garcia (1999), for example, describe many exercises that can be used to increase leaders' awareness, knowledge, and sensitivity when working with multicultural groups.

Assessing Cultural Influences on Group Behavior

It is important for the group leader to recognize that the cultural backgrounds of members can have a profound effect on how they participate in the group. Assessing the cultural influences on group behavior requires constant vigilance throughout the life of a group. Diversity among members from differing cultural backgrounds as well as among members from the same cultural background requires careful consideration. Stereotyping members on the basis of preconceived notions of cultural behavior is an ineffective approach. Members must be individualized and differentially assessed. As Chau (1992) suggests, cultural sensitivity in assessing members is a prerequisite for becoming an effective group leader. Some issues that should be considered when assessing cultural influences on group behavior are described below.

Factors to Consider When Assessing Cultural Influences on Group Behavior

- The match between member and leader backgrounds
- The influence of member backgrounds on group participation
- Members' views of the agency sponsoring the group
- The cultural sensitivity of outreach and recruiting efforts

- The formation of relationships among persons from diverse backgrounds
- The influence of the larger environmental context where members live on their behavior in the group
- Preferred patterns of behavior, values, and languages within the group
- Members' experiences with oppression and their feelings about themselves, their group identity, and the larger society

Early in the planning stage of a group, the benefits of matching member and leader backgrounds should be considered. There is some evidence that minority clients express a preference for ethnically similar workers (Atkinson & Lowe, 2001). However, there is little firm evidence that matching client and worker backgrounds leads to more effective treatment (Atkinson & Lowe, 1995; Proctor & Davis, 1994; Sexton & Whiston, 1994; Sue, Zane, & Young, 1994). Also, there are benefits to having persons with different backgrounds interact, and practical difficulties often limit supervisors' choices in matching leaders and members (Gruenfeld, 1998).

Regardless of whether matching is attempted, some differences in the backgrounds of members and between members and the leader are likely. Therefore, when one plans a group, it is important for the leader to consider how members' backgrounds are likely to affect their participation in it. For example, it is helpful to assess how potential members' differing cultural backgrounds and levels of acculturation and assimilation affect their understanding of the purpose of the group. Members with different backgrounds bring differing expectations and experiences and that can affect how they view the group's purposes and the way work is conducted in the group. Confusion about the purpose of the group can lead to members' frustration and anxiety in the group's early stages.

The leader should also consider how members' backgrounds are likely to interact with the sponsorship of the group. The worker should consider, for example, how the sponsoring agency is viewed by members from different backgrounds. It is also important to consider how accessible the agency is, both physically and psychologically, to potential members. As Davis, Galinsky, and Schopler (1995) note, ethnic and socioeconomic boundaries of neighborhoods may be difficult for members to cross. When the sponsoring agency is perceived as being in a neighborhood that does not welcome persons from differing cultures, the leader may need to reach out to members or deal with members' perceptions of institutional or neighborhood prejudice and discrimination before continuing with further planning efforts.

When recruiting members, the leader should consider how to optimize outreach efforts. For example, in certain ethnic neighborhoods, key community members such as clergy, political leaders, and neighborhood elders may play an important part in helping the worker to gain support for the group and to reach potential members.

When composing a diverse group, the worker should consider how members from differing cultural groups are likely to relate to each other and to the leader. The literature on group composition gives suggestions for composing a diverse group (Brown & Mistry, 1994, 1997; Davis, Galinsky, & Schopler, 1995; Davis, Strube, & Cheng, 1995; McLeod,

Lobel, & Cox, 1996; Mistry & Brown, 1997). Davis, Galinsky, and Schopler (1995) suggest that workers need to be sensitive to racial composition to overcome tension. In addition, they warn that marked imbalance among members with one type of characteristic can cause problems of subgrouping or domination by members of one particular background. When reviewing the strengths of same-sex or same-race groups, Brown and Mistry (1994) noted that same-sex groups have advantages when the group task is associated with issues of personal identity, social oppression, and empowerment or issues of personal and political change.

A complete assessment of group members should consider the larger environmental context in which members live and how that context can influence behavior within the group (Chau, 1992; Lum, 2000; Ramos, Jones, & Toseland, in press). Davis, Galinsky, and Schopler (1995) list several environmental factors that can be considered sources of tension among members from diverse backgrounds—the climate of society, events in the members' neighborhoods, and the sponsoring organization's reputation for responsiveness to racial concerns. In addition, the direct experience of racism, sexism, and other forms of oppression can have profound effects on members' behavior. Still, some commonalities are often present among members with similar backgrounds. This case example describes the impact of one type of experience on open communication and self-disclosure among a group of resettled refugees from Cambodia.

● **CASE EXAMPLE** *Communication and Self-Disclosure*

Despite his efforts to model the skills of open communication and self-disclosure, the leader of a group for resettled refugees from Cambodia often encountered members who were silent when discussions turned to conditions in their homeland. During these discussions, several members had difficulty talking about their experiences and seemed unable to confide in other members of the group. Through encouragement and honest interest, the worker helped several quiet members identify that they had been exposed to a variety of extreme conditions in their homeland, including torture, civil unrest, and government-sponsored violence. One member bravely told her story of watching members of a revolutionary group kill her parents. Her courage in disclosing this to the group helped other silent members to develop trust in the group and to gradually share their own stories. The worker learned how external oppression can profoundly influence communication and interaction within a group.

It is also wise to keep in mind that members bring preferred patterns of behavior, values, and language to the group (Axelson, 1999; Devore & Schlesinger, 1999). They also bring with them experiences with oppression and particular feelings about themselves, their group identity, and the larger society. When problems such as member dissatisfaction or conflict among members occur, the leader should keep in mind that the problems may be caused by cultural differences, not by an individual member's characteristics or flaws in group processes. For example, some members of a group became upset when two African American group members became animated when talking about oppression. The other members talked about their reactions to the anger expressed by these two members. The worker helped the group to discuss what it was like to live with racism and prejudice on a daily basis and the anger that this causes. She acknowledged the white members' difficulty in knowing how to react when this anger is expressed. The worker also helped the group to see that, in some ways, the group reflected difficult and unresolved issues in the community. The interaction that followed the worker's intervention helped all members to become more empathic and understanding, and increased group cohesion.

Several factors can interfere with the process of learning about how cultural background affects members' behavior in the group. The leader may fail to recognize that cultural differences exist or may diminish their importance. Facing difference is a difficult process, and leaders may think recognizing and expressing difference among members will cause conflict within the group. The leader may also fail to recognize differences among members of the same cultural group by assuming that all members of that culture have common behavioral characteristics and thereby overgeneralize and stereotype members with a common cultural heritage. Among Hispanic Americans, for example, there are wide differences in life experiences for people from a Mexican American background and people from Puerto Rico (Ramos, Toseland, Smith, & McCallion, in press). Similarly, there are differences between African Americans with ancestry from different regions of Africa and African Americans with ancestry from Jamaica, Puerto Rico, and South America. It should not be assumed that all members of a common heritage share all perceptions, abilities, and characteristics. It should also be noted that even if members share a common cultural background, major differences in economic status may influence how the members experience the group. Different patterns and degrees of acculturation and assimilation also have a profound impact on the way cultural heritages are expressed in a group (Berry, 1997; Brook, Gordon, & Meadow, 1998; Granrose, 1997). Information on how culture can influence group dynamics follows.

Cultural Influences on Group Dynamics

Communication and Interaction

- Language, symbols, and nonverbal communication patterns of persons from different cultural backgrounds
- Language sensitivity and knowledge of words appropriate to various cultural contexts
- Stylistic elements of communication among diverse groups
- Nonverbal communications and how cultural groups differ in their use of space and distance
- Interaction patterns specific to different cultural groups

Cohesion

- Subgroup patterns among various cultural groups
- Expectations and motivations among persons from diverse backgrounds
- Cultural characteristics that influence common group goals

Social Integration

- Culturally determined normative behavior
- Influence of culture on task and socioemotional role development in groups
- Influence of discrimination and oppression on how members experience power and control within the group

Group Culture

- Shared ideas, beliefs, and values held by members from diverse cultural backgrounds
- Level of group feeling expressed by members as influenced by cultural norms

The leader should assess how members' backgrounds are likely to affect the way they experience communication and interaction patterns, cohesion, social integration, and the overall group culture. To assess communication and interaction patterns, it is important for the leader to understand the language, symbols, and nonverbal communication patterns of people from different cultural backgrounds (Lum, 2000; Ramos, Jones, & Toseland, in press). For example, in leading her first group with Chinese American members, a worker learned that group members from this cultural background felt uncomfortable with some of the attending behaviors she had learned in her social work education. Through some gentle probing and consultation with persons from that community, she learned that her direct eye contact, forward body position, and open body position were intimidating and communicated a level of disrespect to some members.

D. W. Johnson (2003) suggests that assessing communication and interaction patterns requires language sensitivity and knowledge of words and expressions that are appropriate and inappropriate in communicating with diverse groups. The leader should also have an awareness of the stylistic elements of communication, including how members of diverse cultural backgrounds communicate. For example, because of their respect for the authority of the leader's status and position in the group, some Asian Americans rely heavily on the group leader, especially in the first few sessions. Some groups of Native Americans may consider it impolite to give opinions in the group, and such attitudes may be mislabeled as resistance by the leader or by non-Native American members.

The group leader should strive to become aware of the nuances of messages sent by members, including how nonverbal messages differ across various cultures (Ramos, Jones, & Toseland, in press). People from different backgrounds use body language, gestures, and expressions to accompany and define the meaning of the verbal messages they send. In addition, the leader should consider how cultural groups differ in their use of space, that is, whether distance or closeness is the norm, and what other nonverbal communication norms govern interaction in the culture. It is also helpful for leaders to learn the language of members from diverse cultures. Earnest attempts to learn even rudimentary language skills are often respected by group members, an important factor in developing a trusting, professional helping relationship with members.

The leader should be aware of differing interaction patterns used by members of diverse cultural groups. Members from some cultural backgrounds may favor a member-to-leader pattern of interaction; others may favor a member-to-member pattern that supports mutual aid among members in the group. In task groups, members from diverse groups may have differing views of status hierarchies, which can affect interaction patterns between members and the leader. This case example illustrates how culture can influence interaction in a group.

● CASE EXAMPLE *Culture and Group Interaction*

A committee in a community center in a Chinese American section of the city was charged with planning a fundraising event. The leader observed that the Chinese American members of the group hesitated to criticize the behavior of a member who was monopolizing the group. The leader, who was not Chinese American, asked a member after a group meeting about this behavior. The leader learned that the Chinese American members were hesitant to bring up their feelings because the monopolizing member was a person of advanced age and status in the community. According to Chinese American cultural heritage, interactions with older, high-status persons require respect. Criticism was not an acceptable behavior. The leader asked the member for advice about how to handle the situation, and it was suggested that using go-rounds and an agenda that designated other members to give reports could help to reduce the elderly member's dominance because he would then not feel that he had to fill voids or take the lead in loosely structured group discussions. This was tried successfully in subsequent meetings.

When the group has a membership drawn from many cultural groups, the leader should assess how subgrouping patterns may affect the group processes. Sociometric patterns can be influenced by cultural background, and this information is useful in assessing the behavior of members in the group and the behavior of the group as a whole. In a training group for college peer counselors, some members expressed their concerns about why most African American members sat together and communicated among themselves. The leader pointed out that cultural, racial, and ethnic groups often form informal subgroups on the basis of mutual interests and on common characteristics and experiences. The leader helped members to understand that members from minority groups on campus may also have needs for grouping as a protective, security-giving behavior. Through program activities and discussions, the leader helped all members of the group interact and become better acquainted.

Culturally sensitive workers consider the expectations and motivations that members from different cultural backgrounds bring to the group. For example, cohesion can be influenced by member expectations, which, in turn, can be influenced by the cultural background of members. In a support group for caregivers, some members with Hispanic backgrounds did not expect to divulge private family matters or publicly complain about their role as caregivers, and this affected how they bonded with other group members. If the cultural characteristics of members differ widely and are not explicitly taken into consideration, a climate of togetherness and a common sense of group goals can be difficult to achieve and the overall cohesion of the group is affected.

The leader should explore how members' cultural characteristics can affect their views of norms, roles, status, and power within the group. Group norms are often the result of the expectations that members bring to the group from previous experiences. The leader should assess how members' cultural backgrounds influence the norms that are developed in the group. For example, in many African American communities there is a strong belief in the power of spirituality and the "good" Christian life as antidotes to problems such as substance abuse, marital disharmony, difficulties in child rearing, depression, and alienation (Diller, 1999). Members' role expectations, developed within their particular cultural context, also often guide their behavior within the group. Gender-specific role expectations, for example, are prominent among certain ethnic groups. Thus, the leader should consider how members' culture influences their role expectations.

It is also important for the leader to be sensitive to how members from diverse backgrounds experience power and control within the group. Many members from minority groups have had direct experience with oppression, discrimination, and prejudice, which can affect how members feel about the use of power within the group. The leader should understand that these experiences are likely to influence how some members may deal with power and control. It is also imperative for the leader to ensure that patterns of discrimination are not repeated within the group.

The leader should assess how the cultural backgrounds of members contribute to the overall group culture. Shared ideas, beliefs, and values held by group members are, in part, a reflection of what experiences individual members bring to the group. The group culture can include, for example, a heightened sense of spirituality when the group is composed of Native Americans or Hispanic Americans. The strengths of some cultural backgrounds can reinforce other important aspects of group culture. For example, in a caregivers group composed of African Americans, the cultural strength of the extended family as a natural helping network can help create a group culture of networking and mutual aid among members.

The level of group feeling and group morale may also be a function of the cultural context of the group's members. In a group composed of Hispanic Americans, one might expect the expression of a higher level of group feelings and emotions than that in a group composed of Asian Americans because in the latter group, members may believe strong expressions of emotion outside the family are not appropriate (Gray-Little & Kaplan, 2000).

In addition to having an impact on group dynamics such as the culture of the group, it is important for workers to be aware that members' backgrounds can have a profound impact on group development and how leadership emerges in the group. Consider, for example, the impact of gender. Regarding group development, Schiller (1997) points out that affiliation and intimacy often appear earlier in women's groups and that conflict occurs later. Using Garland, Jones, and Kolodney's model of group development, Schiller (1995, 1997) proposes that the first and last stages of group development—preaffiliation and termination—remain the same, but that the three middle stages of group development—power and control, intimacy, and differentiation—would be conceptualized better as establishing a relational base, mutuality and interpersonal empathy, and challenge and change. Schiller (1997) goes on to describe the implications for practice of this alternative conceptualization of group development, which she refers to as the *relational model*.

Regarding leadership, Forsyth (1999) points out that women's leadership skills are often undervalued because they are viewed as socioemotional experts rather than as instrumental experts. Even though it is known that successful leadership depends on both expressive and instrumental skills, group members often overemphasize the instrumental side of leadership (Dodge, Gilroy, & Fenzel, 1995; Nye & Forsyth, 1991). Because of gender stereotypes and leadership prototypes, therefore, men are often viewed by both men and women as having more leadership potential, and men more often emerge as leaders of groups, even in groups that are composed largely of women (Forsyth, 1999). There is evidence, however, that by pointing out these dynamics in both task and treatment groups, workers can provide greater opportunities for women to take on leadership roles (Forsyth, 1999).

Intervening with Sensitivity to Diversity

There are many ways for a group leader to intervene with sensitivity to issues of diversity in the group. Many of these are based on established principles of social work practice. Others are culturally specific practices that can be especially helpful in culturally competent group work practice. Some of these methods follow.

Intervening with Sensitivity to Diversity

- Using social work values and skills
- Using a strengths perspective
- Exploring common and different experiences among members
- Exploring meanings and language
- Challenging prejudice and discrimination
- Advocating for members
- Empowering members
- Using culturally appropriate techniques and program activities

Using Social Work Values and Skills

Developing a culturally sensitive approach to group leadership means using social work values to guide interventions. The values of being nonjudgmental, genuine, and accepting can often compensate for wide differences in cultural backgrounds between the leader and members. Effective communication skills can also make a big difference. For example, good questioning skills, which stress open, nonjudgmental questions, can encourage members to respond in their own cultural styles. Similarly, the leader should be aware that for listening skills to be effective, the skills should be tailored to the cultural background of members. This is illustrated in the following case example.

● CASE EXAMPLE *Culture and Communication*

A leader in a group for substance abusers used active listening skills with a Native American member, often paraphrasing and summarizing the content of the member's statements. When the member's participation became less frequent, the leader wondered if the member was experiencing a relapse of his substance abuse. Despite these initial impressions, the leader learned from his supervisor that his paraphrasing and summarizing might be viewed as offensive by the Native American member. Recognizing that his leadership style might not be the most effective in this situation, he used passive listening skills that conveyed to the member that he was being heard and that his participation was being carefully considered. The member's participation in the group increased. The leader learned that depending on the cultural style of the member, the leader might use active listening skills for some members and passive listening skills for others.

Using a Strengths Perspective

The leader should explore and use the strengths inherent in the cultural backgrounds of members (Appleby, Colon, & Hamilton, 2001). All cultures have strengths, which can be tapped to empower members. A case example of a leader using a strengths-based approach with a group of older adults follows.

● **CASE EXAMPLE** *A Strengths-Based Approach*

In a group for adults who care for relatives with Alzheimer's disease, the leader discussed the strong natural helping networks of several African American members and how these networks supported the efforts of the caregivers. The African American members acknowledged that their networks were resources that they could use for respite care for their relatives. Other members learned about some of the strengths of the African American extended family and realized they could explore some of these arrangements for respite care and emotional support for their own situation. Thus, the understanding of strengths of African Americans greatly contributed to the overall success of the group.

In the same group, a woman of Latino background was criticized by another member for passively accepting the sole responsibility for caregiver in her family. The leader intervened, stressing that the role of caregiver was a culturally assigned one, usually given to a female in the household (Phillips, Torres de Ardon, Komnenich, Killeen, & Rusinak, 2000; Purdy & Arguello, 1992). The leader pointed out that commitment to the care of family members by Latinas was viewed as a core value in Latino culture. Such strong familism in taking care of frail older Latinos was viewed as a strength both within and outside the Latino community (Flores, 2000; Sanchez-Ayende, 1998). Other group members agreed with the leader's perspective. Because she felt her cultural heritage had been acknowledged positively, the woman became more active in the group.

In both task and treatment groups, it is important to point out how the group is strengthened by having members with diverse experiences and perspectives. Unfortunately, although ratings by external evaluations found no differences based on team composition, there is evidence that members of teams that are heterogeneous with regard to gender, racial, and other characteristics perceive themselves to be less effective than teams with homogeneous membership (Baugh & Graen, 1997). It can be helpful, therefore, for workers to emphasize to members the accumulating evidence supporting the notion that diverse perspectives lead to more effective problem solving in groups (Forsyth, 1999). The worker can then go on to encourage members to express diverse perspectives, and to help the group to consider fully and grapple with the implications of each perspective. The worker's ultimate aim is to frame alternative perspectives as benefitting all members by enhancing the information exchange in the group. This will, in turn, enhance the group's ability to accomplish individual member and group goals. For a detailed discussion of how to work with multicultural task groups, see Granrose and Oskamp (1997); and for a review of multicultural work with treatment groups see Brook, Gordon, and Meadow (1998) and Gray-Little and Kaplan (2000).

Exploring Common and Different Experiences among Members

In working with members from diverse backgrounds it is often useful to acknowledge the differences that exist in the group and to explore the experiences that members may have in common. This process can begin by acknowledging diversity in the group and exploring how the cultural backgrounds of members may contribute to that diversity. For example, in a support group for parents who have experienced the death of a child, the leader began by self-disclosing that she was of Irish American background. She explained that, in her family, death was characteristically dealt with by planning large family gatherings, which sometimes took on a festive atmosphere. She also acknowledged that it may be particularly difficult for Irish American men to verbally express their grief. The members used this opportunity to explore their own cultural reactions to death and grieving by noting how different cultures express their feelings about death. The worker's initial disclosure and modeling helped the group explore their differing views of death and grieving and deal with difficult issues held in common by the members.

Exploring common and different experiences can also help overcome barriers to members' self-disclosure. Members are sometimes reluctant to disclose when they believe others may be judgmental about their cultural values, behavior, and lifestyle. As described in the case study, exploring cultural differences and fostering cultural appreciation can help members feel more secure in disclosing their thoughts and feelings.

● **CASE EXAMPLE** *Exploring Cultural Differences*

In a support group for parents, it seemed particularly difficult for participants who came from a Chinese American background to share intimate details of their family life. The worker tried to model self disclosure and also encouraged other members to openly discuss difficult issues that they faced with their children. The developing norm of high self disclosure continued to be difficult for the Chinese American parents. After one meeting, the father met briefly with the worker and noted that in his culture, certain family matters were considered private, to be discussed only among close family members. The worker acknowledged this and promised to help members show sensitivity to this cultural difference during the meetings. The Chinese American family felt more comfortable after that and participated more frequently in some of the group's discussions.

The leader can also model the skill of empathy for members, which, in turn, can increase their responsiveness to differences. Helping members develop empathy allows them to comprehend more fully the experiences that result from diverse lifestyles.

Exploring Meanings and Language

Meaning is expressed through language. Many cultures do not attach common meanings to certain phenomena such as social problems or medical diseases (Dinges & Cherry, 1995). There may be no clear equivalent in the Spanish language, for example, for some psychiatric diagnoses. Likewise, an illness such as Alzheimer's disease may be defined in Spanish using nonmedical terms. The leader should help group members explore the differences in meaning reflected in different languages. Although some rudimentary knowledge of other languages is an asset, the leader should realize that language helps to shape reality. There are instances in which common terms and idiomatic expressions in English have no clear equivalent in another language. The leader should realize that members who speak English as a second language can define social situations, problems, and other conditions in culturally bound ways. It can be very helpful and interesting for all group members to discuss and explore culturally bound definitions, as the case example indicates.

● **CASE EXAMPLE** *The Impact of Language*

In a socialization group for new parents, one of the members had a mobility disability that required her to use a wheelchair. Although other members seemed to be sensitive to the needs of the member with the mobility disability, they used a variety of terms to refer to her during group discussions, including "the handicapped person" and "the disabled person." The leader asked the members to consider using a "person-first" formulation when referring to the member. She suggested that the member was a person with a disability, rather than a disabled or handicapped person. In group discussions, the leader noted that most persons with disabilities are offended when language suggests that they should be primarily defined by the nature of their disability rather than as people first, with all of the same strengths, capabilities, and potential as others. Members became more sensitive to the meanings inherent in language and how language can promote the strengths or weaknesses of people with disabilities.

The leader can help members interpret the significance of certain aspects of their culture to members of the group. In some instances, members may not understand the reasoning behind a cultural practice or phenomenon, which can lead to criticism or insensitivity among members. For example, in a rehabilitation group for spine-injured people, a member from Central America noted that he had visited the local *curandero,* who prescribed native herbs and other remedies. The initial reaction of several members was to discount this practice and accuse the member of going outside the traditional medical establishment. However, the leader and other members explained the importance of folk medicine and traditional healing in the member's culture and how the local healer contributed to the member's mental and physical well-being. Members learned the importance of this cultural practice and the significance of different sources of folk healing for some members (Koss-Chioino, 1995).

Similarly, spirituality may contribute significantly to the well-being of members of a group. It is important to acknowledge the importance of spirituality for particular members of a group and to explain the significance of different religious orientations. Group workers sometimes ignore spirituality because of the belief that it is linked to a specific religious denomination. It is important to take an ecumenical view and emphasize how spirituality transcends organized religion. The worker should avoid proselytizing about a particular religion but should acknowledge the importance of spirituality in the lives of some, if not all, the group members.

Challenging Prejudice and Discrimination

For members of diverse cultures, the realities of prejudice and discrimination can be heightened in a group. Challenging stereotypes and biases is an important leader skill. Some members may deny their individual biases, prejudices, or stereotypes, and it is important for the leader to challenge them to more realistically understand how they feel about people who are different from themselves. There is some evidence, for example, that suggests that psychoeducational group experiences can help members overcome stereotypes and biases (Rittner & Nakanishi, 1993).

Experience also suggests that task groups can help to overcome prejudice. Differences in cultural beliefs (Maznevski & Peterson, 1997; Diaz, 2002), attitudes towards interpersonal interactions (Goto, 1997), differences in attitudes and judgments about the self and others (Earley & Randel, 1997), and language differences (Orasanu, Fischer, & Davidson, 1997) can all be addressed in task groups. The following case example focuses on attitudes towards and judgments about group members based on age stereotypes.

● **CASE EXAMPLE** *Overcoming Prejudice*

In a coalition planning a homeless shelter, several younger members discounted or ignored the suggestions made by older members. This developed as a pattern over the course of the early meetings of the group. Noting this, the leader asked members to spend time giving attention to the group's processes, particularly asking that members discuss how differences in the group might inhibit the group's work. After discussing what she had observed in the group, the leader helped younger members confront their prejudices about the older members and the group became more cohesive and goal oriented.

It is important for the leader to help members understand the discrimination that members have experienced in the past. Almost all minority groups have experienced discrimination and attempts to undermine their power and sense of positive self-identity. Burwell (1998) notes that extermination, expulsion, exclusion, and assimilation have all been used against minority group members. On a more subtle level, society often ignores the views of minorities and marginalizes their contributions. Schriver (1998) suggests, for example, that minorities do not partake of the privileges often accorded to members of the majority group. Access to a privileged status results in unearned advantages accruing to a particular group because of race, gender, socioeconomic status, or some other characteristic. In the United States, for example, white males have a more privileged status than do African American males, which has profound consequences for both groups.

The leader can help members to understand the effects of privilege and discrimination by asking members to identify a situation in which they felt discriminated against and to discuss the experience with other group members. After this exercise, members are better able to appreciate each other's experiences in dealing with discrimination and the effect it has had on their views of themselves, others, and their life position.

Advocating for Members

Members from minority groups may need special assistance in negotiating difficult service systems. Also, they may need help obtaining benefits and services. In a parenting skills group, for example, the leader became concerned about the absence of several Native American members. In investigating the reasons for their absence, she noted that these group members felt guilty about leaving their child-care duties to attend group sessions. The leader secured the support of her agency in providing child care at the agency during group meetings. Because of her efforts, members attended more regularly and their commitment and bond to the parenting group was greatly enhanced. Similarly, Brown (1995) points out that group process considerations are necessary for creating groups that are accessible for members with disabilities.

Leaders may wish to consider engaging in other advocacy activities on behalf of group members such as working with family members and community support systems. For example, in a socialization group for the frail elderly, the leader experienced a good deal of absenteeism from members who nevertheless seemed to enjoy the group. It was discovered that for many members transportation depended on family or friends who were often busy. The leader used this information to advocate on members' behalf with the local Office for the Aging. Eventually, a senior van was assigned to provide transportation for group members. In another instance, a worker built a coalition of members from various gay, lesbian, and bisexual support groups to bring political pressure on city officials to pass adequate antidiscrimination legislation.

Advocating for group members, within and outside the group, is especially important for populations and groups who experience prejudice and discrimination. Persons who are diagnosed with AIDS, for example, often have difficulty obtaining housing, health care, social services, and other community-based services to which they are entitled. Leaders of groups for members experiencing high levels of discrimination should be prepared to spend time outside group sessions to help members gain access to needed services.

Empowering Members

Group intervention can help empower members by raising their cultural consciousness and by developing mutual aid within the group (Chau, 1992; Hopps & Pinderhughes, 1999). Personal, interpersonal, and political power can be fostered by constructive dialogue among all members and by discussions that foster cultural identity and consciousness (Gutierrez & Ortega, 1991; Hopps & Pinderhughes, 1999). The leader can help members obtain a sense of personal power and self-worth by reinforcing positive feelings about their identity and encouraging all members to interact with each other. All levels of system intervention, including larger systems such as institutions and communities, should be included in these efforts. The case example provides a brief illustration of how a social support group engaged larger systems.

● CASE EXAMPLE *Engaging the Community*

A social support group sponsored by Centro Civico decided to sponsor a "senior expo" featuring the contributions of Latino elderly to the local community. The senior expo included ethnic foods, arts and crafts, exhibitions, workshops, and volunteer opportunities. Two other important aspects of the senior expo were a voter registration drive and an opportunity for members of the community to discuss their concerns about public transportation and safety with city council members.

Using Culturally Appropriate Techniques and Program Activities

Culturally sensitive techniques and program activities value diversity within the group, acknowledge how members of minority groups have unique sets of experiences, and allow members to appreciate both minority and majority cultural contexts (Vasquez & Han, 1995). The use of culturally sensitive program activities and other intervention techniques helps members to develop mutual respect for each other. It has been noted, for example, that several curative factors at work in groups for women apply equally to members of other minority groups (Vasquez & Han, 1995). When members have ethnicity or some other characteristic in common, they often feel understood by each other and gain validation for a similar heritage and a similar experience. In addition, such groups help members have compassion for themselves, accept the reality of human frailty, and develop positive perceptions of others. Empowerment can also be a healing factor for members who have lacked power in their lives or who have been unable to act with power in their relationships.

Developing culturally sensitive intervention skills can be fostered by reviewing specialized formats reported in the literature for groups composed of members from specific cultures. Pearson (1991), for example, suggests that leadership skills need to reflect a more structured approach for some Asian and Asian American people. Adopting a traditional Western style, with less structure and reliance on members to take responsibility for group interactions, would cause discomfort for these types of members. In contrast, Rittenhouse (1997) suggests that feminist group work often encourages unstructured out-of-group contact, the minimization of the power distance between leader and member, and a focus on the societal and political factors that contribute to members' problems. Ramos, Toseland, Smith, and McCallion (in press) adapted a health education program for caregivers of frail elderly Latinos. They made provisions to include extended family in the intervention because caregiving among Latinos often involves extended family networks. They also considered cultural nuances regarding the concept of "time." Latinos tend to be present oriented and less concerned about trying to control the future, planning ahead, or being on time (Weaver and Wodarski, 1996). Thus, meeting days were kept flexible and revised during each group meeting and meetings started with a warm-up where members could reacquaint and accommodate members who came late. There was also an informal talk time after the formal end of each group session.

Other writers have also developed culturally sensitive formats for particular minority groups. For example, Mistry and Brown (1997) focus on practice with groupings composed of members from mixed racial backgrounds. Gutierrez and Ortega (1991) report the success of ethnic identity groups and consciousness-raising groups in empowering Latinos. Lopez (1991) suggests that structured activity groups in which members work together on tasks can be helpful for Latino youth. Ramos, Jones, and Toseland (in press) describe how a health education group program for caregivers of the frail elderly can be adapted for Latino caregivers. Lewis and Ford (1990) describe how group leaders can help African American group members use social networks by incorporating traditional strengths of African American families into group work practice. Ashby, Gilchrist, and Miramontez (1987) demonstrate how incorporating traditional Native American "talking circles" into group meetings can be effective in group work with Native American adolescents. Similarly, Kim, Omizo, and D'Andrea (1998) present evidence that culturally consonant group work using a Native Hawaiian healing method and a culturally indigenous form of communication had a more beneficial effect on Native American adolescents' self-esteem than did group work that did not use this approach. Overall, Chau (1992) suggests that group interventions should be directed at helping members enhance ethnic consciousness and pride, develop ethnic resource bases and sources of power, and develop leadership potential. Recently, Hopps and Pinderhughes (1999) have developed a model for working with poor and oppressed populations from various racial and ethnic backgrounds, and textbooks by Appleby, Colon, and Hamilton (2001) and Lum (2003) contain chapters focused on work with Latino, African American, Asian, and other racial/ethnic groups. The following case example provides a brief illustration of how one agency adapted treatment services for Native Americans.

● CASE EXAMPLE *Culturally Sensitive Treatment Services*

Despite many years of working with persons who experienced alcohol and substance abuse, a substance abuse treatment agency recognized that it was less effective when working with persons from Native American backgrounds than with persons from other backgrounds. The executive director of the agency contacted a Native American social worker who had experience in leading a culturally oriented group experience called "The Red Road." This program employed an intensive three-day experience for participants using many aspects of Native American traditions and spirituality, including traditional talking circles, prayers and discussions, traditional drumming and music, and other spiritual aspects such as smudging, pipe ceremonies, and participating in a sweat lodge. In addition, members were able to discuss their people's history of oppression and discrimination, including U.S. social policy toward Native Americans and the effects of the boarding school experience and the reservation system on various Native American nations. This turned out to be a powerful experience for participants, and later qualitative evaluations supported the effectiveness of this culturally relevant treatment method.

Principles for Practice

The group leader has a dual responsibility with regard to diversity. The leader should differentiate among members and individualize each member's strengths but also universalize members' common human characteristics and goals. The leader should help to ensure cultural pluralism, that is, the right of persons from all cultures to adhere to their practices and worldviews. In addition, the leader should seek to promote harmony among members who are different from each other.

The research literature on working with persons from diverse backgrounds is characterized by suggestions for working with particular categories of persons. Group work practitioners can benefit from studying this body of knowledge and applying specific suggestions to their practice with particular groups of people. More broadly, however, the group leader should challenge the group to discover, acknowledge, and deal with its diversity. Often, members are the best source of teaching and learning about diversity. Although this should not be seen as the sole responsibility of members who are from different backgrounds, they can be invited to share their experiences.

To understand diversity and be sensitive to working with persons who come from different backgrounds, group workers should consider the following practice principles:

- Some form of diversity is always present in groups. Workers should acknowledge the diversity in the groups they lead and help members to explore the differences they bring to the group experience.

- Sensitivity to diversity is important for both leaders and members of groups. Leaders who engage in their own process of self-assessment and exploration of feelings about their own identity are in a better position to deliver culturally sensitive intervention than are those with less self-awareness.

- The process of becoming culturally sensitive is an ongoing obligation of all group leaders. Thus, it is important for leaders to continuously seek knowledge about how members define themselves and how their identities affect their participation in the group.

- Being culturally sensitive requires an open mind. Leaders should be nonjudgmental about the differences they encounter among group members and should welcome the richness and positive potential that diversity offers to the group as a whole.

- Persons from diverse backgrounds often have firsthand experience with prejudice, stereotyping, discrimination, and oppression. Leaders should understand and acknowledge the effects of these phenomena and help members to understand how such treatment can affect group participation.

- Diversity and difference can have a profound effect on how groups function. Leaders should recognize that the dynamics of groups vary because of differences in the identities and backgrounds of their members and should consider how diversity is likely to effect the development of groups.

- Member identity and background affects how members work toward their goals. A complete assessment—of group members, the group as a whole, and the group's environment—should consider the diverse characteristics of members and the cultural context in which they have developed.

- Differences in communication styles and language affect the members' overall ability to communicate. Leaders should monitor effects that language and communication have on the conduct of the group and attempt to understand how members from differing cultural groups communicate.

- On the basis of their experiences with environments outside the group, certain members may lack power and may be denied access to society's resources. Empowering members on both an individual and a communitywide basis by using empathy, individualization, support, and advocacy is an important group work skill.

- Persons from differing backgrounds are sustained by their cultural and spiritual traditions. It is important for leaders to acknowledge this and attempt to understand the place of spirituality as well as traditional concepts surrounding illness and healing and should use these factors as much as possible.

- Members who stereotype each other or discriminate against each other should be challenged to confront their biases, prejudices, and stereotypes. These behaviors should not be allowed to continue within the group.

- There are a variety of specialized cultural formats appropriate for use in groups. It is helpful for leaders to develop a repertoire of intervention techniques and program activities relevant to particular cultural groups with whom they are likely to work.

SUMMARY

This chapter focuses on leading task and treatment groups with members from diverse backgrounds. It is important for the group leader to develop a perspective from which to work effectively with members from differing backgrounds. The group leader should develop cultural sensitivity through a process of self-exploration. The leader can also benefit from exploring the identity of others and by gaining knowledge about differing cultural and ethnic groups. An important prerequisite to these activities is openness to differences exhibited by diverse cultures. In planning and composing groups, the leader should consider how persons of differing backgrounds will experience the group and how the group will be affected by their membership. The cultural backgrounds of members can have a profound effect on how members participate in the group. A complete assessment of the group and its members should consider the larger environmental context in which members live and how that context can influence group dynamics.

This chapter also discusses how leaders can intervene with sensitivity to diversity. Suggestions developed in this regard include using social work values and skills, emphasizing a strengths perspective, exploring common and different experiences among members, exploring meanings and language, challenging prejudice and discrimination, advocating for members, empowering members, and using culturally appropriate techniques and program activities. The chapter ends with a description of practice principles to assist leaders working with diverse groups of people.

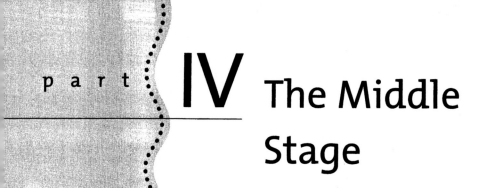

part IV The Middle Stage

chapter 11

Task Groups: Foundation Methods

Task Groups: Foundation Methods

This chapter focuses on the foundation skills, procedures, and methods used in task groups during their middle stage. After a brief discussion of the importance of task groups in social service and health agencies, the first section of the chapter describes nine activities that workers commonly engage in during the middle stage of task group development.

The second section of this chapter describes a six-step model for effective problem solving in groups. The model includes a discussion of the practice skills workers use during each step of the process.

THE UBIQUITOUS TASK GROUP

It has been said that U.S. citizens are involved in committees and other task groups more than any other people (Tropman, 1996). Participation in the decisions that affect their lives is characteristic of a democratic society. Every day millions of meetings take place throughout the United States. Social service agencies could not function without committees, treatment conferences, teams, boards, and other work groups.

Social workers and other helping professionals are often called on to chair committees, teams, and other task groups. For example, social workers are frequently designated team leaders in interdisciplinary health-care settings because social work functions include coordination, case management, and concern for the bio-psychosocial-cultural functioning of the whole person. Workers also are asked to staff task groups (Tropman, 1996). In general, the staff person plays a supportive role in helping the group clarify its goals and carry out its work. Acting under the direction of the task group's leader, the staff person reports directly to the group. The duties and roles of a staff person are quite varied and can include serving as a resource person, consultant, enabler, analyst, implementer, tactician, catalyst, and technical adviser. Despite the importance and widespread use of task groups in social service agencies, with a few notable exceptions (Brill, 1976; Ephross & Vassil, in press;

Fatout & Rose, 1995; Toseland & Ephross, 1987; Tropman, 1996), the human services have paid little attention to how task groups work.

Although task groups can be useful, they can be a source of frustration for their participants when they function ineffectively. For example, Napier and Gershenfeld (1993) describe the "incredible meeting trap" in which little is accomplished and members leave feeling frustrated by the group process. Similarly, Edson (1977) suggests that committee meetings are often dominated by "narrowminded, pigheaded, sly, opinionated, bigoted manipulators" (p. 224). Edson's comments are strongly stated, but they make the important point that many workers are dissatisfied with task group meetings and indifferent to or suspicious about their outcomes. Meetings that are not well run are boring and unsatisfying. They suffer from a lack of participation and corrective feedback from members, who lose interest.

Although task group meetings are often seen as a chore to be endured by members for the good of the organization,[1] well-run meetings can be a positive experience. They help draw people together by creating effective teamwork in which ideas are shared, feelings are expressed, and support is developed for group members and for the decisions made by the group. There are few experiences in the workplace to equal the sense of cohesion, commitment, and satisfaction that members feel when their ideas have been heard, appreciated, and used in resolving a difficult issue and arriving at a decision. The next sections of this chapter describe methods that can help workers lead task groups effectively.

LEADING TASK GROUPS

Although workers perform many similar activities in task and treatment groups during the middle stage, there is a greater emphasis on certain activities because of the differing foci of task and treatment groups. Task groups, for example, are more concerned than are treatment groups with creating new ideas, developing plans and programs, solving problems that are external to the group, and making decisions about the organizational environment.

To lead task groups effectively during their middle stage, it is important to stay focused on the purposes and functions that the group is expected to accomplish. In his classic text on leading task groups, Maier (1963) suggests that the primary purposes of task groups are problem solving and decision making. He goes on to describe methods designed to increase task groups' problem-solving and decision-making abilities.

Although problem solving and decision making are important, several other functions of task groups have been identified in the literature (Napier & Gershenfeld, 1993; Scheidel & Crowell, 1979). Sometimes task groups perform only one function, but usually they attempt to perform several functions simultaneously. These functions may include keeping members informed and involved, empowering members, and monitoring and supervising their performance. For example, in a community agency serving homebound older people,

---

[1]See the film *Meeting in Progress,* Round Table Films, 113 N. San Vincente Blvd., Beverly Hills, CA 90211, for a vivid example of task group members who are ready to end a meeting as soon as a decision is reached.

paraprofessional outreach workers might meet weekly with their supervisor to discuss common problems in obtaining psychological, social, and medical services for their clients. Because workers spend so much time away from the office, a secondary objective of the group might be to help workers identify with the organization for which they work. To accomplish primary and secondary objectives during the middle stage of task groups, workers are called on to help with a variety of activities including the following:

- Preparing for group meetings
- Sharing information, thoughts, and feelings about concerns and issues facing the group
- Involving members and helping them feel committed to the group and the agency in which they work
- Facilitating fact finding about issues and concerns facing the group
- Dealing with conflict
- Making effective decisions
- Understanding the political ramifications of the group
- Monitoring and evaluating the work of the group
- Problem solving

Preparing for Group Meetings

During Meetings

At the beginning of a meeting, the worker is responsible for several tasks. The worker begins by introducing new members and distributing handouts not included with the material distributed before the meeting. Before working on agenda items, the worker should make a brief opening statement about the purpose of the meeting. In this statement, the worker may want to call members' attention to previous meetings and to the mandate of the group as a way to indicate that the meeting will undertake a necessary and important function. Making members aware of the salience of the agenda items to be considered is important for maintaining members' interest and willingness to work during the meeting.

The worker should seek members' approval of written minutes that were distributed before the meeting and request that members raise any questions, changes, or amendments they would like to enter into the minutes. After the minutes are approved, the worker should make announcements and call on group members to make designated reports. Reports should be brief and to the point. Members should verbally summarize written reports that have been circulated with the agenda rather than reading them verbatim because reading lengthy reports can be boring and result in loss of interest and attention of other members.

During the middle portion of the meeting, the worker's task is to help the group follow its agenda. Whatever the purpose of a specific meeting, the middle portion is the time when the group accomplishes much of its most difficult work. To avoid getting stuck on one item of business in meetings that have extensive agendas, details of particular items should be worked out before the meeting. If this is not possible, Tropman (1996) suggests that the group should agree "in principle" on overall objectives and goals about a particular task and then charge a subcommittee or an individual group member with working out the details and bringing them back to the group later.

The worker should model the behavior that is expected of all members. A worker who shows respect, interest, integrity, and responsibility will convey these feelings to members. By encouraging equitable participation, the expression of minority-group opinions, and an appreciation of all sincere contributions to the group's work, the worker sets a positive example for group members to follow.

Jay (1977) suggests that the worker should act more as a servant of the interests of the group as a whole than as a master who imposes his or her will on the group. According to Jay, the worker's self-indulgence is the "greatest single barrier to the success of a meeting" (p. 263). By demonstrating that the good of the group as a whole is foremost when conducting the group's business, the worker gains the respect of members. Authority, control, and discipline should be used only to reduce threats to the group's effective functioning, not to impose the worker's wishes on the group. As members perceive that the worker is committed to accomplishing the group's common objective, the worker will gain the cooperation and the admiration of group members.

The worker should ensure that the pace of the meeting leaves enough time to accomplish the items specified in the agenda. Workers should not rush through important decisions because they are pressed for time at the end of a meeting. Members also become frustrated when they are expected to present or discuss ideas but have no time to do so because the group has spent too much time on earlier agenda items. Part of the responsibility of an effective worker in preparing for a meeting is making sure that the number of agenda items is manageable. Items sometimes take longer to discuss than anticipated, so it is good practice to plan extra time into an agenda. When too many agenda items are submitted for a meeting, the worker should rank the items for importance. Items that are assigned a low priority should be postponed to a later meeting.

Before adjourning, the worker should carry out several actions. These are summarized in the following list.

Ending a Session

- Summarize the meeting's accomplishments
- Praise members for their efforts
- Identify issues and agenda items that need further attention
- Mention where the meeting has placed the group in terms of its overall schedule
- Mention major topics for the next group meeting
- Summarize as clearly as possible the tasks that members agreed to accomplish before the next meeting

These strategies help to clarify responsibilities, reduce confusion, and increase the probability that members will complete assignments that were agreed to during earlier portions of the group's discussion.

Between Meetings

Two major tasks to accomplish between meetings are (1) seeing that decisions and tasks decided on at the previous meetings are carried out, and (2) preparing for the next meeting. The worker can do the first task by reading the minutes of previous meetings. Properly kept minutes include summaries of actions taken, tasks that were assigned, and the time frame for reporting back to the group. It is also helpful for the worker to make brief notes during a meeting or soon after the meeting ends about any decisions made that need to be followed up before the next meeting.

In seeing that the decisions agreed on by the group are carried out between meetings, Tropman (1996) suggests that a worker ensure that members work on and complete reports and other assignments that are necessary for the next group meeting. This does not mean that the worker takes over these tasks, but rather encourages and facilitates the progress of members assigned to carry out particular tasks. For example, the worker might meet with subcommittees of the larger group to provide information or guidance as they carry out their functions.

Between meetings, the worker should also develop and maintain close contacts with administrative staff, governing bodies, and other constituencies that may be affected by the group's work. As spokesperson for the group, the worker should keep in mind that he or she represents the group's public image. A worker should express the officially accepted opinions of the committee, not personal views. The worker should not enter into private agreements or commit to decisions or positions that have not been discussed and accepted by the group. In all but emergency situations, the worker should convene the group and consult with it before making decisions. The only exception is when the group, the agency, or a regulatory body has empowered the worker to act independently without first consulting with the group.

The second major task of the worker between meetings is to prepare for the next group meeting. When there is a written agenda for each meeting, the worker or the member designated as the group's secretary should send a memo to each group member soon after a meeting to request agenda items well ahead of the next meeting. This process allows enough time for the agenda and background or position papers to be completed and sent to members so they can be read before the next meeting. Meeting agendas should be established to facilitate discussion. One effective framework is illustrated in the following meeting agenda outline.

Meeting Agenda Outline

- Examine and approve (with any corrections) brief, relevant minutes from the last meeting
- Make information announcements

- Vote to include special agenda items
- Work on less controversial, easier items
- Work on difficult items
- Break
- Work on "for discussion only" items
- Consider any special agenda items if there is sufficient time
- Summarize
- Adjourn

In preparing for the next meeting, the worker should also organize opening remarks and administrative summaries to be presented. Special care should be taken in preparing for meetings that do not have a written agenda. In such instances, the worker should be clear about how to direct the meeting, what tasks the group will work on, and what goals are to be achieved.

Part of the worker's responsibility in preparing for a meeting is assessing the group's functioning. Questions such as "What is the group's relationship with its outside environment?" "Has the group been functioning smoothly?" "What norms, roles, and interaction patterns have developed in the group?" can stimulate the worker to consider how best to prepare for the next meeting.

In many task groups, the worker acts as both the leader and staff person. However, if a separate staff person is available to a task group, that person can prepare background reports and memos that analyze the group's options, develop resources, set up the meeting arrangements, and attend to other group needs.

Sharing Information

Another important activity of the leader during the middle stage is to help members share information, thoughts, and feelings with one another. For example, medical social workers from different community hospitals organize into an informal support group. Once each month, the leader and the group meet to share information about their work and new techniques for working with people in medical settings.

Teams, committees, delegate councils, and boards use group meetings as a means for members to share their concerns, their experiences, their perspectives, and their expertise. This is an important activity because, as a result of highly differentiated work roles, contact among workers in many agencies is infrequent. Job assignments such as individual treatment sessions and home visits limit opportunities for communication among workers.

Social issues and problems often affect several agencies, and task groups can bring workers from different agencies together. A group meeting is a convenient way for them to share unique viewpoints and differing perspectives on issues, problems, or concerns they face in their own agencies. By providing a forum for sharing knowledge and resources, interagency task groups encourage cooperative and coordinated problem solving.

Open communication and unimpeded sharing of information are prerequisites for task groups to accomplish their objectives. Vinokur-Kaplan (1995) suggests that effective communication within the group and between the group and the organization are key elements of effective teamwork. Empirical findings regarding group productivity and group process confirm that how information is communicated and used in a group has an important effect on the quality and the quantity of a group's productivity (Forsyth, 1999).

The first step in aiding effective communication and sharing information is to ensure that all members have a clear understanding of the topic being discussed and the task facing the group. To stimulate all members' participation in the discussion, the topic must be relevant. If members have little interest in the topic and no stake in the outcome, there is little reason for them to participate. In many groups, members become bored, disinterested, and dissatisfied because they do not understand the importance of a particular topic. The leader should help each member see the relevance and importance of issues as they are brought before the group. When it is clear that a discussion topic is relevant to only a few members of a task group, the worker should consider forming a subgroup to meet separately from the larger group and have the subgroup provide a brief report of its deliberations and recommendations at a later meeting of the entire group.

To focus interest, promote task-relevant discussions, and reduce confusion among members, it is often helpful to develop clear procedural steps such as the six-step, problem-solving model presented later in the chapter. Summarizing and focusing skills can also help the group remain on task. Summarizing can be used to check understanding, to review previously discussed subjects, to go back to items that were not fully discussed, to help separate a problem or issue into several parts, and to bring members' attention to a particularly important aspect of the discussion.

Focusing can be accomplished by suggesting that the group discuss one issue at a time, by pointing out that the group has digressed from the discussion topic, and by making task-relevant statements. Jay (1977) points out that effective workers often have self-imposed rules limiting their communications early in group meetings to allow members the maximum opportunity to participate in the discussion. Often, a few brief summaries and comments that focus the discussion are all that is needed early in the group's work.

Another method of establishing open communication channels and promoting information sharing among all group members is to ensure equitable participation in the group. According to Huber (1980), equitable participation "is the level of participation that is in keeping with the individual's information, knowledge, or other contribution to the group's effort" (p. 185).

The worker can help the group develop a standard of fairness in participation by encouraging the development of rules for participation. Members may agree to keep their comments brief, be attentive to the communication of others when they are speaking, and encourage silent members to participate. The worker can help members follow the rules that are established. This can be accomplished by inviting the participation of other members and asking for feedback about the proposal. The worker can also interrupt long monologues by asking members to summarize their comments briefly or suggesting that members give others a chance to reply.

In some cases it is helpful to structure the discussion by using a round robin procedure or the rules of parliamentary procedure. This is illustrated in the following case example.

● **CASE EXAMPLE** *The Round Robin Procedure*

In a round robin procedure, each group member is asked to present one idea or one piece of information. Going around the group, members take turns presenting one idea. This procedure is continued and each member takes as many turns as needed to share all their ideas with the group. Members who do not have additional ideas simply pass their turn. The round robin is completed when all members have shared all their ideas.

The round robin procedure has several advantages over unstructured, interactive communication procedures. All members have an equal opportunity to participate. Because only one idea is presented at a time, the procedure avoids the boredom that often results when one member enumerates several ideas one after another. By continuing to go around the group until all ideas are heard and by asking members to pass if they do not have any new information to present, a norm is established for sharing as many ideas as possible.

In large task groups, however, round robin procedures are often too time-consuming. Unless the group is divided into subgroups, the procedure is not useful. To facilitate equitable participation in large groups, the worker should consider using parliamentary procedures (Gulley, 1968; Maier, 1963; Scheidel & Crowell, 1979) following *The New Robert's Rules of Order* (Robert, 1983). These procedures, which have been developed over the past 600 years in meetings in business, industry, and political bodies in Britain and the United States, provide for orderly and structured participation in large group meetings.

Group workers should be aware that parliamentary procedures are subject to manipulation by members who are familiar with their complexities. By trading favors for votes before a meeting and calling for votes with few members present, parliamentary procedures can be used to subvert majority rule. Despite these disadvantages, *Robert's Rules of Order* can be helpful in ensuring equitable participation in large meetings. A brief description of parliamentary procedures is included in Chapter 12.

Enhancing Involvement and Commitment

A third important activity during the work stage of task groups is to help members feel that they are a vital part of their agency and the task groups that it sponsors. Because much of any organization's work is done by individuals, there is a danger that staff can become isolated and alienated from an organization. Task groups provide support for their members and a sense of belonging that reduces alienation. For example, a worker in an outreach program for the frail elderly spends much time working with the frail elders who comprise the caseload. Monthly team meetings with other outreach workers provide support and recognition for the worker who is faced with the difficult, often emotionally charged, task of working with frail older adults.

Helping members become involved through their participation in a task group benefits both the organization and its employees. Task groups provide an organized means of developing, implementing, and getting employees to follow policies, procedures, and goals of the agency. They allow employees an opportunity to influence the policies and procedures developed by the agency, which, in turn, helps to make the agency responsive to the needs of its workers. Task groups also help to organize, coordinate, and channel employees' input by clearly delineating how a task group fits into the overall structure of an agency—to whom the group reports and what authority and power the group has to develop or change agency policies. Employees' input can be organized and channeled appropriately.

Several steps can be taken to help task group members feel their input is vital to the agency's sound functioning. First, workers should help members understand the importance of the group's work, its relationship to the agency's purpose, and how the group fits into the agency's administrative structure. This can be accomplished by clearly stating the group's purpose, using flow charts to explain how the group fits into the agency's administrative and decision-making structure, and clarifying the duties, responsibilities, authority, and power that result from membership in the group. Members find this information helpful as they prepare reports and make recommendations or decisions that affect the organization and its consumers.

Second, workers should assign members specific roles in the group. Roles that encourage members to depend on one another for task accomplishment and roles that place them in the position of representing the group to a larger constituency help members feel that they are part of a collective effort that is of vital importance to effective agency functioning.

A third method of enhancing members' involvement and commitment is to invite their input into the agenda and the decision-making processes of the group. This can be done by encouraging members to develop and submit agenda items for future group meetings. Circulating the agenda and any background papers before a meeting can help members prepare their thoughts and concerns before a meeting and increase the chances that they will participate by sharing their views during the meeting. It has been shown that the greater a member's effort and sacrifice in preparing for and working on a task, the more likely the member is to stay involved and committed to the group (Kiesler, 1978). Therefore, asking members to prepare for a meeting by reading background papers, collecting information, and submitting agenda items tends to increase involvement and commitment to the group and the larger organization.

A fourth method of helping members become involved is to encourage them to participate in the decision-making process to the extent possible (Forsyth, 1999). Shared decision making has been found to increase motivation, increase acceptance and understanding of decisions, increase the information available for decision making, and help in processing complex information (Forsyth, 1999).

Although some writers suggest that decision making should always be shared among members (Bradford, 1976), there are some potential disadvantages to giving members decision-making authority. According to Huber (1980), the disadvantages are (1) the great amount of personnel time spent in group decision making, (2) the tendency for groups to produce decisions that are not acceptable to management, (3) expectations that future decisions will also be made through group participation, (4) the tendency for groups to take longer than individuals to reach decisions, and (5) the possibility that group decision making could cause conflict among group members who may have to work together every day. Thus, the decision to delegate decision making to groups should be made only after carefully considering both its advantages and disadvantages in a particular situation. When the advantages of group decision making are questionable, it is often possible to have the group make recommendations but leave the final decision to one person.

Developing Information

A fourth activity of the worker during the middle stage of task groups is to help members generate information and develop creative alternatives for responding to difficult issues and problems facing the group. Although task groups are often thought to be particularly effective for sharing information and developing creative ideas, the available evidence suggests that ordinary interactive group discussions inhibit rather than increase the disclosure of information, ideas, and creative solutions (Hare, Blumberg, Davies, & Kent, 1995).

There are many reasons that group processes may inhibit information sharing and the development of creative ideas.

Group Factors that Inhibit Ideas and Creativity

- Status-conscious group members feel intimidated by members with higher status. Lower-status members tend to share less information and avoid making suggestions that offend higher-status members.

- Norms and social pressures for conformity tend to limit the expression of new and creative ideas.

- Groups have the advantage of the variety of opinions and knowledge offered by all members, but group members may censor controversial opinions.

- Covert judgments are often made but not expressed openly in groups. Members, therefore, become concerned about the effects their self-disclosures will have on future interactions with group members.

- Interacting groups tend to reach premature solutions without considering all available evidence.

The worker can help in several ways to improve group members' opportunities to present new ideas, combine information, and generate creative solutions in interactive groups. First, the worker must clearly indicate to all members that their input is welcome, which means that the worker must be able to address the members' concerns about sanctions that may result from expressing sensitive or controversial ideas in the group. If the worker cannot guarantee freedom from sanctions, he or she should try to be as clear as possible about the boundaries of the discussion. For example, it might be possible for committee members to discuss new policies regarding service delivery, but it might not be acceptable for them to criticize existing supervisory staff who have to follow current policy guidelines. When sanctions are possible from individuals outside the group, the worker can encourage the group to consider keeping their discussions confidential. If lower-status members fear reprisals from higher-status members, the worker can discuss the use of sanctions with higher-status members before the group meeting and gain their cooperation in refraining from applying them. The worker can also suggest that higher-status and lower-status members discuss this issue in the group.

Feedback can both help and hinder the group's development of information and creative solutions. It is commonly thought that all feedback is useful because it helps group members detect and correct errors in information processing, but this is not true in all circumstances. In the early phase of developing information and forming creative solutions, evaluative feedback can have the effect of suppressing further suggestions (Forsyth, 1999). Members fear their ideas may be evaluated negatively and that this will reflect on their competence and their status in the organization. Under these circumstances, few members risk making suggestions, giving opinions, or volunteering information that will not be readily accepted. To encourage free discussion, creative ideas, and new insights about a problem or issue, the worker should ask members to refrain from evaluating ideas early in the group's discussion.

Several other steps can also be taken to help the group develop information and creative ideas to solve a problem.

Developing Information and Creative Ideas

- Encourage the group to develop norms that promote free discussion of ideas
- Point out group pressures that inhibit members' free discussion
- Model an open exchange of ideas by presenting creative, controversial, and thought-provoking ideas
- Encourage members to continue to share unique ideas by praising those who present innovative suggestions
- Encourage lower-status members, who often find it difficult to present their ideas, to share their ideas as early as possible in the group's discussion
- Help the group separate information and idea-generating steps from decision-making steps

When these suggestions are implemented, interacting groups can develop more creative solutions than they would under ordinary conditions.

Dealing with Conflict

It is unlikely that all members of a task group will immediately agree on all aspects of the work of the group. Thus, it is important for workers to realize that conflicts occur even in effective task groups (Forsyth, 1999; Napier & Gershenfeld, 1993). Conflict often emerges at the end of the beginning stage or beginning of the work stage of the group. Earlier in the life of a group, members are just getting to know one another and are less likely to express conflicting viewpoints.

Although some view all conflict as a problem that should be prevented or resolved (Smith & Berg, 1997), most theoreticians and practitioners now make a distinction between what has been called instrumental, substantive, or task conflict and what has been called affective, social, process, or relationship conflict (Guetzkow and Gyr, 1954; Wittman, 1991; Jehn & Chatman, 2000). *Task conflict* is based on members' differing opinions about ideas, information, and facts presented during the task group's work. This type of conflict is often helpful to the development of the group because it stimulates healthy dialogue, the development of solutions that encompass different points of view, and the careful analysis of proposed solutions.

Relationship conflict is based on the emotional and interpersonal relationships among members within and outside of the group. This type of conflict is rarely helpful to the development of the group. In general, relationship conflict is more difficult to resolve than task conflict because it is resistant to persuasive reasoning.

Certain personality characteristics have also been associated with productive and nonproductive conflict. For example, a win-win orientation is often associated with productive conflict, whereas zero-sum orientation is often associated with nonproductive conflict (Jehn & Chatman, 2000; Wall & Nolan, 1987). Similarly, rigidity is associated with conflict escalation, and flexibility is associated with the ability to change perceptions and to accommodate differing points of view (Wall & Nolan, 1987).

Timely intervention into group processes can often help to defuse conflicts. For example, the worker leading a treatment conference in a mental health center might notice that a subgroup of members is not participating as expected. The worker comments on this and discovers that subgroup members are quiet because they disagree with the opinions of a vocal, controlling member. The worker helps the subgroup and the individual member resolve their differences by pointing out the conflict and helping the members confront it. The worker also acts as a mediator to help the subgroup and the member negotiate differences.

Some workers have difficulty dealing with conflict. They avoid, ignore, or minimize it, hoping it will go away. These strategies are generally counterproductive. Avoiding conflict rarely leads to satisfying and meaningful dialogue about the issues facing the group. Most often, when conflicts are avoided, members get the message that they should not express their true feelings and that an honest sharing of information and opinions should be sacrificed so that the group can function "harmoniously." When conflicts are ignored, they sometimes smolder until a particular interaction or event causes them to intensify and erupt. At other times, conflicts subside, but one or more group members are left feeling they have lost the battle. Neither outcome is desirable.

How can the worker handle conflict in a productive and satisfying manner? Substantive and affective conflicts can be reduced by the following procedures.

Suggestions for Handling Conflict in the Group

- View conflict as a natural and helpful part of group development.
- Help members recognize the conflict.
- Encourage group norms of openness and respect for others' viewpoints.

- Encourage group members to suspend judgment until they have listened to the entire group discussion.
- Encourage members to view issues in new ways, to understand situations from other members' vantage points, and to be flexible in their own views of a situation.
- Help members avoid focusing on personality conflicts or personal differences. Instead, help members express the facts and preferences underlying their alternative viewpoints and opinions.
- Emphasize factors that promote consensus in the group discussion.
- Develop information and facts about the situation and seek expert judgments to help resolve conflicting information.
- Follow orderly, preplanned steps for considering alternatives and deciding on solutions.
- Use decision criteria that are mutually agreed on by group members.
- Clarify and summarize the discussion frequently so that all members have a similar understanding of what is being discussed and the decision criteria that will be used.
- Be sensitive to members' personal concerns and needs in developing solutions and arriving at a decision.
- Remain neutral in the conflict and ask questions that seek clarification whenever possible.

In the classic text *Getting to Yes,* Fisher, Ury, and Patton (1997) suggest that the worker should help members (1) separate the person from the issue or problem being addressed, (2) focus on interests or attributes of the problem rather than on members' positions on the issue, (3) generate a variety of possible options before deciding what to do, and (4) insist that the decision about how to proceed be based on some objective standard.

Probably the single most important step in dealing with conflicts in a group is to help members view disagreements as opportunities to gather information and to share views and opinions, rather than as personal attacks or as threats to authority or position. Cooperative processes involve recognizing the legitimacy of others' interests (Ephross & Vassil, in press). Thus, it is important for the leader to welcome differing viewpoints and to encourage the members to do the same. Also, it is helpful to (1) ask members to elaborate on the thinking that led to their viewpoints, (2) suggest that other members listen carefully and ask questions before they react, and (3) highlight points of consensus and mutual interest as they arise. Another step in dealing with conflict involves helping members to avoid turning conflicts into personal attacks. The worker should ask members to keep their comments focused on the issues rather than on members' personal characteristics and should encourage members to make "I" statements and to avoid "you" statements that attack other members or subscribe motives to their behavior. The worker should not react to outbursts and should not encourage members to defend their positions. Instead, the worker should help members in a conflict describe their interests, values, fears, and their goals or objectives. This is illustrated in the following case.

● **CASE EXAMPLE** *Handling Conflicts*

Consider the following two ways of handling a conflict. In the first version, a member of a committee defends his position opposing the development and implementation of a new program by saying, "I don't want my staff to take on this proposed new program because they are already overworked. We were asked just last month to take on more work. I just don't think it is fair to ask us again. What about Joe's department [referring to another member of the committee who is not present]? Why can't Joe and his staff handle this? Joe's not that busy!" In the second version, the member defends his position by using "I" statements. "My interests are in ensuring that the workers in my department don't get so overloaded with work that quality and morale goes down. I appreciate your faith in my department, but I fear that my already overworked staff will become overwhelmed. My objective is to ensure that the workers in my department don't get so burned out that they just throw up their hands and stop trying to do a quality job." The first type of response could be viewed as a personal attack on Joe, who is likely to learn about the member's comments and become angry. The second monologue using "I" statements avoids personalizing the issue. Notice that the second statement lends itself to further discussion and negotiation. For example, the leader might ask the member to describe the workload of his department and how it has changed over the past year. If the workload has increased and concerns about an overload are warranted, the leader might facilitate a discussion among group members about options for getting the work accomplished.

Another useful procedure for dealing with conflict is to help members look beyond their particular positions on an issue and to understand what others hope to accomplish. The worker should encourage members who are having a conflict to state their concerns and their priorities as concretely as possible, but discourage them from defending their positions. Instead, the worker can encourage members to ask questions of each other and to put themselves in each other's positions. The worker should point out shared interests and mutual gains. For example, the worker might point out that all department heads have a stake in ensuring that the members of one department do not become so overloaded that they cannot do a good job. The following case example points out how this can be accomplished.

● **CASE EXAMPLE** *Conflict Resolution*

In the committee where the member is worried about a work overload, the leader might say, "Jim, I understand your concern for your people. They have been working hard. We are all worried about it. Everyone here, and many others, have a stake in your group not getting bogged down, because without the programming your group is doing, none of the other groups could complete their assignments. Let's go around the group and see if we can get some suggestions and ideas about how we could get this new work accomplished without just expecting Joe's group to do it all. I will give you a minute or two to think about it, I will start with the first idea, and then we can go around the group starting with Tom to get everybody's ideas. Okay?"

The worker can help members to reach consensus by agreeing in principle to mutually acceptable goals. As many solutions as possible for achieving the goals should be generated. For example, the committee members might agree that Joe's group should not be asked to take on all the new work, and that the work should be divided up and given to several departments to complete, but first, the worker should ask members to express their preferences for particular options. If a single option is not preferred by all parties, the worker should negotiate a solution by combining options that include some gains and some sacrifices on the part of all parties to the conflict.

Making Effective Decisions

Facilitators of task groups are often called on to help members make effective decisions. For example, a board president helps the board of directors decide whether to expand their agency's geographical service area. A community organizer helps a neighborhood association decide whether to establish a neighborhood watch group to address the crime rate in the community. The leader of an executive council helps the group determine who will be promoted within the organization.

Although groups are often used to make decisions, evidence about their effectiveness is mixed. Groups are better than individuals at influencing opinions and obtaining commitments from members (Kelley & Thibaut, 1969; Lewin, 1948). Napier (1967) found that groups are better at integrating complex perceptual and intellectual tasks because members can rely on one another for assistance. However, for other types of problems, groups may not be any more effective than individuals, and sometimes may be less efficient than individuals working alone (Forsyth, 1999). In summarizing the literature that has compared the problem-solving activities of task groups with the activities of individuals, Hare and colleagues (1995) drew the following conclusions.

Problem Solving: Groups versus Individuals

- Groups are superior to individuals in solving manual problems such as puzzles, particularly when the problem can be subdivided so that each person can use personal expertise to work on a problem component. The superiority of groups has been less consistently documented when the task to be accomplished is of a more intellectual nature, such as a logic problem.

- Although groups are better than the average individual, they are not better than the best individual. Therefore, a group of novices may perform worse than one expert.

- Groups have the advantage of the variety of opinions and knowledge offered by the members, but group members may censor controversial opinions.

- Part of the superiority of group problem solving results from the pooling of individual judgments to converge on a group norm. For some problems, similar accuracy may be achieved by averaging the decisions of noninteracting individuals.

- When groups solve intellectual tasks, members' rational, information-processing orientation may be impeded by socioemotional concerns.

- Because task groups require members to deliberate until they reach a decision, the decisions made in task groups may be more costly than decisions made by one or more individuals working alone.

To improve group decision making, workers should help members avoid the phenomenon known as *group think,* which is mentioned in earlier chapters (Janis, 1972). Group think occurs when group contagion takes over and members fail to express their own thoughts and feelings. Instead, they go along with the predominant sentiment of the group. This phenomenon has been recognized for years. For example, more than 90 years ago, LeBon (1910) referred to *group mind,* a state in which members allow an emotion generated from their participation in a group to dominate their intellectual powers. Similarly, more than 80 years ago, Freud (1922) wrote about the power that the group has over an individual's ego. *Group think* continues to be an important topic in the literature (see, e.g., Flippen, 1999; Forsyth, 1999; Paulus, 1998; Turner & Pratkanis, 1998). For example, the concept of *group think* has been used to compare the coercive power and the malevolent authority of cults and gangs (Knox, 1999b). Recently, a videotape has also been made to illustrate group decision making and the processes which inhibit creativity and foster "group think" (Katten & Janis, 2000).

Before 1960, it was generally thought that problem-solving groups make more conservative decisions than do individuals. Experiments by Stoner (1968) and Ziller (1957), however, indicated that groups make riskier decisions than individuals. Stoner (1968) called this phenomenon the *risky shift.* As evidence began to accumulate, it became clear that the shift may be toward greater or lesser risk. Riskier decisions are made when a group's members approve of risk taking (Teger & Pruitt, 1967; Wallach & Wing, 1968), when persuasive information is presented (Ebbesen & Bowers, 1974), when the responsibility for the decision is shared among group members (Myers & Arenson, 1972; Zajonc, Wolosin, & Wolosin, 1972), or when the leader approves of a risky decision (Myers & Arenson, 1972). On the other hand, risk taking is discouraged in some groups, and members are rewarded for developing conservative solutions (Stoner, 1968).

Several steps can be taken to help members avoid group think and risky shifts. Norms and a group climate that encourages free and open discussion of ideas tend to discourage conformity and to decrease group think. Procedures that clarify how a group will use information and arrive at a decision also tend to reduce conformity. An example, shown in the following case, illustrates this point.

● CASE EXAMPLE *Avoiding "Group Think"*

In a family service agency, the personnel committee was charged with the hiring of a new clinical supervisor. Many applications were received for the position, and a cursory review suggested that many appeared to be well qualified. However, some of the members of the committee favored one particular applicant and other members started to agree, mentioning the skills of this person. The leader cautioned the group against deciding before giving all candidates careful consideration. In order to avoid deciding on one applicant before carefully considering all others, the leader of the personnel committee suggested that the group come up with a set of decision criteria that they could apply evenly to all candidates. The leader indicated that these decision criteria should include all the factors that the members of the committee felt were important for the new clinician to possess. The committee came up with criteria that included clinical and supervisory experience, ability to speak Spanish, and familiarity with the type of psychotropic medications typically used by clients of family service agencies.

To arrive at a final group decision, a procedure for choosing among alternatives is needed. Most groups make their final decisions using consensus, compromise, or majority rule. In certain situations, each procedure can result in quite different decisions. To avoid the suspicion that a particular decision-making procedure is being chosen to influence a decision about a particular issue, a method of choosing among alternatives should be agreed on as early as possible in a task group's deliberations.

Consensus is often considered the ideal way to select among alternatives because all group members commit themselves to the decision. When reviewing conditions for effective work with groups, Whitaker (1975) suggests that helping a group achieve consensus reduces conflict within the group and makes the group more effective. Consensus does not, however, necessarily imply agreement on the part of all group members. Napier and Gershenfeld (1993) point out that consensus requires that individuals be willing to go along with the group's predominant view and carry it out in good faith.

Although other decision-making procedures are quicker, reaching consensus often brings considerable support for a decision because members are more likely to cooperate in implementing decisions that they have thoroughly discussed and agreed on. Consensus is sometimes difficult to achieve in groups. It can be time-consuming and tension-provoking because each alternative must be discussed thoroughly along with dissenting viewpoints. Also, there is the danger that members will acquiesce and decision quality will be sacrificed to arrive at a solution that is acceptable to all group members (Napier & Gershenfeld, 1993). Nevertheless, reaching consensus rather than deciding by majority rule builds group cohesion and member satisfaction.

When issues are controversial and there is much dissenting opinion, it is often possible to reach consensus by modifying original proposals. To develop amendments to proposals that are acceptable to all group members, the discussion of each alternative should focus on the reasoning behind members' objections to the alternative. This process helps all group members identify the acceptable and unacceptable parts of each alternative. After a discussion of all the alternatives, the acceptable parts of several alternatives can often be combined into one solution that is acceptable to most, if not all, members.

Majority rule is a frequently used procedure to decide between alternatives in task groups because it is less time-consuming than consensus or compromise procedures, and when the vote is done by secret ballot, it protects the confidentiality of members. Majority rule is an excellent procedure for deciding routine and relatively minor questions. However, because a significant minority may not agree with the final outcome, majority rule is a less appealing procedure when the issue is important and when the support and cooperation of the entire group are needed for successful implementation. For important decisions, a two-thirds majority vote is an alternative to simple majority rule. A two-thirds majority vote ensures at least substantial support for a decision made by the group.

Understanding Task Groups' Political Ramifications

Although much of this chapter and the next are focused on problem solving and decision making, task groups also have political functions that are frequently overlooked or ignored by group workers because they are uncomfortable with the notion of behaving in a political fashion. Levinson and Klerman (1973) recognized this stance when they said the cultivation of power is viewed by many professions, including social work, "as vulgar, as a sign of character defect, as something an upstanding professional would not be interested in or stoop to engage in" (p. 66). Yet, politics are an important part of the dynamics that govern the functioning of task groups during the middle stage.

An essential step in becoming more aware of the political functions of task groups is to develop an orientation that views political behavior as an essential ingredient of all task groups. Gummer (1987) points out that rather than viewing political behavior as symptomatic of a character defect, it may be better viewed "as the quest of the mature personality for the resources needed to affect increasingly larger areas of one's world" (p. 36).

Gummer suggests that task groups should be analyzed and understood in terms of how they are used to exercise and enhance the power of the members who participate in them. Although the overt exercise of power is generally frowned on in our society, there are many symbolic ways that task groups help managers exercise their power and position within an organization. In a power-oriented analysis of task groups, Gummer (1987) focused on four elements: (1) the physical setting, (2) membership, (3) the agenda, and (4) procedural rules.

In regard to the physical setting, Gummer suggested considering the symbolic meaning of the meeting location. For example, is the meeting taking place in a neutral place, or in a place that is "owned" by the leader or a particular member? Is the meeting taking place in a symbolic setting such as an outreach office or a new building to symbolize the importance of the setting? Gummer also suggested analyzing the symbolism attached to how the meeting room is arranged. For example, does the setting promote work or comfort? Are chairs set up around a table with paper, pencils, overhead projectors, and other work-oriented aids? Or is the setting filled with couches, soft chairs, food, and other items that convey a relaxed, informal atmosphere?

Who is invited to participate in a meeting is also important from a political perspective. Participation in meetings is the organizational equivalent of enfranchisement. Gummer (1987) stated "whether an organization is run along autocratic, oligarchic, or democratic lines, whatever rights members are entitled to are accorded by their inclusion in certain organizational groups. Conversely, limits on one's organizational position are established by exclusion from certain groups" (p. 30).

Determining who can participate is an important source of power because it "organizes into attention" the interests and positions associated with the included individuals (Forester,

1981). For example, the character of a task group might be changed when consumers are included on advisory boards. Similarly, the substantive deliberations of a committee examining staffing ratios and workloads is likely to change when both nonprofessional and professional staff are included in the meetings.

Meeting agendas can also be used for political purposes. Bachrach and Baratz (1962) suggested that power can be exercised by confining the scope of decision making to relatively safe issues. The ordering of items on the agenda may also be used for political purposes. For example, the leader or certain members may take a long time to discuss several trivial issues at the beginning of a meeting as a way to leave little time to work on issues that they would rather not address. Similarly, how agenda items are presented often has political ramifications. Gummer (1987) suggests that politically oriented individuals who want certain items tabled, defeated, or changed encourage their proponents to present their issues in the broadest terms possible so that the specifics of the issue are not discussed, and thus the specifics become confused or obfuscated by a general discussion of the philosophical principles of the organization. Conversely, items that these members would like to see acted on and accepted by the group are presented as specifically and noncontroversially as possible.

Procedures governing how the group conducts its business can also be developed with political purposes in mind. In democratic organizations it is expected that, at a minimum, procedural rules should (1) provide task group members with sufficient time to deliberate the issues the group is charged to address and (2) provide for adequate representation of minority opinions. However, procedural rules can be manipulated by politically minded individuals. For example, important decisions may be deferred to the executive committee of a board rather than taken up during a full board meeting. Similarly, the membership of a nominating subcommittee or a finance subcommittee may be stacked to favor the wishes of the board chairperson or a certain subgroup of powerful members.

Monitoring and Evaluating

The worker is also often called on to help task groups to monitor and evaluate their efforts. Monitoring by the group leader should focus on both group processes and group outcomes. The leader monitors group processes to ensure that they are leading to a satisfying experience for group members while at the same time facilitating the group's work. The duel focus on members' satisfaction and goal accomplishment has long been identified as an effective means of working with task groups (Bales, 1954, 1955). It continues to be an important focus for the leadership of task groups in contemporary society.

Task groups may monitor and evaluate their own performance or be called on to monitor and evaluate other systems. For example, an outpatient mental health team may monitor and evaluate its own performance by reviewing recidivism data on all former clients at three-month, progress-review meetings (Vinokur-Kaplan, 1995).

Task groups may also monitor and evaluate the functioning of other entities. For example, boards of social service agencies are responsible for monitoring and evaluating the functioning of the entire agency. Because boards are ultimately responsible and legally liable for the proper conduct of social service agencies, monitoring and evaluating functions are a critical component of an effective board's work (Blackmon & Holland, 2000; Chait, Holland, & Taylor, 1993; Hughes, Lakey, & Bobowick, 2000; Wolf, 1990).

For effective monitoring and evaluation during the middle stage, task groups must be clear about their mandate from the agency and the ethical, moral, and legal obligations as expressed by regulatory agencies, professional societies, legislative bodies, and the larger society. Sometimes these items are clearly specified in the bylaws of the sponsoring organization. Often, however, it is the responsibility of the task group to develop a set of standards, rules, or guidelines that can be used to monitor and evaluate performance. An example presented in the following case illustrates this function of a board.

● **CASE EXAMPLE** *Development of an Institutional Research Review Board*

A large, private social service agency decided to encourage evaluations of several of its service programs. To ensure that the research would serve a useful purpose, protect the rights and the confidentiality of their clients, and meet state and federal rules and regulations, an institutional research review board was formed. The first meeting of this group focused on reviewing the procedures of similar review boards at other agencies and examining state and federal regulations. The group then prepared guidelines governing its own operation and guidelines for researchers to use when preparing proposals to be reviewed by the board. The guidelines were, in turn, modified and ratified by the executive staff and the board of the social service agency.

To fulfill their monitoring and evaluating functions adequately, task groups develop feedback mechanisms to help them obtain information about the results of a decision and take corrective actions when necessary (Nadler, 1979). The type of feedback useful to a task group depends greatly on the group's mandate and the monitoring and evaluating required in the particular situation. A board, for example, may require periodic reports from the agency director, the director of clinical services, the agency executive, and the coordinator of volunteer services. In addition, the board may review program statistics, quarterly financial statements from a certified accountant, and reports from funding sources about the performance of the agency. In other cases, a task group may use formal data-gathering procedures to perform its monitoring and evaluation functions. A discussion of these methods is presented in Chapter 13.

Problem Solving

Problem solving has been given more consideration in the group work literature than any other function of task groups. Task groups spend much time performing other functions, but problem solving is often seen as a task group's major function. The next section describes a generic, six-step, problem-solving model that can be used effectively in a variety of task groups.

A MODEL FOR EFFECTIVE PROBLEM SOLVING

The effectiveness of problem-solving efforts depends on the extent to which an optimal solution is developed and implemented. Effective problem solving involves six steps:

1. Identifying a problem
2. Developing goals
3. Collecting data
4. Developing plans
5. Selecting the best plan
6. Implementing the plan

As shown in Figure 11.1, the steps are not discrete. In practice, they tend to overlap. For example, preliminary goals are often discussed during problem identification, and goals are modified and refined as data collection continues.

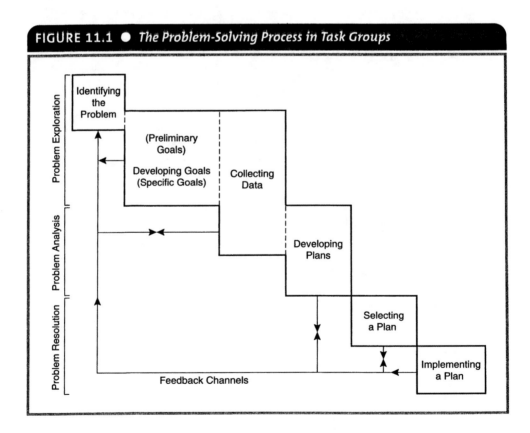

FIGURE 11.1 ● *The Problem-Solving Process in Task Groups*

Problem-solving processes are used repeatedly by groups as they conduct their business. A task group may have to use two or more cycles of a problem-solving process to accomplish a single task. The process is represented in Figure 11.2.

● **CASE EXAMPLE** *Problem Solving*

An adult protective services team spends three meetings developing a plan for emergency evening coverage for all clients on team members' caseloads. The plan is then implemented for three months on a trial basis. After the trial period, the team may reconsider aspects of the plan. Using the problem-solving process a second time, the team decides on a modified version of the plan that includes greater cooperation with police and emergency health and mental health providers in the county.

Identifying a Problem

How a problem is identified and defined is crucial to effective problem solving. It affects what data will be collected, who will work on the problem, what alternatives will be considered, and who will be affected by the problem's resolution. When they are first identified, problems are often unclear and muddled. For example, the staff of a social service agency perceives a problem in serving a large group of Mexican Americans who live in the area. The problem could be defined in several ways, including (1) not having Spanish-speaking workers, (2) not conducting any outreach efforts to this population, (3) having a poor public image with Mexican Americans in the community, (4) not having the financial resources to develop programs, and (5) providing the wrong services to meet the needs of the population.

FIGURE 11.2 ● *Two Cycles of a Problem-Solving Process*

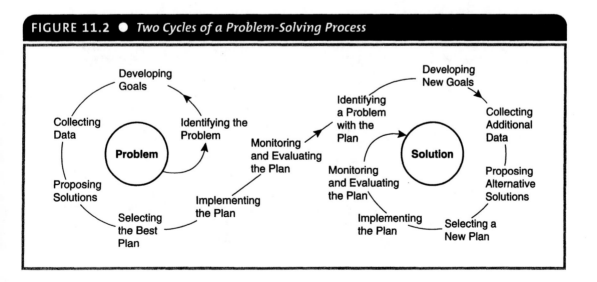

Several steps can be taken to help a group define a problem to promote problem solving. These include (1) clarify the boundaries of the problem, (2) seek out members' perceptions of the problem and their expectations about how it will be solved, (3) develop a problem-solving orientation, (4) define a solvable problem, and (5) specify the problem as clearly as possible.

Clarifying Boundaries

The first issue that confronts workers and members as they define the boundaries of a problem is how to handle large problems that may have several interrelated components. One method of handling a large problem is to partialize it. Partializing problems gives members a sense of direction and helps them to avoid feelings of being overwhelmed by the enormity of the problem.

As problems are partialized, they should have clear boundaries. Boundaries refer to the extent and scope of a problem or issue facing the group. Defining clear boundaries helps problem solvers focus and clarify their thoughts and suggestions about a problem, which leads to more effective solutions (D'Zurilla & Goldfried, 1971).

When setting boundaries, workers are in a delicate position. On the one hand, they do not want to hamper the group's creative problem-solving ability. The worker wants the group to consider all the relevant options for problem resolution. On the other hand, the worker is often in a better position than is any other group member to recognize what is politically, economically, and organizationally feasible. The following case example may help to illustrate this point.

● **CASE EXAMPLE** *Setting Boundaries*

In a community group working on ways to increase services for Mexican Americans, the worker informs members that potential solutions to the problem should not commit the agency sponsoring the group to new services that require additional funding this year. The worker goes on to explain how funding for new programs is obtained and that all funds requested for the current fiscal year are already committed to other projects. The worker continues to explain that although the proposed solutions should not require new funds, the group might consider making recommendations to the agency's administrative staff about seeking additional funding during the next fiscal year.

Whenever possible, the boundaries of the problem-solving process should be as broad and as flexible as possible so as not to stifle creative problem solutions. The worker should point out members' freedom within the boundaries and the importance of accomplishing the task within specified limits. The group should be given a convincing rationale for limiting the scope of a problem and the scope of the efforts used to resolve it. Without guidelines, the group may arrive at a solution that is unacceptable to persons who must implement it. Members who spend their time and energy developing a solution that is not feasible will feel frustrated and disappointed when they realize their recommended solution was not implemented.

Members' Perceptions and Experiences

Members' perceptions of problematic situations and their expectations about how the situations should be resolved determine the way the members approach a problem. If the members of a group are to be satisfied with the group's problem-solving process and committed to the solution that is reached, the members' views about problems facing the group must be respected. There is no better way to show respect than to solicit their views and ensure that they are given a fair hearing by all members. Failure to clarify members' expectations and perceptions about a problem often leads to difficulties later in the group's problem-solving process. Hidden agendas can develop, in part, because unclarified expectations are acted on by members. An open discussion often causes a modification of members' perceptions and expectations and forms the basis for mutually agreed-on goals.

Careful consideration of the views of individual group members does not mean that every opinion or bit of information should be treated as equally correct or important. Although there is a tendency to associate equality of ideas with equal treatment of group members, the concepts should not be confused (Kiesler, 1978). Members should be treated equitably in the group process, but the importance of their contribution changes as the work of the group changes.

Problem-Solving Orientation

During the process of identifying a problem it is important for the worker to help members develop a problem-solving orientation (D'Zurilla & Goldfried, 1971). Such an orientation includes (1) minimizing irrational beliefs about problematic situations, (2) recognizing and being willing to work on problems as they occur, and (3) inhibiting tendencies to respond prematurely on the first impulse or do nothing. Irrational beliefs about "how the world should be" can inhibit members from recognizing problematic situations and can also interfere with problem resolution (Ellis, 1962). Members should be guided to use evidence, logic, and sound reasoning as they identify and define a problematic situation (Barker, 1979; Gouran, 1982; Harnack & Fest, 1964; Stattler & Miller, 1968).

An effective problem-solving orientation includes recognizing problems that need attention and being willing to work on them. It is sometimes difficult for task groups to confront and work on problems facing them. For example, a team in a psychiatric hospital may avoid discussing problems in its own functioning for fear that the discussion will be viewed as an attack on individual members. In this case, the team leader should help by facilitating the development of a group climate that encourages problems to be viewed as shared concerns whose resolution will benefit all team members.

In developing a problem-solving orientation within the group, it is important to help members reduce their tendency to make immediate and automatic responses (Toseland, 1977). Frequently, members suggest solutions without carefully considering the problem. It has been found that less effective problem solvers are impulsive, impatient, and quick to give up (Bloom & Broder, 1950). Therefore the workers should encourage members to stop to think about the problem, collect data, and analyze alternative solutions before deciding what to do.

There should be sufficient time during a meeting agenda to grapple with difficult problems. According to Tropman (1996), difficult items should be placed in the middle third of the agenda. At this point, members are at the peak of their (1) psychological focus,

(2) physiological awareness, (3) attention, and (4) attendance. Easier items should be placed earlier in the agenda. Because they require less energy, items for discussion only can be placed at the end, when members have little energy for problem solving.

Defining a Solvable Problem

Groups are sometimes blocked in their problem-solving ability because they fail to frame the problem correctly (Maier, 1963). Group members may fail to identify the correct actors, the correct systems, or the correct obstacles that constitute the problem situation. In the early stages of problem solving, the group should be tentative and flexible with its problem definition so that the definition can be modified when new data are collected.

The worker can use several techniques to improve the group's ability to define a solvable problem. Maier (1963) suggests that, whenever possible, problems should be stated in institutional rather than personal terms. For instance, in the example presented earlier, a definition that attributed the problem of lack of services for Mexican Americans to an inept director of clinical services would have alienated the director of clinical services and thus have made the problem more difficult to solve. However, identifying the problem as a lack of service hours for Mexican Americans would have opened possibilities for modifying service delivery patterns. Similarly, defining the problem as a lack of knowledge and expertise about Mexican American clients would have suggested that the committee consider assessing members' willingness to learn more about the Mexican American population.

To help the group obtain a new perspective on a problem, the worker can use the reframing technique described in Chapter 10 and illustrated in the following example.

● CASE EXAMPLE *Reframing*

Some of the members of the committee considering services for Mexican Americans are not convinced that services for this population are lacking. The worker asked members to imagine going to an agency where no one speaks English and where all workers and most clients have different cultural backgrounds from their own. The exercise encouraged skeptical members to reconsider their stand on the question of whether something should be done to improve services for Mexican Americans.

Reframing may also be done by focusing on the positive aspects of a problem. For example, a problem that is experienced as anxiety provoking may be reframed as one that motivates the group to improve a situation. In these ways, members' motivation to solve problems can be increased.

Specifying the Problem

Having a clearly defined and mutually understood problem is essential if members are to work effectively together. When problems are first expressed in a meeting, they are often stated as partially formulated concerns. For example, a committee member might say, "I get a sense that some of our staff may be having difficulty with the new record-keeping system." Many terms in this statement are vaguely defined. Terms such as "get a sense," "some of our staff," and "difficulty" can have different meanings for each member of the group.

As concerns are raised by members, the worker should help them clarify vague or ambiguous terms. The statement in the previous paragraph, for example, could be clarified to indicate that three members of the community team and one member of the day treatment team expressed concerns that the new record-keeping forms took too long to fill out. Further, the phrase "took too long to fill out" should be clarified so that it becomes clear what it is the group is being asked to consider. For example, "took too long to fill out" could mean "cannot complete the case record in the 15 minutes allocated for that purpose," or could mean "being asked to collect data that are not needed to work with clients." Sometimes members of the task group may find that they cannot specify the problem further without collecting additional information.

After the group has clarified the problem, the worker should summarize it in a clear, brief statement. Ideally, the problem should be defined in objective terms that have similar meanings for all members. Objective terms with clear, observable referents help members arrive at a common understanding of the situation. When summarizing, the worker should restate the boundaries of the problem and the group's authority and responsibility so that members have a clear idea of their role in resolving the problem.

Developing Goals

The second step in the problem-solving process is goal setting. Goal setting does not occur only once in the problem-solving process. Tentative goals are formulated soon after the problem has been identified and aid in data collection because they help shape the scope of the information to be collected. Goals are often modified and specified as information is accumulated. Initial goals may sometimes be abandoned entirely, with new goals developed on the basis of the data accumulated. Through a process of exploration and negotiation, the worker and the members share their perspectives about the goals the group should achieve relative to a particular problem. The emphasis should be on formulating goals that are mutually acceptable.

Goal statements should be as clear and specific as possible. Desired changes in problem situations should be stated as objective tasks. For example, goals to increase services to Mexican Americans might include (1) providing eight hours of training for each outreach worker during the next six months, (2) increasing the number of Mexican Americans served by the agency from an average of three per month to 15 per month by the next fiscal year, (3) translating program brochures into Spanish within three months, and (4) printing 400 bilingual Spanish-English brochures at the beginning of the next fiscal year. Each goal is specific and easily understood.

Group workers can use several other principles for developing effective goals. These are presented in the following list.

Principles for Developing Goals

- Goals should be directed at the mutual concerns of all members.
- Goals should be consistent with the group's mandate, its overall objectives, and the values that have been agreed on by the group as a whole.

- Goals should be attractive enough to gain the commitment, cooperation, and investment of all group members.
- Goals should be realistic and attainable through the resources available to the group and its members.
- Goals should be time limited.
- The goal-setting process should set a supportive, encouraging climate for goal attainment.

At the end of the goal-setting process, members should be clear about the tasks they must perform to achieve the goals. It is important for the worker to summarize the goals that have been decided on by the group and to review each member's role in their achievement. This process avoids misunderstandings about who is responsible for what during a specified time period. Members should be clear about the time frame for accomplishing goals and about the mechanisms for reporting their achievements to the group.

Collecting Data

Data collection is the third step in the problem-solving process. Groups sometimes arrive at hasty, ill-conceived solutions because they rush to implement initial ideas without carefully exploring the situation, the obstacles to problem resolution, and the ramifications of a proposed solution. Data collection is concerned with the generation of ideas. This process should be kept separate from analyzing facts and making decisions because analysis and evaluation tend to inhibit idea generation.

The group should have as much information as possible about the problem as it analyzes data and prepares alternative solutions. Knowing the history of the problem helps the group develop a longitudinal perspective on the problem's development and course. Comparing the state of affairs before and after a problem has occurred can often point to potential causes and possible solutions. While gathering data about the history of the problem, the group should become familiar with previous attempts to solve it. This information can help the group avoid repeating past failures.

Scheidel and Crowell (1979) list five conditions that help to create a group climate that encourages members to share information and views about a problem: (1) maintaining the group's openness to speculation, (2) encouraging an open search for all pertinent data, (3) encouraging all group members to present their ideas, (4) demonstrating genuine appreciation of differences, and (5) refraining from evaluation. A supportive group climate reduces the need for members to defend their positions. Gibb (1961) points out that communications should be expressed (1) nonjudgmentally, (2) genuinely, (3) without the intent of controlling others, (4) with tentativeness rather than certainty, and (5) as an equal rather than as a superior contribution. Facilitating this type of communication in a group increases problem exploration and contributes to high-quality solutions.

Members occasionally can become stuck in the ways they explore and review a problem (Napier & Gershenfeld, 1993). To develop new approaches, members should be encouraged to (1) view problems flexibly, (2) expand the way information is collected and combined, (3) recognize and fill gaps in available information, (4) generate new ideas by viewing situations from alternative perspectives, and (5) use both lateral and vertical thinking processes.

Vertical thinking processes are often associated with rational problem-solving strategies. *Vertical thinking* relies on inductive and deductive reasoning. Evidence and reason are used in a logical fashion until a solution is reached. Solutions are grounded in facts that are built one on another in an orderly, systematic, and linear fashion.

Lateral thinking processes are particularly useful when vertical thinking processes have not yielded a creative solution. Lateral thinking helps free ideas that have been blocked by stale, routine ways of conceptualizing a problem and its potential solutions. Instead of relying on an orderly, linear combination of facts, *lateral thinking* is characterized by the use of analogies, metaphors, similarities, contrasts, and paradoxes. Seemingly disparate facts, thoughts, and ideas are put together in new and creative ways. Analogies, for example, help bring out similarities between objects or situations that were previously considered to be different. For example, solutions found to be helpful in analogous situations might be tried by group members in their current problem-solving situation. For further information about the lateral thinking process, see De Bono (1968, 1971, 1972).

Developing Plans

Data collection encourages divergent thinking processes, but preparing plans for problem resolution encourages convergent thinking processes (Scheidel & Crowell, 1979). The worker calls on members to organize, analyze, and synthesize facts, ideas, and perspectives generated during problem exploration. Displaying the data for all members to see can be helpful. It is difficult for members to keep a large amount of information in mind as they attempt to develop alternative solutions. Displaying information on newsprint or a blackboard helps to ensure that all members are aware of the full range of information shared during a discussion. Ordering and clarifying the information generated by the group can also be helpful. Useful techniques for doing this are presented in the following list.

Handling Information Generated by the Group

- Separate relevant from irrelevant facts
- Combine similar facts
- Identify discrepancies
- Look for patterns across different facts
- Rank facts from most important to least important

During the process of organizing data, members should be encouraged to discuss the logic behind their reasoning. Members should be encouraged to give each other a chance to explain why they see things the way they do, rather than to defend their own choices. Defending choices often entrenches group members' opinions, whereas a discussion of how members think information should be used often brings out commonalities and similarities in their views of the situation.

Before making a decision, members should be encouraged to develop as many alternative solutions as possible. Because critical and evaluative comments tend to inhibit the production of creative ideas, workers should caution members not to criticize each other's solutions as they are presented.

Selecting the Best Plan

After all members have presented their alternatives, the group should review each one. The review serves several purposes. It helps ensure that all members understand each alternative. Misunderstandings at this point can cause conflict and reduce the chances for achieving closure in the problem-solving process. When reviewing each alternative, members can be encouraged to discuss how they would overcome obstacles and challenges likely to be encountered if the alternative were implemented.

When selecting among alternatives, members should be encouraged to consider the overall likelihood that a plan will resolve the problem in a manner that is valued by all group members. For this purpose, it is helpful for members to develop criteria that can be used to judge each plan. Rational methods based on multiattribute utility analysis (see Chapter 12) have been developed to help members develop decision criteria. Although much has been written about these methods (Baron, 1994; Clemen, 1996; Watson & Buede, 1987), they have not been widely applied in the human services. (For exceptions, see Dalgleish, 1988; Milter and Rohrbaugh, 1988; and Toseland, Rivas, and Chapman, 1984.)

Sometimes groups rely on decision criteria developed by experts. For example, a task group formed by the U.S. Department of Health and Human Services was charged with distributing funds for health maintenance organizations in medically underserved areas. By using panels of experts, the committee developed four criteria for deciding among programs that applied for funds in medically underserved areas. These criteria were (1) the number of physicians per 1,000 people, (2) the percentage of families in the area with less than $5,000 annual income, (3) the infant mortality rate in the area, and (4) the percentage of the area's population over age 65 (Health Services Research Group, 1975).

In most situations, groups rely on the expertise of their own members to develop decision criteria. This is frequently done by having members rate the advantages and the disadvantages of each alternative. Alternatives may be combined or modified to maximize advantages and minimize disadvantages. As members decide among alternatives, they should keep in mind the group's mandate, its goals, and the ideal situation they would like to see result if the problem were resolved successfully. Members may also want to consider other factors, such as the benefits and costs of implementing alternative solutions, the comfort and ease with which particular solutions are likely to be implemented, and the political ramifications of alternative solutions. The most effective solution to a problem may not be the most desirable solution if it is too costly or if it is likely to offend, inconvenience, or otherwise upset persons who will be asked to implement it.

Implementing the Plan

Excellent decisions can be worthless if they are not implemented properly. Effective problem solving requires that a task group actively oversee the implementation of its plan.

Input from persons who will be influential in implementing the plan should be solicited as early as possible in the problem-solving process. Once a solution is decided on, members should begin to gain support for it from constituencies outside the group. Members should seek the support of persons who will be accountable for the decision and with authority to implement it. For example, the committee that decided to improve outreach efforts to Mexican Americans by training staff and publicizing agency programs in the community sought the cooperation of the board of directors, the agency's executive director, the directors of programs responsible for implementing staff training and publicity campaigns, all the direct service staff who were going to be involved in the program, and the leaders of the Mexican American community.

When seeking the support of others, members may have to educate people about the value of a new approach to a problem. Motivating people to cooperate with the implementation of a decision is not an easy task. Persuasion, lobbying, and other tactics may be necessary to gain support for the proposed solution (Rothman, Erlich, & Tropman, 1995).

Once the receptivity of persons responsible for implementing the decision is ensured, the group can begin to organize and supervise the plan's implementation. With a large plan, a division of labor is often helpful—each member may be assigned specific responsibilities. There may also be a need for training to educate persons who will implement the plan.

It is often helpful to delineate steps in the implementation sequence and to develop a time line. Objectives can be specified for each step, and the group can obtain periodic feedback about implementation progress. Feedback channels should be established to keep the group apprised of the solution's utility in terms of its expected outcome. Feedback can be used to overcome obstacles, stabilize change, and meet the challenges of a continually changing environment.

Implementing the proposed solution also includes identifying, contacting, and utilizing available resources. A heterogeneous group can be advantageous in this process because of the resources a diverse membership brings to the group. It is also important to prepare members for opposition. Obstacles may include inertia, passive resistance, or active attempts to block implementation of a proposed solution. Chapter 9 contains information on how to overcome inertia and resistance.

SUMMARY

This chapter focuses on the foundation skills, procedures, and methods needed to work effectively with task groups. Task groups have an important place in all human service organizations. Each day, meetings take place that have an important effect on what services are provided and how they are delivered. Social workers and other helping professionals are frequently called on to chair or staff committees, teams, and other task groups. When meetings are well run, members become a satisfied and cohesive team committed to achieving its objectives. Poorly run meetings, however, often lead to boredom and frustration.

During the work stage of task groups, the worker often is called on to engage in the following activities: (1) preparing for group meetings, (2) helping members share information, (3) helping all members get involved in the work of the group, (4) helping members develop ideas and information, (5) dealing with conflict, (6) helping members make effective decisions, (7) understanding the political ramifications of task groups, (8) monitoring and evaluating, and (9) problem solving.

Problem solving is probably the single most important function of task groups. The chapter concludes with a six-step, problem-solving model: (1) identifying a problem, (2) developing goals, (3) collecting data, (4) developing plans, (5) selecting the best plan, and (6) implementing the plan. In practice, these steps overlap and they are interconnected by feedback channels. Task groups repeat variations of problem-solving processes during the life of the group as they perform their functions and work on the tasks that confront them.

● CASE EXAMPLE

Lola's supervisor reviewed her accomplishments as a group leader in preparation for her annual review. Two years ago Lola was assigned to chair the organization's long-range planning committee. Lola felt she had been an active group leader. Lola lived in a rural part of West Virginia called Blair County. She worked for Join Together, an outreach and community development organization. The organization's long-range planning committee was composed of representatives from all levels of the organization, including administration, client services, program development, and finance. Over the course of her tenure as leader, the group had achieved a high level of functioning. Lola's supervisor identified several activities and skills that helped the group to function effectively and achieve its purpose.

Lola spent a good deal of time preparing for group meetings. In addition to reviewing and monitoring the work of the subcommittees, she researched issues for future meetings, prepared an agenda, and made numerous personal contacts with group members. Lola hoped that her level of activity between meetings served as a model for all members. After evaluating the amount of work done by members outside of meetings, Lola's supervisor concluded that her modeling behavior had helped to establish a group norm of hard work.

One of the most impressive aspects of the group meetings was the sharing of information that occurred among members. Lola encouraged all members to keep the group updated on existing programs and ideas for new services. Between meetings Lola shared important information with all members of the committee. At the beginning of each meeting, members shared updates and suggestions with each other. Lola's supervisor noted to herself that through this process, the group had achieved a high level of communication and interaction. Members were familiar and comfortable with the roles they played in the group. Her assessment was that these factors fostered group cohesiveness and raised the productivity of group members.

Lola also helped the group develop a clear structure for the monthly meetings. She helped establish clear procedures for developing information, solving problems, and making decisions. She encouraged members to participate actively during meetings by modeling good member skills such as listening, asking good questions, and giving support. She also helped members feel that their feedback and recommendations were taken seriously by the organization. Lola worked carefully with the administrators to ensure that group deliberations would be influential on the future directions of organizational policy and programs. Group members felt empowered by this knowledge.

Lola's organizational skills helped the group adopt a clear structure for solving problems and making decisions. She helped the group decide on a standard format for problem solving. For example, when faced with having to decide how to find funding for a new volunteer outreach program in the local school, the group followed the steps of identifying the problem, setting goals, collecting data, developing plans, and selecting and implementing the plan. The group learned and relied on this format in many of its problem-solving discussions. During decision-making activities, Lola suggested clear guidelines about how to proceed. These were discussed, modified, and adopted by the group. She encouraged the group to develop decision criteria and procedures before making important decisions. Although this took some time, Lola's organizational skills helped the group decision-making process become easier and more systematic. Lola was also good at helping the group build consensus by finding common interests and points of agreement. Consensus building helped members be more committed to the group decision.

Lola spent time monitoring and evaluating the group. She devoted a regular portion of each meeting agenda to discussions of members' ef-

forts and their effectiveness. She also developed a survey form to obtain members' feedback about her leadership skills and for gathering suggestions about how the group could be improved. Lola shared the results of the survey with members and incorporated members' suggestions into the work of the group.

The long-range planning committee had some history of disagreements and conflicts. Several of the members had strong personalities. Others felt that their departments should have more control over the projects chosen for future funding and implementation. Lola's greatest difficulty was her ability to deal with the conflicts that arose in the group. Her supervisor noted that she seemed uncomfortable with conflict in the group. She suggested that Lola listen carefully to both sides of discussions and remain neutral in the face of pressure to agree with one side or the other. Lola helped the group recognize that some disagreements about issues were healthy for group discussions. Lola's supervisor suggested that she help the group differentiate these substantive conflicts from affective conflicts, in which members personalized conflicts with other members. At different times, Lola helped the group resolve both types of conflicts. Still, she worked hard to more fully develop her skills of listening, mediating, negotiating, and compromising.

As Lola's supervisor reflected on the group's accomplishments, she noted that Lola had guided the group by providing it with many of the elements it needed to function effectively. Lola felt a sense of pride in knowing that she had used her talents and skills to guide the development of an effective task group. Through her efforts, the group identified several service needs and helped to implement programs for persons living in rural West Virginia.

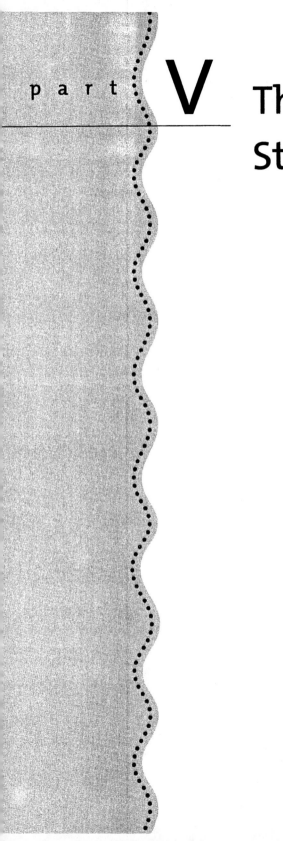

part **V** The Ending
Stage

Evaluation

Evaluation is the process of obtaining information about the effects of a single intervention or the effect of the total group experience. Workers can use informal or formal measures to obtain such information. In conducting an informal evaluation, a worker might ask the members of a group to evaluate how the group is progressing. To complete a formal evaluation, a worker might collect information systematically using preplanned measurement devices before, during, or after the group has met. In either case, the worker uses the information to evaluate the group. This chapter explores many ways to obtain information about a group and guides the worker in deciding what evaluation methods will be most useful in various situations.

THE PRACTITIONER'S DILEMMA

Increasingly in social work and allied disciplines, there has been a push toward accountability and empirically validated practice. Workers have been urged to become practitioner-researchers to improve their work as they practice (Thomas, 1990). The push for evaluating practice has occurred even though group workers sometimes fail to keep adequate records, let alone perform systematic evaluations of their practice.

The dilemma for many practicing group workers is that other demands of practice seem to be more pressing than evaluations, which require valuable time and energy. Further, many practitioners find it difficult to understand the logic of evaluation methods or their day-to-day usefulness. It has been proposed that practitioners (1) leave research to researchers, (2) become consumers of research, and (3) concentrate on developing experience and expertise as group leaders (Trotzer, 1999). However, Trotzer and most others urge group workers to evaluate their own practice whenever possible. Recently, the focus has been on developing evidence-based practice guidelines that describe the most effective interventions for particular problems (Howard & Jenson, 1999; Rosen & Proctor, 2003). For example, practice guidelines for the treatment of depression indicate that the most effective method for treating it is a combination of pharmacotherapy and psychotherapy (American Psychiatric Association, 2002).

The push toward accountability and empirically validated group work practice has made a difference. In a review of the literature in 1986, Feldman (1986) found that compared with a review completed 20 years before (Silverman, 1966), the number of research studies had more than doubled. However, Feldman noted that the number of research studies was still small and that much needed to be done before group workers could claim that their practice is well grounded in scientific research. For reviews of the history of group research, see the special issue of *Group Dynamics, Theory, Research and Practice* edited by Forsyth (2000), Barlow, Burlingame, and Fuhriman (2000), or Forsyth and Corazzini (2000).

WHY EVALUATE? THE GROUP WORKER'S VIEW

When evaluating their work with a particular group, workers should consider the resources they have available for conducting an evaluation. For example, it is important to assess the encouragement they will receive from their agency for evaluating their own practice. It is also important to consider the time they have available for an evaluation. Matching resources and available time with an appropriate method for evaluating their practice is essential.

Reasons for Conducting Evaluations

Workers' reasons for wanting information about a group depend on how they believe they can use the information. Some of the benefits of evaluation for group workers are presented here.

Benefits of Evaluations

- Evaluations can satisfy workers' curiosity and professional concerns about the effects of specific interventions they perform while working with a group.
- Information from evaluations can help workers improve their leadership skills.
- Evaluations can demonstrate the usefulness of a specific group or a specific group work method to an agency, a funding source, or society.
- Workers can assess the progress of group members and see whether the group is accomplishing agreed-on purposes.
- Evaluations allow group members and others who may be affected to express their satisfactions and dissatisfactions with a group.
- Workers can gather knowledge that can be shared with others who are using group methods for similar purposes and in similar situations.

- Workers can systematize and make overt the covert hypothesis-generating and hypothesis-testing processes they routinely engage in as they practice.
- Evaluations can examine the cost-effectiveness of group work services.

Organizational Encouragement and Support

To evaluate their practice with a group, workers should begin by assessing the willingness of the organization for whom they work to provide the resources to conduct an evaluation. Some organizations do little or nothing to encourage evaluations and may even penalize the worker for attempting one. Agency norms, peer pressure, or administrative directions may suggest to workers that other tasks are more important than evaluating their practice. In other cases, high caseloads may inhibit workers' abilities to evaluate their practice.

Without active encouragement by an organization's administrators, workers are left to rely on their own motivations for evaluating their work with a group. Organizations can increase workers' opportunities for evaluation by including evaluation tasks as a part of workers' practice responsibilities, by providing the time for evaluations, and by encouraging workers to discuss evaluations during regularly scheduled staff meetings. Rather than requiring workers to fill out forms and records that they do not use and often do not see again after administrative processing, organizations can instead help by developing and implementing information systems that can be used by workers to evaluate their practice. A well-designed information and evaluation system can provide feedback for group work practitioners as well as for agency administrators.

Time Considerations

Workers should consider how much time they have available to conduct an evaluation. Most workers collect some information about the groups they lead, and this information can often be the basis for an evaluation if it is collected appropriately. Little additional time is needed for evaluation beyond the time necessary to make modifications in the original data-collection system.

In other situations, workers may want information that is not routinely collected. They should estimate the amount of time it will take them to collect, process, and analyze the additional information. They can then compare the time needed for the evaluation with the time they have available and decide whether the evaluation is feasible.

When workers have valid reasons for evaluating their practice, they may be able to persuade their organization to allow them sufficient time to conduct the evaluation, particularly when a worker is developing a new, innovative program to achieve the goals the organization has set as a priority for service delivery.

Selecting an Evaluation Method

After determining how much time is available for an evaluation, workers should consider how to match their information needs and available time to an appropriate evaluation method.

This chapter reviews the major types of evaluations. Each evaluation method is discussed in terms of its strengths and weaknesses, time requirements, and flexibility.

Workers must also decide what data-collection instruments they will use in conjunction with a particular evaluation method. The major types of data-collection instruments used by group workers follow.

Data Collection Instruments

- Progress notes
- Self-reports or personal interview data from workers, members, and observers
- Questionnaires
- Analysis of reports or other products of a group's work
- Review of audiotapes and videotapes of group meetings
- Observational coding schemes
- Role play or in vivo performance tests
- Reliable and valid scales

These data-collection instruments can be used with any of the major types of evaluation methods. Some measures, however, are frequently associated with one type of evaluation. For example, progress notes are often used in monitoring evaluation methods; reliable and valid scales are more frequently used in effectiveness and efficiency evaluations. As each type of evaluation method is reviewed, the methods of collecting data that are often associated with each method are described.

EVALUATION METHODS

Workers can use four broad types of evaluation methods to obtain data: evaluations for (1) planning a group, (2) monitoring a group, (3) developing a group, and (4) testing the effectiveness and efficiency of group outcomes. Workers can use any of the evaluation methods to obtain information about the process or the outcome of a group. Process evaluations focus on the interaction in a group; properties of a group such as cohesion, norms, roles, and communication patterns; how the group is being conducted; or other aspects of the functioning of a group. Outcome evaluations focus on the products or tasks achieved by individual members or the group as a whole.

Regardless of the type of evaluation employed or whether the evaluation focuses on processes or outcomes, workers should be able to use evaluations to receive feedback about their practice. Instead of viewing practice evaluations as useless administrative requirements, workers should see them as a way to help them become more effective, and as a way to develop new knowledge that can be shared with other group workers.

EVALUATIONS FOR PLANNING A GROUP

Evaluations used for planning a group are seldom mentioned in the group work literature. This section discusses two important evaluation methods for planning: (1) obtaining program information, technical data, and materials for specific groups that the worker is planning to lead and (2) conducting needs assessments to determine the feasibility of organizing a proposed group.

Obtaining Program Information

The worker can often benefit from information about methods previously used in working with similar groups. Workers may be able to obtain some information from colleagues or from workers in other agencies in which similar groups have been conducted. Workers may also find it useful to utilize the sources listed here.

Ways to Obtain Program Information

- Examine records from previous groups that focused on similar concerns
- Attend workshops and conferences where group workers share recent developments in the field
- Review relevant journals[1] and books using computerized or manual search procedures
- Read the minutes of previous group meetings
- Read the bylaws of the sponsoring organization
- Read any operating procedures that may exist from previous meetings of the task group
- Be clear about the charges and responsibilities of the group
- Obtain information about how similar objectives and goals were accomplished in other organizations and by other task groups
- Attend meetings of groups working on similar concerns

Library literature searches have been made much easier and much less time-consuming in recent years by the availability of online CD-ROM computerized databases. Two databases that are particularly relevant to social group workers are Social Work Abstracts Plus and PSYCLIT (psychology). Also, group workers in health settings may find MEDLINE (medicine) useful; group workers in school settings may find ERIC (education) useful; and group workers in forensic settings may find NCJRS (National Criminal Justice Reference Service) useful. There are also specialized bibliographies that can be helpful in developing new group work services. For example, John Ramey (1999) has prepared a comprehensive bibliography of social group, with supplements from 1999 until the present.

---

[1]Some of the most important journals that focus on specific groups and specific group work methods are *The Group, Group and Organization Management, International Journal of Group Psychotherapy, Journal for Specialists in Group Work, Small Group Research,* and *Social Work with Groups.*

Needs Assessment

Workers might also find it useful to have some information about potential members of a proposed group as illustrated in the following case. This information might include (1) potential members' willingness to attend the group, (2) their motivations for attending, and (3) their capabilities for helping the group achieve its purposes. In treatment groups, workers may want to conduct a needs assessment by asking other workers whether clients with whom they work might be appropriate for the group or whether workers have received requests for a particular group service they have been unable to meet.

● CASE EXAMPLE *Evaluating the Need for a Group*

In order to assess the need for a support group for teen parents, the worker began by consulting existing research from several government organizations, including the local Department of Health and the state Department of Children and Family Services. Data suggested that the incidence and prevalence of teen parenting was particularly high in the local community. The worker also conducted "key informant" interviews with community leaders and executive directors of several local social service organizations. Information obtained during the interviews confirmed the results found in the initial analysis of existing data. In addition, several interviewees suggested that they would be interested in referring potential members to the group; the worker sent them copies of a survey designed to obtain information about the number of potential referrals to the group and any other information about the interests and motivation of potential members.

Data from community needs assessments designed for multiple purposes can be useful in obtaining information about potential group members. Contacting people or organizations in the community may also provide access to potential members. When workers have identified the clients, they can contact them directly by a personal interview, a telephone call, or a letter. Toseland (1981) has described methods of reaching out to clients in more detail.

In some task groups, membership may result from elections, appointments, or the person's position in an organization. A planning evaluation can familiarize a worker with rules and regulations governing a task group's composition and operation. Planning evaluations can also help a worker collect information and assess the potential contributions that members can make in helping the group achieve its objectives (Rothman, 1974). For more information about conducting planning evaluations, see Rossi, Freeman, and Lipsey (1999).

EVALUATIONS FOR MONITORING A GROUP

Monitoring refers to keeping track of the progress of group members and group processes. Monitoring is discussed in Chapter 8 as an assessment device, but it can also be used to evaluate group work practice. Monitoring methods have received more attention in the group work literature than has any other type of evaluation method. Monitoring is the least demanding and most flexible of the evaluation procedures described in this chapter. It can be useful for obtaining information for process or outcome evaluations.

Monitoring Methods

The first step in the monitoring process is to decide what information to collect. For example, persons who work with remedial groups designed for clients with psychological disorders may be interested in monitoring changes in individual members over the course of the group on the five axes presented in the *Diagnostic and Statistical Manual of Mental Disorders* (American Psychiatric Association, 2000). A worker asked to lead an interdepartmental committee of a large public welfare agency may be interested in monitoring the extent to which individual committee members complete assigned tasks.

Whatever information group workers decide to collect, they must be clear about how they define it so it can be monitored with appropriate measures. Concepts that are ambiguous, obscure, or unspecified cannot be measured accurately.

The next step in monitoring is to decide how the needed information will be collected. Data can be collected by administering questionnaires; asking for verbal feedback about the group; or by recording information about the group through written records, tape recordings, or video recordings of group sessions.

In treatment groups, members may be asked to record information about their own behavior or the behavior of other group members. Self-monitoring methods include (1) counting discrete behaviors; (2) keeping a checklist, a log, or a diary of events that occur before, during, and after a behavior or a task that is being monitored; and (3) recording ratings of feeling states on self-anchored rating scales. These types of monitoring methods are described in Chapter 8 because they are often used for assessment. As illustrated in the following sections, in the monitoring process, collecting data can be the task of the worker or of the group members.

Monitoring by the Group Worker

One of the easiest methods of monitoring a group's progress is to record the activities that occur during or after each meeting. This form of record keeping involves writing or dictating notes after a meeting (Wilson, 1980). The worker may use a process-recording method of monitoring or a summary-recording method. Process recordings are narrative, step-by-step descriptions of a group's development. Wilson and Ryland (1949) noted that process recordings can help a worker analyze the interactions that occur during a group meeting. However, process recordings are time-consuming and, therefore, are rarely used by experienced group workers. They are, however, useful in the training and supervision of beginning group workers because they provide rich detail and give trainees an opportunity to reflect on what occurs during group meetings.

Summary recording is less time-consuming, more selective, and more focused than process recording. Summary recording focuses on critical incidents that occur in a group and involves using a series of open-ended questions. The questions are most frequently used for monitoring a group's progress after each group session, although they may be used at less frequent intervals during a group's development. Figure 13.1 is an example

FIGURE 13.1 ● *Group Recording Form*

Group name: _____   Beginning date: _____

Worker's name: _____   Termination date: _____

Session number: _____   Date of session: _____

Members present: _____

_____

_____

_____

Members absent: _____

_____

_____

Purpose of the group: _____

_____

Goals for this meeting: _____

_____

_____

Activities to meet these goals: _____

_____

_____

_____

Worker's analysis of the meeting: _____

_____

_____

_____

_____

Plan for future meetings: _____

_____

_____

_____

_____

of a summary recording form used to record a meeting of a family life education group for foster parents.

When using either summary or process recordings, it is important for the worker to record the information as soon as possible after the meeting so that events are remembered as accurately as possible. The meaning of the open-ended summary-recording questions should be as clear as possible so that workers' recordings are consistent from group to group. Ambiguous questions open to several interpretations should be avoided. The amount of time required for summary recordings depends on the number of questions to which the worker responds and the amount of analysis each question requires. The next case provides an example of how a group recording form can be employed.

The open-ended questions of summary-recording devices sometimes fail to focus or define the recorded information sufficiently, especially when the worker wants similar information about all clients. Summary-recording devices are usually not designed to connect the group worker's activities to specific goals and outcomes.

● CASE EXAMPLE *Audiotape Evaluations*

In a family life education group for foster parents, the worker wanted to systematically analyze whether the group was achieving its goals. Using a group recording form after each meeting, she spent time writing down the goals of the group, the activities to accomplish the goals, and the quality of the interaction. She also recorded her analysis of how well the group worked toward achieving its overall purpose (see Figure 13.1). After several group sessions, she reviewed the completed weekly recordings in order to obtain a summary of how well the group was achieving its purpose. Based on her weekly analyses of meetings, the worker concluded that although members appeared to achieve a high degree of learning about family life, they failed to create significant supportive relationships with each other. Based on these conclusions, the worker increased program activities that provided members with opportunities to develop closer and more supportive relationships.

Recording systems such as the problem-oriented record (Kane, 1974), have been designed to overcome this problem. In the problem-oriented record-keeping system, problems to be worked on by the group are clearly defined, goals are established, and data are collected and recorded in relation to each specified problem. The system enables workers to show how group work interventions designed to accomplish a certain goal are connected to a specific assessment of the problem.

In task groups, the minutes of a meeting serve as the record of the group's business. They are often the official record of the proceedings of a group. Minutes are prepared from notes taken during the meeting by a person designated by the worker or elected by the group's membership. A staff person, the secretary of the group, or another person may take notes regularly. Sometimes, members rotate the task. The minutes of each meeting are usually distributed to members before the next meeting and are approved by members, with any revisions, during the first part of the next meeting.

Workers may also want to use audiotape or videotape recorders to obtain information about a group. Recordings have the advantage of providing an accurate, unedited record of the meeting. In remedial groups, audiotapes provide immediate feedback about members' verbal behavior. Members may want to replay a segment of the tape if there is a discrepancy about what was said during some portion of the meeting.

● **CASE EXAMPLE** *Audiotapes to Improve Coleadership*

Bonnie and Fred decided to audiotape a new employment skills group they were coleading in a day treatment program for persons recently discharged from inpatient mental health settings. With the members' permission, they taped the meetings; they then listened to the tapes between meetings to identify ways they might improve their leadership of future group meetings.

In educational and other groups, videotapes can be used to demonstrate appropriate behavior and critique inappropriate behavior. Videotaping is especially useful during program activities, such as role playing, that are designed to increase skills or change behavior patterns. Video feedback helps members review their behavior during role-play practices to discuss alternative ways of behaving. For example, members of an assertion training group might watch videotapes of themselves in a situation requiring an assertive response. They may analyze voice tone, facial expressions, body posture, and the verbal interactions that occurred. Audiotapes and videotapes provide the worker with a permanent record that can be shared with the group, with supervisors, or in educational workshops.

There are some disadvantages to taping a group. A recording's absolute quality makes it difficult for members to make statements off the record, which may inhibit the development of trust in the group. The worker may not find it necessary or even desirable to have the level of detail provided by a tape. The worker may have to spend too much time reviewing irrelevant portions of a tape to find information that could have been obtained quickly if brief, summary recordings had been used instead. However, if a worker is interested in monitoring the group's interaction patterns in a thorough and precise fashion or if an entire transcript of the group session is needed, audio or videotapes are ideal.

Sometimes it is desirable to use specialized coding systems to obtain reliable and valid data from tape-recorded group sessions, particularly when the worker wishes to obtain a detailed and accurate picture of group processes for research. Coding systems can be used by one or more raters of the tapes to determine the frequency and content of a group's interactions. Coding systems described by Bales (1950), Bales, Cohen, and Williamson (1979), Budman et al. (1987), Hill (1977), and Rose (1989) are examples of methods that can be used to analyze specific group interactions. Other coding systems are described in comprehensive reviews of group process instruments prepared by Fuhriman and colleagues (Fuhriman & Barlow, 1994; Fuhriman & Packard, 1986).

Monitoring by Group Members

The most common use of monitoring by group members occurs in treatment groups in which individual members keep a record of their behavior between group meetings and report back on the behaviors during the next meeting. An illustration of the steps in the self-monitoring procedure appears in Figure 13.2. During this procedure, the worker and the group

FIGURE 13.2 ● *The Self-Monitoring Process*

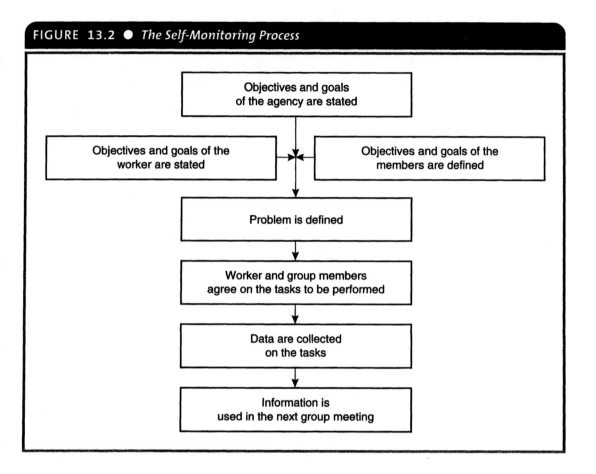

members together decide (1) what data to collect, (2) when to collect the data, (3) how much data to collect, (4) how to collect the data, and (5) when the information collected by members should be analyzed by the group. As these questions are discussed and answered, the worker reviews each member's monitoring plan.

Members can also monitor a group's progress at the end of each meeting or at intervals during the life of the group. Members may use a short questionnaire devised for this purpose or they can discuss the group's performance orally with the worker. Monitoring of this type encourages members to provide periodic feedback that can be used by workers to improve their practice throughout the life cycle of a group.

Group members also benefit from self-monitoring procedures. Members can share ideas about the group's performance and how it might be improved, which gives them a sense of control and influence over the group's progress and increases their identification with the group's purposes. Also, members who believe their ideas are valued, respected, and listened to are more likely to feel satisfied with their participation in the group. See, for example the following case example.

● **CASE EXAMPLE** *Monitoring the Progress of a Single Parent's Group*

In an educational group for single parents, the worker asked each member to complete a session evaluation form during the last five minutes of each meeting. The form was composed of short, closed-ended questions using a Likert scale, as well as open-ended questions designed to obtain qualitative data about member satisfaction with the group meetings (see Figure 13.3). At several intervals during the life of the group, the worker did a quantitative analysis of members' ratings on the level of helpfulness of information obtained from the group sessions as well as members' satisfaction with the group and with its leader. These data indicated a steady positive progression in how members valued the

---

FIGURE 13.3 ● *Session Evaluation Form*

Was the information presented about child development helpful to you in understanding your child's behavior?

4	3	2	1
Very Helpful	Somewhat Helpful	A Little Helpful	Not at All Helpful

What information did you find most helpful? _____

_____

_____

Rate the effectiveness of the leader in this group session.

4	3	2	1
Very Helpful	Somewhat Helpful	A Little Helpful	Not at All Helpful

What did you find most helpful about the group during this session? _____

_____

_____

What did you find least helpful about the group? _____

_____

_____

Overall, rate your satisfaction with today's group meeting.

4	3	2	1
Very Helpful	Somewhat Helpful	A Little Helpful	Not at All Helpful

Additional comments: _____

_____

_____

information they received and how they rated the group and the leader. Data collected about what members liked most and least about each session suggested that members particularly disliked some of the guest speakers brought in by the leader and preferred sessions where they could practice child management skills.

Verbal evaluations of a group's performance do not provide a permanent record. An evaluation form consisting of closed-ended, fixed-category responses and open-ended items can be used if the worker, group members, or the agency wants written feedback about the group. Figure 13.3 shows a session evaluation form developed by a worker leading a group for single parents. The form contains several easily understood closed- and open-ended questions. The closed-ended questions are Likert-type scales that require respondents to record their opinions on an ordered scale. Because the same scale values are used for all group members, responses made by each member can be compared with one another. Open-ended items are designed to allow each member to reply uniquely; responses may vary considerably from member to member. An alternative session evaluation form to the one shown in Figure 13.3 can be found in Rose (1998).

In task groups, members often make oral reports of their progress. Although the reports are often not considered to be evaluation devices, they are an important means by which the worker and the members monitor the group's work. At the completion of a task group, minutes, documents, final reports, and other products that result from the group's efforts can also be used to evaluate the success of the group.

In treatment groups, an important indicator of the group's performance is the completion of contracts that individual members make with the group or the worker about tasks to be done during the week to resolve a problem or change a particular behavior. Another indicator is the completion of between-session tasks. Rose (1989) calls the completion of between-session tasks the "products of group interaction." He suggests that the rate of completion of tasks is an important indicator of the success of the group.

EVALUATIONS FOR DEVELOPING A GROUP

A third method of evaluating group work practice, developmental evaluation, is useful for the worker who is interested in preparing new group work programs, developing new group work methods, or improving existing group programs. Developmental research, as it has been called by Thomas (1978), is similar to research and development in business and industry. It allows practicing group workers to create and test new group work programs.

The process of developmental evaluation includes developing, testing, evaluating, modifying, and re-evaluating intervention methods as new groups are offered. Developmental evaluations are especially appealing for workers who offer the same or similar group programs repeatedly because the evaluations require workers to evaluate group programs in a sequential manner. A developmental evaluation occurs as successive group programs are offered.

Unlike monitoring evaluations, which are relatively easy for group workers to conduct, developmental evaluations are rather complex. They require careful thought, planning, and design by the worker. The steps for conducting a developmental evaluation are presented in the following list.

Steps in a Developmental Evaluation

- Identifying a need or problem
- Gathering and analyzing relevant data
- Developing a new group program or method
- Evaluating the new program or method
- Modifying the program or method on the basis of the data obtained

As shown in Figure 13.4, the process may be conducted several times as new group programs are offered and evaluated by the worker. Although developmental research requires careful thought as well as time and energy, it yields improvements in programs and methods that can make group work practice more effective and more satisfying.

In developing and evaluating a new group program or a new group method, the worker can select from a variety of research designs, depending on the type of program or method being developed and the context in which the evaluation will occur. Single-system methods

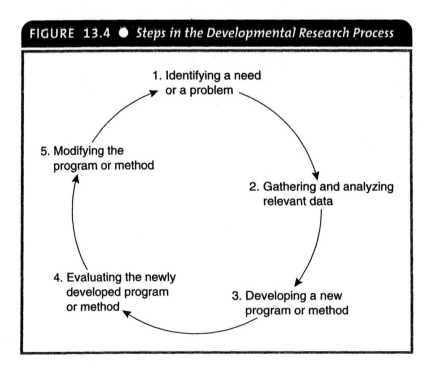

FIGURE 13.4 ● *Steps in the Developmental Research Process*

1. Identifying a need or a problem

2. Gathering and analyzing relevant data

3. Developing a new program or method

4. Evaluating the newly developed program or method

5. Modifying the program or method

and case study methods are particularly useful for developmental evaluations. Although quasi-experimental design methods are also frequently used in developmental research, in this chapter the methods are described in relation to effectiveness and efficiency evaluations because they are also frequently used in evaluations of group outcomes. For a more thorough discussion of the issues involved in choosing an appropriate method for developmental research, see Bailey-Dempsey and Reid (1996), Fortune and Reid (1998), Kirk and Reid (2002), Rothman and Tumblin (1994), and Thomas and Rothman (1994).

Single-System Methods

Single-system methods (often called single-subject designs) have been developed to evaluate data collected over time from a single system such as a group. The data obtained by using single-system designs may include information about a single group member or the group as a whole. Single-system methods compare baseline data to data collected when an intervention is made in the group. The baseline period occurs before the intervention period. Data collected during the preintervention or baseline periods are intended to represent the functioning of the group as a whole or a group member on a particular variable. After the baseline period, an intervention occurs, which may cause a change in the data collected during the baseline period.

As shown in Figure 13.5, a change in level or in slope of the data collected may occur after the intervention. Observations before and after the intervention are compared to see how the change has affected what the group worker is measuring. For example, after collecting baseline data and finding that members of a group were talking almost exclusively to the worker rather than to each other, the worker may intervene by discussing the issue with the group, prompting members to talk with one another more frequently, and praising them when they initiate conversation with one another.

After the intervention, communications between members and the worker decrease, and communications between members increase. Figure 13.6 graphs the results of such an intervention. The single-system method illustrated in Figure 13.6 is often called an *AB design,* in which A is the baseline period before intervention and B is the postintervention, data-collection period.

Various single-system designs are multiple baseline, withdrawal, reversal, and changing criterion. These types of single-system designs are more complicated to apply for the practicing group worker than is the AB baseline-intervention design, but they are also more effective than the AB design in reliably evaluating practice outcomes. They are especially useful when workers have the time, energy, interest, and resources to test the efficacy of a new or alternative intervention to improve practice with future groups working on similar problems. For additional information about single-system methods, see Bloom, Fisher, and Orme (2003).

Case Study Methods

Case studies rely on precise descriptions, accurate observations, and detailed analyses of a single example or case. Case studies were developed by researchers interested in qualitative

FIGURE 13.5 ● *Changes in Baseline Data after an Intervention in a Group*

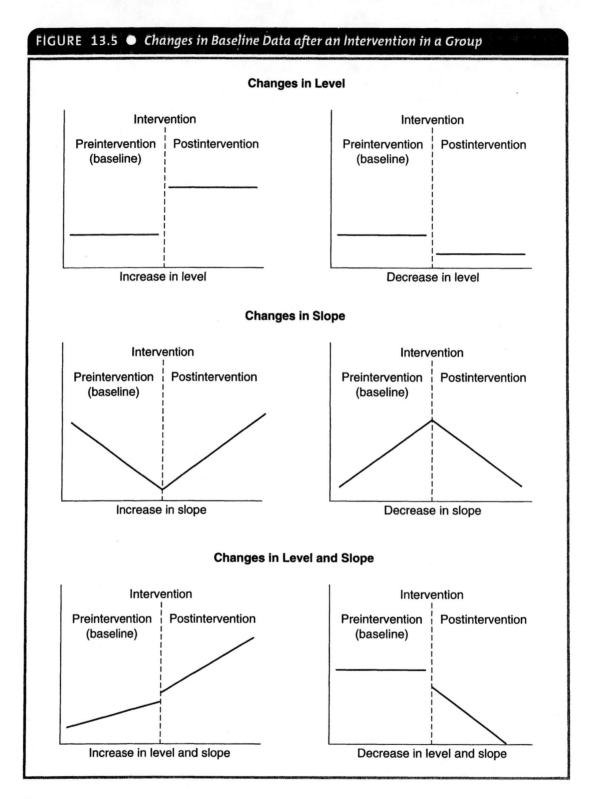

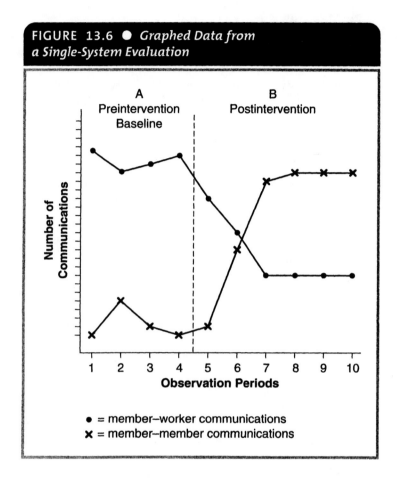

FIGURE 13.6 ● *Graphed Data from a Single-System Evaluation*

A
Preintervention
Baseline

B
Postintervention

Number of Communications

1   2   3   4   5   6   7   8   9   10
Observation Periods

● = member–worker communications
✕ = member–member communications

research methods. Because group workers are accustomed to keeping records and analyzing their work in detail, these methods may have more appeal for some group workers than the quantitatively oriented, single-system research methods.

As with single-system methods, case study methods are based on intensive analysis of a single case. Therefore, the data collected may not be as internally or externally valid as data collected using classic control-group designs. Nevertheless, the strengths of case studies are that they can provide a clear, detailed, vivid description of the processes and procedures of a group in action, and they are often more feasible to apply in practice settings than in control-group designs.

Case study methods include participant and nonparticipant observation (Marshall & Rossman, 1999; Padgett, 1998; Patton, 2000), case comparison methods (Butler, Davis, & Kukkonen, 1979), ethnographic methods (Scheneul, Lecompte, Borgatti, & Nastasi, 1998), and focus group interviews (Greenbaum, 1998; Krueger & Casey, 2000; Morgan, 1997). The following example illustrates the use of case study methods.

● **CASE EXAMPLE** *Using Case Study Methods*

A group worker who was planning on leading a health and wellness group for cardiac patients found it useful to "sit in" on several other wellness groups conducted in the community. She obtained permission to observe several groups in hospital and nonhospital settings and was able to videotape some of these. Using case study methods to analyze the content of the video recordings as well as her own notes made from observing each group, she concluded that most of the groups not only provided important education information, but also provided a strong sense of "universality" among members, that is, helping members to understand that they were not unique or alone in experiencing particular problems. She also concluded that members provided a strong component of mutual aid to each other in these groups. She used this information to develop a new group in her own setting.

Using a case comparison method, a worker who has developed a group program for alcoholics may want to compare the program with similar programs, perhaps those offered by Alcoholics Anonymous and a county alcoholism program. A comparison of the three programs along prespecified dimensions created by the worker to answer specific information needs could lead to innovations in the worker's program. The worker may also want to conduct focus group interviews with individuals who have participated in each program to determine the most- and least-valued features of each program. These features could then be evaluated for their efficacy, as described in the process shown in Figure 13.4.

Group workers might also want to use case study methods in working with task groups. For example, a worker might want to use nonparticipant observation to compare the methods that other day-treatment mental health agencies use when reviewing clients in treatment-team meetings.

Both single-system methods and case study methods offer workers the opportunity to continually develop and improve their practice. Rigorous application of these methods requires that workers spend time designing and implementing evaluation methods and collecting data that are not routinely available. The worker must decide whether the extra effort spent in organizing and carrying out a developmental evaluation is worth the new or improved programs that may result.

EVALUATIONS FOR DETERMINING EFFECTIVENESS AND EFFICIENCY

Effectiveness evaluations focus on the extent to which a group accomplishes its objectives. They give workers the opportunity to gain objective feedback about the helpfulness of the methods being used and the outcomes achieved. Efficiency evaluations compare the benefits of a group program with its cost. They attempt to place a monetary value on the outcomes of a group and to compare this cost with the costs incurred by conducting a group.

Effectiveness and efficiency evaluations rely on experimental and quasi-experimental designs, reliable and valid measures, and statistical procedures to determine the significance of an intervention on the outcome of task or treatment groups. Compared with the other types of evaluations mentioned in this chapter, effectiveness and efficiency evaluations are less flexible, more technically complex, and more difficult to conduct. Because of the nature of the methods employed and the precision and rigor necessary to apply them, a flexible and cooperative setting is needed to conduct effectiveness and efficiency evaluations. The sponsoring agency must be willing to supply the needed resources and the technical assistance necessary for conducting such evaluations.

One method for evaluating outcomes that is less difficult to apply than many other effectiveness evaluation methods is called *goal attainment scaling* (Kiresuk & Sherman, 1968). Using this method, the worker can obtain information about the achievement of goals by individual group members or the group as a whole. An example of goal attainment scaling is shown in Figure 13.7.

FIGURE 13.7 ● *Example of Goal Attainment Scaling*

Scale Levels	Problem Areas		
	Anxiety	**Depression**	**Loss of Appetite**
1. Most unfavorable expected outcome	Four or more self-rated occurrences of feeling anxious each day	Suicide	Refuses to eat any daily meals
2. Less than expected outcome	Three self-rated occurrences of feeling anxious each day	One or more attempts at suicide	Eats one meal each day
3. Expected outcome	Two self-rated occurrences of feeling anxious each day	No attempts at suicide, discusses feelings of depression	Eats two meals each day
4. More than expected outcome	One self-rated occurrence of feeling anxious each day	No attempts at suicide, discusses possible causes of depression	Eats three meals each day
5. Most favorable expected outcome	No self-rated occurrence of feeling anxious each day	No attempts at suicide, identifies two causes for depression	Eats three meals a day and snacks between meals
Weight	5	25	5
Goal Attainment Score	4	3	3
Weighted Goal Attainment Score	20	75	15

Members and the group leader can work together to develop outcome measures for each scale level. For example, a group may decide that the most unfavorable outcome for the problem of depression is suicide. Similarly, the group may decide that the most favorable outcome for loss of appetite is to eat three meals a day and to snack between meals. After work on the problem areas is completed, goal attainment can be measured by using the scales that have been developed for each problem area. In the example in Figure 13.7, goal attainment is indicated by a box around the actual outcome. For the problem of anxiety, the outcome was one self-rated occurrence of feeling anxious each day. This outcome was given a score of 4.

As shown in Figure 13.7, it is possible to weight each scale differentially so that attaining more important goals receives greater emphasis in the overall evaluation than does attaining less important goals. Thus, the goal attainment score of 4 obtained for the problem of anxiety is multiplied by its weight of 5 to yield a goal attainment score of 20. Even though the goal attainment score on the problem area of depression is a 3, after it is multiplied by its weight (25), the weighted goal attainment score for the problem of depression (75) is much greater than that obtained on the problem of anxiety (20). Goal attainment scores on each scale can be added together to form a composite score for individual or group goal attainment.

Statistical procedures have been developed to compare goal attainment scores across individual group members and across groups (Garwick, 1974). Although goal attainment scaling has received some methodological criticism (Seaberg & Gillespie, 1977), the procedure remains an important tool for group workers to consider when conducting effectiveness evaluations.

A variation on goal attainment scaling that has been used successfully in several studies of the effectiveness of group treatment is the pressing problem index (Toseland, Labrecque, Goebel, & Whitney, 1992; Toseland, et al., 2001; Toseland, McCallion, Smith, & Banks, in press). During the intake interview, potential group members are asked to describe several problems they would like to work on in the group. These problems, plus any other problems known to commonly affect the individuals targeted for the intervention, are listed in an inventory of pressing problems. Before meeting and again at the end of the group, participants are asked to rate the stress caused by each pressing problem and their efficacy in coping with the problem. Change in stress and efficacy in coping with the pressing problems are assessed by adding up the responses to all pressing problems at each time of measurement.

Effectiveness evaluations rely on experimental and quasi-experimental designs to determine whether a group accomplishes its objectives. A true experimental design employs random assignment of participants to treatment and control groups. It compares the treatment and control groups on specific outcome variables to measure differences between treatment and control group subjects. In *quasi-experimental designs,* participants cannot be randomly assigned to treatment and control groups. It is often difficult to assign subjects randomly to treatment and control groups in practice settings. Therefore, quasi-experimental designs are often used in effectiveness evaluations even though they are subject to possible biases because nonrandomly assigned subjects are more likely to be nonequivalent on important variables that may affect the outcome variables being measured.

It is especially difficult to conduct adequate effectiveness evaluations in group research projects. To do valid statistical analyses of data from experimental designs, the observations or measures on each unit of analysis must be independent. Researchers testing the effectiveness of group treatment sometimes assume that individual group members are the unit of analysis. However, individual members are not independent of one another in a group setting because they are affected by other members of the group. For example, while members are taking a questionnaire, a lawn mower might go past the window and disturb all members of the group. Members' scores are not totally independent of one another; that is, the lawn mower affects all members in a similar manner. One way to overcome this problem is to ensure that all evaluation instruments are given to group members on a one-to-one basis outside of the group meeting.

The requirement for independent observations is also violated by researchers interested in group-level phenomena such as cohesion and leadership. Glisson (1986) has pointed out that some statistical procedures such as analysis of variance (ANOVA) are not robust to this violation, which can lead to serious overestimates of the effectiveness of group procedures (Eisenhart, 1972). Because there must be a relatively large number of units of analysis to obtain valid statistical comparisons of a group-level phenomenon, effectiveness evaluations of group work practice require that a relatively large number of groups be conducted. Evaluating large numbers of groups is often difficult to do in practice settings because of the limitations on resources, group participants, and competent group leaders. For these reasons, alternatives to using the group as the unit of analysis have been proposed (Bonito, 2002; Burlingame, Kircher, & Honts, 1994; Hoyle & Crawford, 1994).

Efficiency evaluations can be complex and time-consuming, but they can also be useful to persons who want to assess whether their programs are cost-effective. For example, a nonprofit health agency employs a group worker to conduct a smoking-cessation group program. The worker conducts an effectiveness evaluation and finds that 60 percent of the group members become nonsmokers after the group program. The worker also collects data about the costs of the program and the costs to employers who have employees who smoke. These data provide the basis for the worker's efficiency evaluation.

Figure 13.8 shows the worker's calculations and illustrates that at a success rate of 50 percent, the smoking-cessation group program saves the employer $220 each year, beginning one year after the program ends. Savings to the employer last for as long as the employee remains with the company as a nonsmoker. Because the smoking-cessation program has a success rate of 60 percent, employers who have long-term employees are likely to save more than $220 each year for each employee who participates in the smoking-cessation program. This information would be helpful to the nonprofit health agency in motivating large employers whose workers' average length of employment exceeds one year to offer smoking-cessation group programs to their employees.

A description of the methodology for effectiveness evaluations can be found in Babbie (2002) or Rossi, Freeman, and Lipsey (1999), and a description of efficiency evaluations can be found in Drummond, Stoddart, and Torrance (1987), Gold, Siegel, Russell, and Weinstein (1996), Levin and McEwan (2001), or Nas (1996). Group workers should have a basic understanding of these methods to be able to assess the efficacy of their own practice and to be able to critically evaluate methodologies used in published reports about the effectiveness and efficiency of group work methods and group programs.

FIGURE 13.8 ● An Efficiency Evaluation of a Group Program for Smoking Cessation

Costs of Smoking to the Employer per Employee per Year*

Insurance:	
Health	$220.00
Fire	10.00
Workers' Compensation and other accidents	40.00
Life and disability	30.00
Other:	
Productivity	166.00
Absenteeism	100.00
Smoking effects on nonsmokers	110.00
Total cost of smoking	$660.00

Per Employee Cost of the Smoking-Cessation Program

Smoking-cessation program	$120.00
Employee time to complete the program	100.00
Total Cost for Each Employee	$220.00

Total Cost of Achieving One Nonsmoker
(based on a projected success rate of 50%) $440.00

Savings to Employers

Total cost of smoking	$660.00
Total cost of the smoking-cessation program	−440.00
	$220.00

*Cost figures taken from Marvin Kristein, "How Much Can Business Expect to Earn from Smoking Cessation," presented at the Conference of the National Interagency Council on Smoking and Health, Chicago, Illinois, January 9, 1980.

EVALUATION MEASURES

The four broad types of evaluation methods provide a framework that workers can use to collect information for planning, monitoring, developing, or assessing the efficacy or efficiency of their practice with a group. In applying these methods, workers can choose from a variety of measures to collect the necessary information for an effective evaluation. Numerous measures have been developed for evaluating group work practice; some specifically focus on properties of the group as a whole, and others may be useful to the worker in evaluating changes in members of specific groups. Decisions about which measures to use depend on (1) the objectives of the evaluation, (2) properties of the measures being considered for use, (3) the form in which the data will be collected, and (4) what constructs will be measured.

Choosing Measures

The first and most essential step in choosing appropriate measures is to decide on the objectives of the evaluation. Clarifying the information that is needed, what the information collected will be used for, and who will use the information can help the worker choose the appropriate measures for the evaluation. For example, if the worker is interested in obtaining feedback from members about their satisfaction with a particular group, the worker may be less concerned about the reliability and validity of a measure than about the difficulties members might experience in providing the information. The worker may also be concerned about members' reactions to the evaluation and the time needed to administer it, particularly if the worker has a limited amount of group time available for conducting an evaluation.

The worker should be familiar with two properties of measures that govern the quality of the data to be collected. *Reliability* refers to the extent to which an instrument measures the same phenomenon in the same way each time the measure is used. A reliable measure is consistent. When measuring the same variable, it yields the same score each time it is administered. *Validity* refers to the extent to which a data-collection instrument measures what it purports to measure. A valid measure is one that yields a true or actual representation of the variable being measured. The ideal situation is for a group worker to use a reliable and valid measure that has already been constructed. When such measures exist, they are generally superior to measures developed quickly by the worker without regard to reliability or validity.

Constructing reliable and valid measures takes a considerable amount of time. Workers should decide what level of measurement precision and objectivity is needed when deciding how much time to spend constructing and validating a measure. For additional information about constructing reliable and valid measures, see Hopkins (1998), Nunnally (1994), or Sax (1996).

Another consideration in choosing appropriate evaluation measures is to decide what form of data collection would be most useful to the group worker and most convenient for group members. Data can be collected by interviewing members, by written response to a questionnaire, or by audio or video recordings. The data-collection form that will be most helpful to the worker depends on how the data will be used and the extent to which group members are willing and able to cooperate with the data-collection procedures used. In evaluating group work with children, older people, and disabled people, for example, audiotaped responses can often overcome any difficulties the individuals might have in making written responses.

Finally, the worker must decide how a particular property or concept will be measured. For example, after deciding that the objective of an evaluation is to test the effectiveness of a particular group, the worker must decide whether information is sought about changes in the behavior, cognition, or the affect of individual group members. In task groups, the worker may want to measure both the extent to which a group completes its tasks and the quality and the quantity of the products or tasks achieved.

When one conducts evaluations, it is often helpful to have multiple measures of the property being measured. When measuring the effectiveness of a group program for drug abusers, for example, the worker might want to measure reductions in drug intake, changes in self-concept, and changes in beliefs about the effects of drug abuse. Multiple measures, such as blood tests, attitude scales, and a questionnaire concerning information about drug use, might be useful in assessing the group's effectiveness in helping members become drug free.

Types of Measures

A wide variety of reliable and valid measures are available for group workers to use when they are evaluating interventions with specific groups (Fisher & Corcoran, 1994; Kramer & Conoley, 1992; Robinson & Shaver, 1973). These sources include self-report measures, observational measures, and measures of the products of group interaction. In the description of each type of measure, the text indicates particular measures that have often been used in evaluations of group work.

Self-Report Measures

Perhaps the most widely used evaluation measures are written and oral self-reports, in which group members are asked to respond to questions about a particular phenomenon. Although they may focus on any phenomenon, self-report measures are particularly useful in measuring intrapersonal phenomena such as beliefs or attitudes, which cannot be measured directly by observational measures. Group workers can also construct their own self-report measures for specialized situations in which no published self-report measures exist. However, it is difficult to construct a reliable and valid self-report measure. Fortunately, a variety of published self-report measures are available, including measures of anxiety, depression, assertiveness, self-concept, and locus of control. Five published measures that may be of particular interest to group workers are the Group Atmosphere Scale (Silbergeld, Koenig, Manderscheid, Meeker, & Hornung, 1975), Hemphill's Index of Group Dimensions (Hemphill, 1956), the Hill Interaction Matrix (Hill, 1977), Yalom's Curative Factors Scale (Lieberman, Yalom, & Miles, 1973; Stone, Lewis, & Beck, 1994) and the Therapeutic Factors Inventory (Lese & MacNair-Semands, 2000).

The Group Atmosphere Scale (GAS) was designed to measure the psychosocial environment of therapy groups. It consists of 12 subscales: (1) aggression, (2) submission, (3) autonomy, (4) order, (5) affiliation, (6) involvement, (7) insight, (8) practicality, (9) spontaneity, (10) support, (11) variety, and (12) clarity. Each subscale contains 10 true-false items. The GAS has been assessed to have acceptable reliability and validity (Silbergeld et al., 1975).

Hemphill's Index of Group Dimensions measures 13 properties of groups: (1) autonomy, (2) control, (3) flexibility, (4) hedonic tone, (5) homogeneity, (6) intimacy, (7) participation, (8) permeability, (9) polarization, (10) potency, (11) stability, (12) stratification, and

(13) viscidity. The measure consists of 150 items to which group members respond on a five-point scale from definitely true to mostly false.

The Hill Interaction Matrix (HIM-A, HIM-B, HIM-G) is a self-report measure in which a group leader, a group member, or an observer responds to 72 items about group process. The measure is designed to discriminate between types of group interactions on two dimensions: the content discussed and the level and type of work occurring in the group.

Yalom's Curative Factors Scale is a widely used, 14-item measure that assesses 12 therapeutic dimensions in treatment groups: (1) altruism, (2) catharsis, (3) cohesiveness, (4) existentiality, (5) family re-enactment, (6) guidance, (7) hope, (8) identification, (9) interpersonal input, (10) interpersonal output, (11) self-understanding, and (12) universality. Stone, Lewis, and Beck (1994) have reported some psychometric properties of the instrument.

The Therapeutic Factors Inventory is a 99-item scale that measures Yalom's (1995) therapeutic factors. It contains 11 subscales that measure (1) altruism, (2) catharsis, (3) cohesiveness, (4) corrective enactment of the primary family group, (5) development of socializing techniques, (6) existential factors, (7) imitative behavior, (8) imparting information, (9) instillation of hope, (10) interpersonal learning, and (11) universality. The scale has good reliability, but validity testing is needed (Lese & MacNair-Semands, 2000).

Observational Measures

Unlike self-report measures that rely on the accuracy of a respondent's memory, observational measures use independent, objective observers to collect data as they occur or as they are replayed from video or audio recordings. Although observational measures are less susceptible to biases and distortions than are self-report measures, observational measures are used less frequently than self-report measures because they require the availability of one or more trained observers to collect the data. The observers code discrete group interactions into categories that are mutually exclusive and exhaustive; that is, during each observation period, only one observation is recorded and it can be recorded in only one category.

The most well-known observational measure for groups is called Bales' Interaction Process Analysis (Bales, 1950). This observational index consists of 12 categories. Interactions are coded by assigning each person a number. For example, when an interaction occurs from member 1 to member 4 or from member 3 to member 1, the interaction is marked 1-4 or 3-1 in the appropriate category. With well-trained observers, Bales' Interaction Process Analysis can be a useful tool for the evaluation of group interactions.

More recently, Bales (1980) and Bales, Cohen, and Williamson (1979) have developed a measure called Systematic Multiple Level Observation of Groups (SYMLOG). As explained in Chapter 8, SYMLOG is a method for analyzing the overt and covert behaviors of group members. With SYMLOG, a three-dimensional graphic presentation or field diagram of the interaction of group members is made. Through the field diagram, group members can analyze the way they interact with one another to improve the ability of the group to accomplish its tasks. An example of the use of SYMLOG for assessing group functioning can be found in Chapter 8. As an evaluation tool, SYMLOG can be used to measure several variables affecting both the socioemotional and the task aspects of members' behavior in groups.

Other observational measures have also been used for evaluating changes in a group over time. For example, Moreno's (1934) scales of sociometric choice and sociometric preference, described more fully in Chapter 8, assess relationships among members of a group by having each member rank other members on certain dimensions such as their preference for working with other group members or their liking for other group members.

Products of Group Interaction

A worker may be able to measure the products of group interaction in a simple and straightforward manner. In task groups, products of the group's work are often tangible. For example, a team may develop a written document that governs how services will be delivered to clients. The work of a delegate council may be evaluated by the number of agenda items it acts on during its monthly meeting. In both instances, group products can be used for purposes of evaluation. In treatment groups, products of group interaction may also be useful measures. Rose (1989) suggests that measurable products of group interaction include behavior change, the number of between-meeting tasks generated at a group meeting, and the number of tasks actually completed.

Evaluation measures from which workers can choose when evaluating their practice with a group range from measures consisting of a few open-ended questions made by a worker who wants to get some feedback from group members to sophisticated observational measures requiring highly trained observers. Workers develop or select measures in relation to the evaluation design they are going to use and, ultimately, in relation to the information they hope to obtain. Although selecting appropriate measures and implementing effective evaluations is time-consuming for the practicing group worker, it is often well worth the effort because it may result in improved service and in new and innovative group programs.

SUMMARY

Evaluation is the method by which practitioners obtain information and feedback about their work with a group. In the current age of accountability and fiscal constraints by which difficult program choices are made, evaluation methodologies are useful tools for practitioners. This chapter discusses some reasons that group workers may choose to use evaluation methods in their practice.

Practitioners are often faced with a dilemma when considering whether to evaluate their practice. They must decide whether the demands of serving clients are compatible with developing and conducting evaluations. This chapter describes the strengths and weaknesses of a number of evaluation methods that may be used in differing practice situations and settings.

Four broad types of evaluation methods are evaluations for (1) planning a group, (2) monitoring a group, (3) developing a group, and (4) testing the effectiveness and efficiency of a group. These methods are used with a variety of evaluation measures to help practitioners develop, test, and implement more effective group work methods. Evaluation methods can also be combined with knowledge accumulated from practice experiences (sometimes referred to as *practice wisdom*) to improve the methods used by group workers to meet a variety of needs in diverse practice settings.

● **CASE EXAMPLE**

Despite telling his group work students always to monitor and evaluate their practice with groups, Bob knew that they would be caught in the classic practitioner's dilemma. The demands of service delivery would make it difficult for them to spend the time and resources needed to formally evaluate their work with groups. He was surprised, however, when a former student returned with good news about research funding and a request for help. Maureen had been awarded a demonstration grant of $5,000 to develop an evaluation of her violence reduction group. In addition, the state's education department suggested that if her research project was successful, Maureen could apply for a much larger grant to implement and evaluate additional groups. She hoped that Bob could give her some helpful ideas for a research design.

Maureen's violence reduction group was aimed at sensitizing elementary students to the types of violence in their school environment and helping them find nonviolent ways of behaving. It had an educational component that consisted of a series of standardized lessons about violence. In addition, it had a growth component in which members learned new ways of handling themselves when confronted with anger from their peers.

Based on her conversations with Bob, Maureen decided to use the Achenback Child Behavior Checklist (Achenback, 1991) in her evaluation because it had been found to be a reliable and valid measure of children's behavior by researchers who had examined its psychometric properties. Al-

though there is both a parent and a teacher version of the Achenback Child Behavior Checklist, she decided to use only the parent form because she was concerned that teachers were too busy to spend the time to fill out the form for each student involved in the project. Instead, she designed a short questionnaire aimed at collecting feedback from teachers about students' behaviors in the classroom.

Maureen decided to use a partial-crossover control group design to evaluate the impact of the group. She would start a new group from the waiting list and use some of the students who were still on the waiting list as a control group. In a partial-crossover design, after the intervention is conducted with the experimental group, the control group is then offered the intervention.

Although the design would provide good information about the effectiveness of the group, it posed several ethical issues. First, Maureen had to secure written permission from the parents of the children who would participate in both the experimental and control groups. Second, Maureen had to discuss and justify the use of the waiting list as a control group with the children's parents and with school administrators. Confidentiality and voluntary participation were also issues. As a result of her discussions with students, parents, and administrators, Maureen secured permission to proceed with the research.

To help ensure the equivalence of the experimental and control groups, Maureen randomly assigned students on the waiting list to either of the two groups. When the groups were composed, she asked the parents of children in both groups to fill out the behavior checklist. This measurement served as a pretest for both the experimental and control groups and provided important baseline information. She triangulated these data with information obtained from teachers who filled out the short questionnaire she had developed. Maureen then conducted the violence reduction sessions with the experimental group. At the end of the group, she again administered the Achenback checklist to parents of children in the experimental and control groups and again collected data from teachers. She then compared the pretest and posttest results for both groups. Students in the experimental group achieved positive movement on their checklist scores whereas scores for the control group members did not change significantly. Using the control group scores as a second pretest, Maureen then ran the violence reduction group for the members of the control group. Posttest scores for this crossover group were significantly higher than their pretest scores.

The parents of students who participated in Maureen's violence reduction groups reported fewer incidents of acting out behavior of a violent nature, especially related to school. In addition, teachers reported that students who participated in the violence reduction groups had more control over their feelings of anger and used more positive measures for mediating their personal disputes in the classroom.

Maureen spent a good deal of time preparing a final report on her research project. She made sure to document both the results of her findings as well as the nature of the intervention that took place within the violence reduction groups. School administrators were pleased at the outcome of her evaluation efforts. With a sense of pride and gratefulness, Maureen sent a copy of the final report to her former research teacher with a note of thanks for helping her with the project. She later learned that her research report was the highlight of the state education department's review panel's deliberations on funding new initiatives aimed at reducing violence in schools.

Guidelines for Ethics

American Group Psychotherapy Association, Inc.[1]

INTRODUCTION

The American Group Psychotherapy Association is a professional multidisciplinary organization whose purpose is to "provide a forum for the exchange of ideas among qualified professional persons interested in group psychotherapy and to publish and to make publications available on all subjects relating to group psychotherapy; to encourage the development of sound training programs in group psychotherapy for qualified mental health professionals; to encourage and promote research on group psychotherapy and to establish and maintain high standards of ethical, professional group psychotherapy practice."

Membership in the American Group Psychotherapy Association presumes strict adherence to standards of ethical practice. As a specialty organization, AGPA supports the ethical codes of the primary professional organizations to which our members belong. Providing guidelines for the ethical behavior of group psychotherapists serves to inform both the group psychotherapist and public of the American Group Psychotherapy Association's expectations in the practice of group psychotherapy.

---

[1]Reprinted with the permission of the American Group Psychotherapy Association, Inc., 25 East 21st Street, 6th Floor, New York, NY 10010, Telephone: (212) 477-2677.

GENERAL GUIDELINES

Ethics complaints about AGPA members will be directed to the primary professional organization of the members. AGPA's response as to sanctions will parallel that of the primary organization. For example, if the primary organization concludes that an individual's membership should be suspended for one year, AGPA will suspend membership for one year. Should an ethical complaint be received regarding a member of AGPA who does not belong to a primary professional organization, the complainant will be directed to the state licensing board and/or the state or federal legal system. If the member is found guilty, AGPA's sanctions will parallel the sanctions of the state licensing board, other governmental agencies or courts of law as to the person's ability to practice; the AGPA cannot parallel such sanctions as fines, penalties, or imprisonment.

For those members of the American Group Psychotherapy Association who are psychiatrists, the principles of ethics as applied by the American Psychiatric Association shall govern their behavior; members who are clinical psychologists shall be expected to comply with the principles of ethics laid down by the American Psychological Association; members who are clinical social workers shall be expected to comply with the ethical standards established by the National Federation of Societies for Clinical Social Work; members who are clinical specialists in nursing shall be expected to comply with the principles of ethics of the American Nurses' Association; members who are pastoral counselors shall be expected to comply with the ethical standards of the American Association of Pastoral Care; and members of other professional disciplines having published principles of ethics shall follow those principles. Members of the Association who do not belong to one of the above professional groups having a published standard of ethics shall follow the principles of ethics laid down by the American Psychological Association.

GUIDELINES OF GROUP PSYCHOTHERAPY PRACTICE

The following guidelines of group psychotherapy practice shall serve as models for group therapists' ethical behavior.

Responsibility to Patient/Client

1. The group psychotherapist provides services with respect for the dignity and uniqueness of each patient/client as well as the rights and autonomy of the individual patient/client.

    1.1 The group psychotherapist shall provide the potential group patient/client with information about the nature of group psychotherapy and apprise them of the risks, rights, and obligations as members of a therapy group.

   1.2 The group psychotherapist shall encourage the patient/client's participation in group psychotherapy only so long as it is appropriate to the patient/client's needs.

   1.3 The group psychotherapist shall not practice or condone any form of discrimination on the basis of race, color, sex, sexual orientation, age, religion, national origin, or physical handicap, except that this guideline shall not prohibit group therapy practice with population specific or problem specific groups.

2. The group psychotherapist safeguards the patient/client's right to privacy by judiciously protecting information of a confidential nature.

   2.1 The group shall agree that the patient/client as well as the psychotherapist shall protect the identity of its members.

   2.2 The group psychotherapist shall not use identifiable information about the group or its members for teaching purposes, publication, or professional presentations unless permission has been obtained and all measures have been taken to preserve patient/client anonymity.

3. The group psychotherapist acts to safeguard the patient/client and the public from the incompetent, unethical, illegal practice of any group psychotherapist.

   3.1 The group psychotherapist must be aware of her/his own individual competencies, and when the needs of the patient/client are beyond the competencies of the psychotherapist, consultation must be sought from other qualified professionals or other appropriate sources.

   3.2 The group psychotherapist shall not use her/his professional relationship to advance personal or business interests.

   3.3 Sexual intimacy with patients/clients is unethical.

   3.4 The group psychotherapist shall protect the patient/client and the public from misinformation and misrepresentation. She/he shall not use false or misleading advertising regarding her/his qualifications or skills as a group psychotherapist.

Professional Standards

The group psychotherapist shall maintain the integrity of the practice of group psychotherapy.

1. It is the personal responsibility of the group psychotherapist to maintain competence in the practice of group psychotherapy through formal education activities and informal learning experiences.

2. The group psychotherapist has a responsibility to contribute to the ongoing development of the body of knowledge pertaining to group psychotherapy whether involved as an investigator, participant, or user of research results.

3. The group psychotherapist shall accept the obligation to attempt to inform and alert other group psychotherapists who are violating ethical principles or to bring those violations to the attention of appropriate professional authorities.

Ethical Guidelines for Group Counselors[1]

Association for Specialists in Group Work[2]

ETHICAL GUIDELINES

1. **Orientation and Providing Information:** Group counselors adequately prepare prospective or new group members by providing as much information about the existing or proposed group as necessary.

2. **Screening of Members:** The group counselor screens prospective group members (when appropriate to their theoretical orientation). Insofar as possible, the counselor selects group members whose needs and goals are compatible with the goals of the group, who will not impede the group process, and whose well-being will not be jeopardized by the group experience. An orientation to the group (i.e., ASGW Ethical Guideline #1) is included during the screening process.

3. **Confidentiality:** Group counselors protect members by defining clearly what confidentiality means, why it is important, and the difficulties involved in enforcement.

4. **Voluntary/Involuntary Participation:** Group counselors inform members whether participation is voluntary or involuntary.

---

[1]Reprinted with the permission of the Association for Specialists in Group Work, a Division of the American Counseling Assocation, 5999 Stevenson Avenue, Alexandra, VA 22304. No further reproduction authorized without written permission of the American Counseling Association.

[2]These guidelines were approved by the Association for Specialists in Group Work (ASGW) Executive Board, June 1, 1989.

5. **Leaving a Group:** Provisions are made to assist a group member to terminate in an effective way.

6. **Coercion and Pressure:** Group counselors protect member rights against physical threats, intimidation, coercion, and undue peer pressure insofar as is reasonably possible.

7. **Imposing Counselor Values:** Group counselors develop an awareness of their own values and needs and the potential effect they have on the interventions likely to be made.

8. **Equitable Treatment:** Group counselors make every reasonable effort to treat each member individually and equally.

9. **Dual Relationships:** Group counselors avoid dual relationships with group members that might impair their objectivity and professional judgment, as well as those which are likely to compromise a group member's ability to participate fully in the group.

10. **Use of Techniques:** Group counselors do not attempt any technique unless trained in its use or under supervision by a counselor familiar with the intervention.

11. **Goal Development:** Group counselors make every effort to assist members in developing their personal goals.

12. **Consultation:** Group counselors develop and explain policies about between-session consultation to group members.

13. **Termination from the Group:** Depending upon the purpose of participation in the group, counselors promote termination of members from the group in the most efficient period of time.

14. **Evaluation and Follow-Up:** Group counselors make every attempt to engage in ongoing assessment and to design follow-up procedures for their groups.

15. **Referrals:** If the needs of a particular member cannot be met within the type of group being offered, the group counselor suggests other appropriate professional referrals.

16. **Professional Development:** Group counselors recognize that professional growth is a continuous, ongoing, developmental process throughout their career.

Standards for Social Work Practice with Groups[1]

Association for the Advancement of Social Work with Groups, Inc., an International Professional Organization (AASWG)

These standards reflect the distinguishing features of group work as well as the unique perspective that social workers bring to their practice with groups. Central to social work practice with groups is the concept of mutual aid. The group worker recognizes that the group, with its multiple helping relationships, is the primary source of change. The group worker's role is one primarily of helping members work together to achieve the goals that they have established for themselves.

By design, these standards are general, rather than specific. They are applicable to the types of groups that social workers encounter in the full range of settings in which they practice. Further, the standards allow the individual practitioner to apply a variety of relevant group work models, within the more general mutual aid framework.

Section I identifies essential knowledge and values that underlie social work practice with groups. In Sections II through V, worker tasks in the pre-group, beginning, middle, and ending phases of the group are identified, as is specific knowledge that may be needed by the worker in each phase.

---

[1]Reprinted with the permission of AASWG.

I. **Core Knowledge and Values**

    A. Familial, social, political, cultural context of member identity, interactional style, and problem
- members are viewed as citizens
- members are capable of change and capable of helping one another

    B. Attention to the whole person
- systems perspective used in assessment and intervention
- person and environment
- bio-psycho-social perspective
- member-in-group
- group-in-community

    C. Competency-based assessment
- emphasis on member strengths as well as deficits

    D. Mutual aid function
- group consists of multiple helping relationships
- worker's primary role is one of helping members to help one another

    E. Groups characterized by democratic process
- members are helped to own the group
- equal worth of members and worker
- worker is not all powerful "expert"
- worker to group and worker to members
- relationships characterized by egalitarianism and reciprocity

    F. Emphasis on empowerment
- group goals emphasize individual member growth and social change
- group worker promotes individual and group autonomy

    G. Worker's assessment and interventions characterized by flexibility and eclecticism

    H. Small group behavior
- group as an entity separate and distinct from individual members
- phases of group development foster change throughout the life of the group
- recognition of how group process shapes and influences individual member behavior

    I. Groups formed for different purposes and goals
- group type (e.g., education, problem-solving, social action) influences what worker does and how group accomplishes its goals

    J. Monitoring and evaluation of success of group in accomplishing its objectives through observation and measurement of outcomes and/or processes

II. Group Work in the Pre-Group Phase

Tasks:

A. Identify common needs of potential group members

B. Plan and conduct outreach, recruitment of members

C. Secure organizational support and sanction for group, if needed

D. Address organizational resistance to groups, if needed

E. Screen and prepare members for group, when appropriate

F. Secure permission for members' participation, when needed

G. Develop compositional balance, if appropriate

H. Select appropriate group type, structure, and size

I. Establish meeting place, time, etc., that promotes member comfort and cohesion

J. Develop and articulate verbally and/or in writing a clear statement of group purpose that reflects member needs and, where appropriate, agency mission

K. Develop and articulate clear statement of worker role that reflects the group's purpose

L. Use preparatory empathy to tune into members' feelings and reactions to group's beginning

Knowledge Needed:

A. Organization's mission and function and how this influences nature of group work service

B. Social and institutional barriers which may impact on the development of group work service

C. Issues associated with group composition

D. Human life cycle and its relationship to potential members' needs

E. Cultural factors and their influence on potential members' lives and their ability to engage in group and relate to others

F. Types of groups and their relationship to member needs

G. Specific types of individual and social problems that lead to a need for group

III. Group Work in the Beginning Phase

Tasks:

A. Provide clear statement of group (and, if necessary, agency) purpose and worker role

B. Elicit member feedback regarding perception of needs, interests, and problems

C. Encourage members to share concerns and strengths with one another

D. Facilitate connections between members and members and worker

E. Encourage awareness and expression of commonalities among members

F. Monitor group for manifestations of authority theme and, when needed, respond directly

G. Assess impact of cultural differences between members and between members and worker and address directly when needed

H. Assist group in establishing rules and norms that promote change and growth

I. Use of self to develop cohesion among members and comfort with worker

J. Assist members in establishing individual and group goals

K. Clarify link between individual and group goals

L. Help members to establish a beginning contract which provides clarity and direction to their work together

M. Promote individual autonomy and empowerment of members

N. Create and maintain environment of sociocultural safety

Knowledge Needed:

A. Group dynamics in beginning stage of group

B. Causes/manifestations of resistance to change among members and in external environment

IV. Group Work in the Middle Phase

Tasks:

A. Point out commonalities among members

B. Reinforce connection between individual needs/problems and group goals

C. Encourage and model supportive, honest feedback between members and between members and worker

D. Use here and now/process illumination to further group's work

E. Help members use role playing, behavioral rehearsal, and other verbal and non-verbal activities to accomplish individual and group goals

F. Monitor norms that govern group's work

G. Assess group's progress toward its goals

    H. Re-contract with members, if needed, to assist them in achieving individual and group goals

    I. Identify obstacles to work within and outside group's boundaries and deal with directly

    J. Clarify and interpret communication patterns between members, between members and the worker, and between the group and others external to the group

    K. Identify and highlight member conflict, when needed, and facilitate resolution

    L. Summarize sessions

Knowledge Needed:

    A. Group dynamics in the middle phase

    B. Role theory and its application to members' relationships with one another and with worker

    C. Communication theory and its application to verbal and non-verbal interactions within group and between group and others external to group

    D. Member interactions as manifestations of sociocultural forces of race, class, gender, sexual orientation, etc.

    E. Member interactions as manifestations of psychodynamic factors

    F. Purposeful use of verbal and non-verbal activities

V. Group Work in the Ending Phase

Tasks:

    A. Identify and point out direct and indirect signs of members' reactions to ending

    B. Share worker's ending feelings with members

    C. Assist members in sharing their feelings about endings with one another

    D. Help members identify gains they have made and changes that have resulted from their participation in the group

    E. Assist members in applying new knowledge and skills to their daily lives

    F. Encourage member feedback to worker

    G. Help members honestly reflect on and evaluate their work together

    H. Develop plans for continuation of service or referral of members, as needed

    I. Assess individual member and group progress

    J. Evaluate impact of group experience on individual members and external environment

Knowledge Needed:

A. Group dynamics in the ending phase

B. Formal and informal resources which maintain and enhance members' growth

C. Influence of past losses and separations in lives of members and worker on group's ending

Films and Videotapes

Blue Sky Productions. (1997). *Discovering community: A future search as a spring-board for action in Santa Cruz County.* Blue Sky Productions, 39201 Schoolcraft Road, Suite B-12, Livonia, MI 48150.

Len Brown. *Problem Solving.* Rutgers University, School of Social Work, 536 George Street, New Brunswick, NJ 08903.

Len Brown. *Termination.* Rutgers University, School of Social Work, 536 George Street, New Brunswick, NJ 08903.

M. R. Carroll. *Group Work: Leading in the Here and Now.* American Counseling Association, 5999 Stevenson Avenue, Alexandria, VA 22304-3300.

Tom Casciato. *Circle of Recovery, with Bill Moyers.* Circle of Recovery, Box 2284, South Burlington, VT 05407.

Center for Psychological Issues in the Nuclear Age. *Meetings That Lead to Action.* Center PINA, 475 Riverside Drive, New York, NY 10115

Edmund S. Muskie Institute of Public Affairs. *Mattering . . . A Journey with Rural Youth.* The Clearinghouse, Muskie School, PO Box 15010, University of Southern Maine, Portland, ME 04112.

Naomi Feil. *Looking for Yesterday.* Edward Feil Productions, 4614 Prospect Avenue, Cleveland, OH 44103.

Naomi Feil. *The More We Get Together: How to Form a Validation Group.* Edward Feil Productions, 4614 Prospect Avenue, Cleveland, OH 44103.

Mel Goldstein. *Reflections on Group Work: The Video Curriculum to Teach Social Group Work.* School of Social Work, State University of New York at Stony Brook, Health Sciences Center, Stony Brook, NY 11794.

Mary Goulding. *Brief therapy-redecision model.* The Milton H. Erickson Foundation, 3606 North 24th Street, Phoenix, AZ 85016.

Mary Goulding. *One-session group therapy with six clients from the audience.* The Milton H. Erickson Foundation, 3606 North 24th Street, Phoenix, AZ 85016.

Insight Media. *Groups and Group Dynamics.* Insight Media, 121 West 85th Street, New York, NY 10024.

Institute for Mental Health Initiatives. (2000). *Learning to manage anger: The RETHINK workout for teens.* Research Press, P.O. Box 9177, Champaign, IL. 61826.

International University College. *Group dynamics in the electronic environment.* Jones Digital Century. Englewood Company, 9697 East Mineral Avenue, Englewood, CA 80112.

Sandra Janoff, Allan Kobernick & Yvonne Agazarian. *Systems-centered psychotherapy—module II—discussion around shame in a shamed group.* Blue Sky Productions, 39201 Schoolcraft Road, Suite B-12, Livonia, MI 48150.

Paul Kadis & Vernessa Gipson. *Dealing with anger: Givin' it, takin' it, workin' it out.* Research Press, P.O. Box 9177, Champaign, IL 61826.

Steven Katten & Irving Janis. *Groupthink.* CRM Learning, 2215 Faraday Avenue, Carlsbad, CA 92008.

Allen Kobernick. *Self-differentiation: A day with John and Joyce Weir.* Blue Sky Productions, 39201 Schoolcraft Road, Suite B-12, Livonia, MI 48150.

William Lauzon. *Staff Groups: Wellness in the Workplace.* Office of Television and Radio, Building 4048–Kilmeer, Rutgers University, New Brunswick, NJ 08903.

Walter Lifton. *Just Like a Family.* University Film Service, University at Albany, State University of New York, 1400 Washington Avenue, Albany, NY 12222.

Marsha Linehan. *Understanding borderline personality disorder: The dialectical approach.* Guilford Press, 72 Spring Street, New York, NY 10012.

Andrew Malekoff. *A Sense of Alienation or Belonging: Building Bridges through Group Involvement.* Institute for Group Work with Children & Youth, 480 Old Westbury Road, Roslyn Heights, NY 11577-2215, Attn: Jane Yazdpour.

Edward Mason. *Chrysalis '86: The Development of a Therapeutic Group.* Penn State AudioVisual Services, 1127 Fox Hill Road, University Park, PA 16803.

Vivian Nelson & Bill Roller. *The promise of group therapy: A live to tape demonstration of a time-limited group.* Jossey Bass, 989 Market Street, San Francisco, CA 94103-1741.

Robert Pasick. *Men in Therapy: Men's Issues and Group Treatment.* AGC United Learning, Menninger Video Productions, 1560 Sherman Avenue, Suite 100, Evanston, IL 60201.

William Piper. *Helping People Adapt to Loss: A Short-Term Group Therapy Approach.* Guilford Publications, Catalog #2498, 72 Spring Street, New York, NY 10012.

Public Broadcasting Video. *Frontline: The Color of Your Skin.* PBS Video, 1320 Braddock Place, Alexandria, VA 22314. No. Fron-9211K. (This is not a film about group work, but a film showing group dynamics at the U.S. Army's Defense Equal Opportunity Management Institute. This film can be used to discuss sensitivity training or race relations in groups.)

Research Press. *Skills & techniques for group counseling with youth.* Research Press, Dept. 23W, P.O. Box 9177, Champaign, IL 61822.

Sheldon Rose. *The Best of the Children's Groups.* School of Social Work, University of Wisconsin–Madison, 425 Henry Mall, Madison, WI 53706.

Sheldon Rose. *Common Problems in Parent Training Groups.* School of Social Work, University of Wisconsin–Madison, 425 Henry Mall, Madison, WI 53706.

Sheldon Rose. *The Golden Eagles.* School of Social Work, University of Wisconsin–Madison, 425 Henry Mall, Madison, WI 53706.

Sheldon Rose. *Problem Solving in Groups.* School of Social Work, University of Wisconsin–Madison, 425 Henry Mall, Madison, WI 53706.

Round Table Films. *Meeting in Progress.* Round Table Films, 113 North San Vincente Boulevard, Beverly Hills, CA 90211.

Saul Scheidlinger & Cary Sandberg. *Reunion with the Mother of Abandonment: A Group Fantasy.* Insight Media, 121 West 85th Street, New York, NY 10024.

Lawrence Shulman. *Skills of Helping: Leading a First Group Session.* Instructional Communication Center, McGill University, Montreal, Quebec, Canada H3A 2K6.

Lawrence Shulman. *Skills of Helping: The Married Couples Group.* Instructional Communication Center, McGill University, Montreal, Quebec, Canada H3A 2K6

Rosemary Snead. *Skills and Techniques for Group Counselling with Youth.* Research Press, 2612 North Mattis Avenue, Champaign, IL 61821.

David Spiegel & Pat Fobair. *Supportive-Expressive Group Therapy for People with Cancer and Their Families.* Center for Media and Independent Learning, University of California Extension, 2000 Center Street, 4th Floor, Berkeley, CA 94704.

David Spiegel & Pat Fobair. *Tape I, The Process of Forming a Support Group and Detoxifying Death; Tape II, Taking Time and Fortifying Families; Tape III, Dealing with Doctors and Controlling Pain through Self-Hypnosis; Tape IV, A Model Session.* Center for Media and Independent Learning, University of California Extension, 2000 Center Street, 4th Floor, Berkeley, CA 94704.

Roberta Starzecpyzl. *Shooting Stars.* Dragon Rising Productions, P. O. Box 629, Village Station, New York, NY 10014.

Irving Yalom. *Understanding Group Psychotherapy.* Center for Media and Independent Learning, University of California Extension, 2000 Center Street, 4th Floor, Berkeley, CA 94704.

Irving Yalom. *Understanding group psychotherapy: Volume II. Inpatient group psychotherapy. Tape A: Orientation and agenda formation. Tape B: Agenda filling and summary.* Brooks/Cole Publishing Company, 511 Forest Lodge Road, Pacific Grove, CA 93950.

Irving Yalom. *Inpatients.* Center for Media and Independent Learning, University of California Extension, 2000 Center Street, 4th Floor, Berkeley, CA 94704.

Irving Yalom. *Outpatients.* Center for Media and Independent Learning, University of California Extension, 2000 Center Street, 4th Floor, Berkeley, CA 94704.

Irving Yalom. *Yalom: An interview.* Center For Media and Independent Learning, University of California Extension, 2000 Center Street, 4th Floor, Berkeley, CA 94704.

OTHER FILM RESOURCES

Interviews of Saul Bernstein, Giesela Konopka, Helen Northen, Helen Phillips, Mary Lou Sommers, and Gertrude Wilson as well as other films are available in VHS format from David Klaassen, Social Welfare History Archives, University of Minnesota, 1012 Walter Library, 117 Pleasant Street, SE, Minneapolis, MN 55455.

Group Announcements

SUPPORT GROUP FOR NEW PARENTS

You are invited to join a support group of parents who have children ages 6 months to 2 years. The group will discuss concerns identified by its members including such possible issues as infant care, sharing household responsibilities, disciplining your child, toilet training, and child-care resources.

Sponsor

Greenwich Community Mental Health Center
49 Cambridge Avenue
Greenwich, NY
(212) 246-2468

Group Leaders

George Oxley, ACSW, clinic director
Marybeth Carol, BSW, clinic social worker

Membership

Open to all parents with children from ages 6 months to 2 years

Dates and Times

March–April–May, Thursday evenings from 7:30 to 9:30 P.M.

Child Care

Parents are encouraged to bring their children to the center. Child care will be available from human service interns of Hudson Center Community College.

Cost

Enrollment fee for the three-month group, total $90.00 per couple, payable monthly

For further information, call Mr. Oxley or Ms. Carol at (212) 246-2468.

YOUTH CENTER INTEREST MEETING

The residents of the Johnsonville, Pittstown, and Valley Falls area are invited to discuss the proposed establishment of a youth center for these communities. Issues to be discussed include cost of service, fundraising, need for service, and support for such a service.

Sponsor

Rensselaer Council of Community Services

Meeting Place

Johnsonville Firehouse

Date and Time

Thursday, March 25, from 7 to 9 P.M.

Further Information

Call Jim Kesser, ACSW
(212) 241-2412

Refreshments will be served.

Outline for a Group Proposal

Treatment/Task

Abstract

Short statement summarizing major
points of group

Purpose

Brief statement of purpose
How the group will conduct its work
Job description of the worker

Agency Sponsorship

Agency name and mission
Agency resources (physical facilities, financial,
staff)
Geographic and demographic data on agency

Membership

Specific population for the group
Why population was chosen

Recruitment

Methods to be used

Composition

Criteria for member inclusion/exclusion
Size, open or closed group, demographic
characteristics

Orientation

Specific procedures to be used

Contract

Number, frequency, length, and time of meeting

Environment

Physical arrangements (room, space, materials)
Financial arrangements (budget, expense,
income)
Special arrangements (child care, transportation)

appendix E

An Example of a Treatment Group Proposal

ADOLESCENT DISCHARGE GROUP

The Children's Refuge Home

Abstract

This is a proposal for a social skills training group for adolescents who are about to be released into the community from the children's refuge home.

Purpose

The group will discuss what each member expects to be doing on release to the community. The group will reinforce social learning that has taken place during the residential placement and will help members learn new social skills that will be needed to successfully relate to parents, siblings, teachers, and employers. Role playing, behavior rehearsal modeling, and reinforcement will be employed as methods of teaching social skills.

Agency Sponsorship

The Children's Refuge Home, a residential treatment facility for delinquent youth, serves teenage boys who cannot live at home because of law-breaking activities. About 200 boys reside here in 15 cottages. The agency has a 200-acre campus with an on-campus school. Staff ratio is about one staff member per four boys; direct-care staff include child care workers, social workers, nursing staff, psychologists, psychiatrists, and clergy.

Membership

Approximately 10 boys are released to the community each month. The discharge group will be composed from a population of boys for whom discharge is planned within the next three months.

Recruitment

Because this group represents a new service for the institution, members will be recruited by asking cottage parents for volunteers from their respective cottages. An announcement will be printed and delivered to the senior cottage parents for all cottages. In addition, teachers and social workers will be contacted to suggest possible candidates for the group.

Composition

The group will be composed of six to eight boys from 12 to 14 years old who anticipate discharge from CRH within the next three months. In addition, this first group will include only children who will be returning to natural parents or relatives rather than to foster care or group homes. The group will be closed and will not add new members because it is important that social skills be learned in a gradual and cumulative fashion.

Orientation

Each member will be interviewed by the leaders. During this interview, the members will view a videotape on group treatment for children, and the details of the tape will be discussed to demonstrate how group meetings will be conducted.

Environment

The ideal location for this group is the diagnostic classroom within the campus school. Proximity to videotaping equipment is necessary so group members can tape and view role plays. A small budget is required ($120) for proposed field trips, charts, and materials for listing skills and posting individual and group progress, and for refreshments after meetings. Additional expenses include two color videotapes ($60). Special arrangements will have to be made so that each member's afterschool recreation schedule is free for Monday afternoon meeting times.

An Example of a Task Group Proposal

TASK FORCE ON RESEARCH UTILIZATION IN PROBATION

Abstract

This is a proposal for establishing an interagency task force to study how research and research procedures are used in three county probation offices. The group will issue a report with recommendations for increasing research use in probation settings.

Purpose

This group will be formed to study the use of research in county probation offices. The group will meet to discuss the results of surveys taken on each probation office regarding the extent to which probation workers use published research to inform their practice and the extent to which they conduct research in conjunction with their practice. The group will be convened by Robert Rivas, ACSW, at Siena College.

Agency Sponsorship

The task force will be sponsored by the tri-county consortium of probation agencies. The Rockwell County agency will provide physical facilities for meetings. Financial costs will be shared by all county agencies.

Membership

Each county agency will nominate three representatives to attend meetings to ensure equal representation among agencies.

Recruitment

Mailings will be sent to all agency directors. Members of the tri-county association will be informed by an announcement in the newsletter. Each agency director will be requested by letter to appoint three representatives to the task force.

Composition

The task force will require that each agency appoint one representative from each of the following categories: probation administrator, probation supervisor (or senior officer), and probation officer. The task force will include nine representatives from agencies and two research consultants from local colleges. All members of the task force should have some knowledge about research methods. This will be a closed group, although interested people may attend specific meetings after obtaining permission from the group's leader.

Orientation

The group will be given several research reports to read to prepare for discussions. The group leader will contact each member individually to get ideas for composing an agenda.

Contract

The task force will meet once a month for six sessions. Meetings will last for three hours and will take place every fourth Monday of the month from 9 A.M. to noon. The group will be required to compose and issue a preliminary report on research use within one month after the final meeting.

Environment

The Rockwell County agency will provide the use of its staff meeting room, which is equipped with tables and blackboards, for the group's work. Copying facilities will be provided by Rockwell County, and each county will be billed for one third the expenses (limit $30.00 per county). About $100 will be required to prepare and distribute the task force's final report and recommendations (contributed by the county association). Agency directors for each county have been requested to provide travel allowance (25 cents a mile) for all travel in conjunction with the work of the task force.

appendix G

Suggested Readings on Program Activities

PROGRAM ACTIVITIES FOR GROUPS OF CHILDREN AND ADOLESCENTS

Allen, J. S., & Klein, R. J. (1996). *Ready, set, relax: A research-based program of relaxation, learning, and self-esteem for children.* Watertown, WI: Inner Coaching.

Borba, M., & Borba, C. (1993). *Self-esteem: A classroom affair.* (2nd ed.). San Francisco: Harper.

Carrell, S. (1993). *Group exercises for adolescents: A manual for therapists.* Newbury Park, CA: Sage Publications.

Cartlege, G., & Milbrun, J. F. (Eds.). (1980). *Teaching social skills to children.* Elmsford, NY: Pergamon Press.

Duncan, T., & Gumaer, J. (1980). *Developmental group for children.* Springfield, IL: Charles C. Thomas.

Ehly, S., & Dustin, R. (1989). *Individual and group counseling in the schools.* New York: Guilford Press.

Ferrara, M. (1992). *Group counseling with juvenile delinquents: The limit and lead approach.* Newbury Park, CA: Sage Publications.

Goldstein, A. P., Sprakin, R. P., Gerhaw, N. J., & Klein, P. (1980). *Skill streaming the adolescent. A structured learning approach to teaching prosocial skills.* Champaign, IL: Research Press.

Hazel, J. S., Schumaker, J. B., Sherman, J. A., & Sheldon, J. (1999). *A social skills program for adolescents.* Champaign, IL: Research Press.

Kaufman, G., & Lev, R. (1999). *Stick up for yourself: Every kid's guide to personal power and positive self-esteem.* Minneapolis, MN: Free Spirit.

Mandell, G., & Damon, L. (1989). *Group treatment for sexually abused children.* New York: Guilford Press.

Mannix, D. (1993). *Social skills activities for special children.* West Nyack, NY: The Center for Applied Research in Education.

McElherne, L. M. (1999). *Jumpstarters: Quick classroom activities that develop self-esteem, creativity and cooperation.* Minneapolis, MN: Free Spirit.

McGinnis, E., & Goldstein, A. P. (1984). *Skill streaming the elementary school child: A guide for teaching prosocial skills.* Champaign, IL: Research Press.

McGinnis, E., & Goldstein, A. P. (1990). *Skill streaming in early childhood.* Champaign, IL: Research Press.

Middleman, R. (1982). *The non-verbal method in working with groups: The use of activity in teaching, counseling, and therapy.* An enlarged edition. Hebron, CT: Practitioners Press.

Morganett, R. (1990). *Skills for living: Group counseling activities for young adolescents.* Champaign, IL: Research Press.

Norem-Hebeisen, A. A. (1976). *Exploring self-esteem.* New York: National Humanities Education Center.

Paulson, L., & van den Pol, R. (1998). *Good talking Words: A social communication skills program for preschool and kindergarden classes.* Longmont, CO: Sporis West.

Payne, L. M. (1997). *Just because I am: A child's book of inspiration.* Minneapolis, MN: Free Spirit.

Payne, L. M., & Rohling, C. (1997). *We can get along: A child's book of choices.* Minneapolis, MN: Free Spirit.

Pfeiffer, J. W., & Goodstein, L. (Eds.). (2001). *The annual: Developing human resources.* San Diego, CA: University Associates, Inc.

Pope, A. W., McHale, S. M., & Craighead, W. E. (1988). *Self-esteem enhancement with children and adolescents.* New York: Pergamon Press.

Rathjen, D. P., & Foreyt, J. P. (Eds.). (1980). *Social competence: Interventions for children and adults.* Elmsford, NY: Pergamon Press.

Rose, S. (1998). *Group psychotherapy with troubled youth: A cognitive behavioral approach.* Thousand Oaks, CA: Sage Publishing.

Rose, S., & Edleson, J. (1998). *Working with children and adolescents in groups.* San Francisco: Jossey-Bass.

Simons, L. (2000). *Taking "No" for an answer and other skills children need.* Seattle, WA: Parenting Press, Inc.

Smith, M. A. (1977). *A practical guide to value clarification.* La Jolla, CA: University Associates.

Teolis, B. (2002). *Ready-to-use conflict resolution activities for elementary students.* West Nyack, NY: Center for Applied Research in Education.

Wells, H. C., & Canfield, J. (1976). *One hundred ways to enhance self-concept in the classroom.* Englewood Cliffs, NJ: Prentice-Hall.

Whitehouse, E., & Pudney, W. (1996). *A volcano in my tummy: Helping children to handle anger. A resource book for parents, caregivers, and teachers.* Gabriola Island, BC: New Society.

PROGRAM ACTIVITIES FOR GROUPS OF OLDER PEOPLE

Beisgon, B. (1989). *Life enhancing activities for the mentally impaired elderly.* New York: Springer.

Birren, J., & Deutchman, D. (1991). *Guiding autobiography groups for older adults.* Baltimore: John Hopkins Press.

Booth, H. (1986). Dance/movement therapy. In I. Burnside (Ed.), *Working with the elderly: Group processes and techniques* (2nd ed., pp. 211–224). Boston: Jones and Bartlett.

Clark, P., & Osgood, N. J. (1985). *Seniors on stage: The impact of applied theater techniques on the elderly.* New York: Praeger.

Clements, C. (1994). *The arts/fitness quality of life activities program: Creative ideas for working with older adults in group settings.* Baltimore: Health Professions Press.

Dickey, H. (1987). *Intergenerational activities.* Buffalo, NY: Potentials Development for Health & Aging Services.

Fisher, P. (1989). *Creative movement for older adults.* New York: Human Sciences Press.

Flatten, K., Wilhite, B., & Reyes-Watson, E. (1988). *Exercise activities for the elderly.* New York: Springer.

Flatten, K., Wilhite, B., & Reyes-Watson, E. (1988). *Recreation activities for the elderly.* New York: Springer.

Foster, P. (Ed.). (1983). *Activities and the "well elderly."* New York: Haworth Press.

Fry, P. (1983). Structured and unstructured reminiscence training and depression among the elderly. *Clinical Gerontologist, 1*(13), 15–37.

Goodwin, D. (1982). *Activity Director's bag of tricks.* Chicago: Adams Press.

Helgeson, E., & Willis, S. (Eds.). (1987). *Handbook of group activities for impaired older adults.* New York: Haworth Press.

Hennessey, M. (1986). Music therapy. In I. Burnside (Ed.), *Working with the elderly: Group processes and techniques* (2nd ed., pp. 198– 210). Boston: Jones and Bartlett.

Houten, L. (1990). *Moving for life: Movement, art & music.* Buffalo, NY: Potentials Development for Health & Aging Services.

Hurley, O. (1996). *Safe therapeutic exercise for the frail elderly: An introduction* (2nd ed). Albany, NY: Center for the Study of Aging.

Ingersoll, B., & Goodman, L. (1983). A reminiscence group for institutionalized elderly. In M. Rosenbaum (Ed.), *Handbook of short-term therapy groups* (pp. 247–269). New York: McGraw-Hill.

Ingersoll, B., & Silverman, A. (1978). Comparative group psychotherapy for the aged. *The Gerontologist, 18*(2), 201–206.

Jacobs, R. (1987). Older women: Surviving and thriving. Milwaukee, WI: Family Service America.

Kamin, J. (1984). How older adults use books and the public library: A review of the literature. Occasional papers number 165 (ERIC Document Reproduction Service No. ED 247954).

Karras, B. (1994). *Say it with music: Music games and trivia.* Mt. Airy, MD: Eldersong Publications.

Killeffer, E., Bennett, R., & Gruen, G. (1985). *Handbook of innovative programs for the impaired elderly.* New York: Haworth Press.

King, K. (1982). Reminiscing psychotherapy with aging people. *Journal of Psychosocial Nursing and Mental Health Services, 20*(2), 21–25.

Lesser, J., Lazarus, L., Frankel, R., & Havasy, S. (1981). Reminiscence group therapy with psychotic geriatric in-patients. *The Gerontologist, 21*(3), 291–296.

Lewis, M., & Butler, R. (1974). Life review therapy: Putting memories to work in individual and group psychotherapy. *Geriatrics, 29*(11), 165–173.

Lowman, E. (1992). *Arts & crafts for the elderly.* New York: Springer.

McMorde, W., & Blom, S. (1979). Life review therapy: Psychotherapy for the elderly. *Perspectives In Psychiatric Care, 17,* 292–298.

Schlenger, G. (1988). *Come and sit by me: Discussion programs for activity specialists.* Owings Mills, MD: National Health Publishing.

Schulberg, C. (1986). *The music therapy sourcebook.* New York: Human Sciences Press.

Sherman, E. (1987). Reminiscence groups for the community elderly. *Gerontologist, 27*(5), 569–572.

Sherman, E. (1990). Experiential reminiscence and life review therapy. In G. Lietaer, J. Rombauts, & R. Van Balen (Eds.), *Client-centered and experiential psychotherapy in the nineties*. Leuven, Belgium: Leuven University Press.

Suchan, C. (1985). *Edible activities*. Buffalo, NY: Potentials Development for Health & Aging Services.

Thurman, J., & Piggins, C. (1996). *Drama activities with older adults: A handbook for leaders*. New York: Haworth Press.

Toseland, R. (1995). *Group work with the elderly and family caregivers*. New York: Springer.

Wilson, M. (1977). Enhancing the lives of aged in a retirement center through a program of reading. *Educational Gerontology, 4*(3), 245–251.

Wolcott, A. (1986). Art therapy: An experimental group. In I. Burnside (Ed.), *Working with the elderly: Group process and techniques* (pp. 292–310). North Scituate, MA: Duxbury Press.

Zgola, J. (1987). *Doing things: A guide to programming activities for persons with Alzheimer's disease and related disorders*. Baltimore: Johns Hopkins Press.

Bibliography

Aaker, D., Kunar, V., & Day, G. (2001). *Marketing research* (7th ed.). New York: John Wiley & Sons.

Abels, P. (1980). Instructed advocacy and community group work. In A. Alissi (Ed.), *Perspectives on social group work practice* (pp. 326–331). New York: The Free Press.

Abramson, J. (1983). A non-client-centered approach to program development in a medical setting. In H. Weissman, I. Epstein, & A. Savage (Eds.), *Agency-based social work* (pp. 178–187). Philadelphia: Temple University Press.

Abramson, J. (1989). Making teams work. *Social Work with Groups, 12*(4), 45–63.

Achenbach, T. (1991). *Manual for the Child Behavior Checklist: 4–18 and 1991 Profile.* Burlington, VT: University Associates in Psychiatry.

Achenbach, T. (1997). *Child Behavior Checklist.* Burlington, VT: University Medical Education Associates.

Adam, E. (1991). Quality circle performance. *Journal of Management, 17*(1), 25–39.

Addams, J. (1909). *The spirit of youth and the city streets.* New York: Macmillan.

Addams, J. (1926). *Twenty years at Hull House.* New York: Macmillan.

Al-Assaf, A., & Schmele, J. (Eds.). (1997). *The textbook of total quality in healthcare.* Boca Raton, FL: St. Lucie Press.

Alberti, R., & Emmons, M. (2001). *Your perfect right* (8th ed.). San Luis Obispo, CA: Impact Press.

Aldarondo, E., & Mederos, F. (Eds.). (2002). *Programs for men who batter: Intervention and prevention strategies in a diverse society.* Kingston, NJ: Civic Research Institute.

Alemi, F., Mosavel, M., Stephens, R., Ghaderi, A., Krishnaswamy, J., & Thakkar, H. (1996). Electronic self-help and support groups. *Medical Care, 34,* OS32–OS44.

Alimo-Metcalfe, B., & Alban-Metcalfe, R. (2001). The development of a new transformational leadership questionnaire. *Journal of Occupational and Organizational Psychology 74,* 1–27.

Alinsky, S. (1971). *Rules for radicals.* New York: Random House.

Alissi, A. (Ed.). (1980). *Perspectives on social group work practice.* New York: The Free Press.

Alissi, A. S. (2001). The social group work tradition: Toward social justice in a free society. *Social Group Work Foundation Occasional Papers,* 1–25.

Allport, F. (1924). *Social psychology.* Boston: Houghton Mifflin.

American Association of Group Workers. (1947). *Toward professional standards.* New York: Association Press.

American Psychiatric Association. (2002). *Diagnostic and statistical manual of mental disorders* (4th ed.). Washington, DC: Author.

Anderson, B. F. T. (2000). "The nominal group technique." *Quality Progress 33*(2): 144.

Anderson, J. (1979). Social work practice with groups in the generic base of social work practice. *Social Work with Groups, 2*(4), 281–293.

Anderson, J. (1997). *Social work with groups: A process model.* New York: Longman.

Anderson, J., & Carter, R. W. (2003). *Diversity perspectives for social work practice: Constructivism and the constructivist framework.* Boston: Allyn and Bacon.

Aponte, J., Rivers, R., & Wohl, R. (2000). *Psychological interventions and cultural diversity* (2nd ed.). Boston: Allyn and Bacon.

Appleby, G., Colon, E., & Hamilton, J. (2001). *Diversity, oppression, and social functioning: Person-in-environment assessment and intervention.* Boston: Allyn and Bacon.

Aronson, H., & Overall, B. (1966). Therapeutic expectations of patients in two social classes. *Social Work, 11,* 35–41.

Asch, P. (1957). An experimental investigation of group influences. In Walter Reed Army Institute of Research, *Symposium on preventive and social psychiatry.* Washington, DC: Walter Reed Army Institute of Research.

Asch, S. (1952). *Social psychology.* Englewood Cliffs, NJ: Prentice Hall.

Asch, S. (1955). Opinions and social pressures. *Scientific American, 193*(5), 31–35.

Asch, S. (1957). *An experimental investigation of group influence.* Paper presented at the Symposium on Preventative and Social Psychiatry, Walter Reed Army Institute of Research, Washington, D.C.

Ashby, M., Gilchrist, L., & Miramontez, A. (1987). Group treatment for sexually abused Indian adolescents. *Social Work with Groups, 10*(4), 21–32.

Asher-Svanum, H. (1991). *Psychoeducational groups for patients with schizophrenia.* Gaithersburg, MD: Aspen.

Association for the Advancement of Social Work with Groups. (1998). *Standards for social work practice with groups.* Akron, OH: AASWG.

Atkinson, D., & Lowe, S. (1995). The role of ethnicity, cultural knowledge, and conventional techniques in counseling and psychotherapy. In J. Ponterotto, J. Casas, L. Suzuki, & C. Alexander (Eds.), *Handbook of multicultural counseling* (2nd ed., pp. 387–414). Thousand Oaks, CA: Sage.

Axelson, J. A. (1999). *Counseling and development in a multicultural society* (3rd ed.). Pacific Grove, CA: Brooks/Cole.

Babbie, E. R. (2001). *The practice of social research* (9th ed.). Belmont, CA: Wadsworth Thompson Learning.

Bachrach, P., & Baratz, M. S. (1962). Two faces of power. *American Political Science Review, 56,* 947–952.

Back, K. (1951). Influence through social communication. *Journal of Abnormal and Social Psychology, 46,* 9–23.

Bailey, D., & Koney, K. M. (1996). Interorganizational community-based collaboratives: A strategic response to shape the social work agenda. *Social Work, 41,* 602–611.

Bailey-Dempsey, C., & Reid, W. J. (1996). Intervention design and development: A case study. *Research on Social Work Practice, 6*(2), 208–228.

Bales, R. (1950). *Interaction process analysis: A method for the study of small groups.* Reading, MA: Addison-Wesley.

Bales, R. (1954). In conference. *Harvard Business Review, 32,* 44–50.

Bales, R. (1955). How people interact in conference. *Scientific American, 192,* 31–35.

Bales, R. (1980). *SYMLOG: Case study kit.* New York: The Free Press.

Bales, R., Cohen, S., & Williamson, S. (1979). *SYMLOG: A system for the multiple level observations of groups.* New York: The Free Press.

Balgopal, P., & Vassil, T. (1983). *Groups in social work: An ecological perspective.* New York: Macmillan.

Bandura, A. (1977). *Social Learning Theory.* Englewood Cliffs, NJ: Prentice-Hall.

Bandura, A. A. (1995). *Exercise of personal and collective efficacy in changing societies.* New York: Cambridge University Press.

Bandura, A. A. (1997a). *Self efficacy: Exercise and control.* New York: Freeman.

Bandura, A. A. (1997b). *Self-efficacy in changing societies.* New York: Cambridge University Press.

Banker, R. D., Field, J. M., Schroeder, R. G., & Sinha, K. K. (1996). Impact of work teams on manufacturing performance: A longitudinal field study. *Academy of Management Journal, 39*(4), 867–890.

Barker, L. (1979). *Groups in process: An introduction to small group communication.* Englewood Cliffs, NJ: Prentice-Hall.

Barker, V., Abrams, J., Tiyaamornwong, V., Seibold, D., Duggan, A., Park, H., & Sebastian, M. (2000). New contexts for relational communications in groups. *Small Group Research, 31*(4), 470–503.

Barlow, C., Blythe, J., & Edmonds, M. (1999). *A handbook of interactive exercises for groups.* Boston: Allyn and Bacon.

Barlow, S. H., Burlingame, G. M., & Fuhriman, A. (2000). "Therapeutic application of groups: From Pratt's "Thought control classes" to modern group psychotherapy." *Group Dynamics, Theory Research, and Practice 4*(1): 115–134.

Baron, J. (1994). *Thinking and deciding* (2nd ed.). New York: Cambridge University Press.

Barrick, M., & Alexander, R. (1987). A review of quality circle efficacy and the existence of positive-findings bias. *Personnel Psychology, 40,* 579–593.

Barth, R. P., Yeaton, J., & Winterfelt, N. (1994). Psychoeducational groups with foster parents of sexually abused children. *Child and Adolescent Social Work Journal, 11*(5), 405–424.

Bass, B. M. (1985). *Leadership and performance beyond expectations.* New York: The Free Press.

Bass, B. M. (1998). *Transformational leadership: Industry, military, and educational impact.* Mahwah, NJ: Erlbaum.

Bass, B. M., & Avolio, B. J. (1990a). The implications of transactional and transformational leadership for individual, team, and organizational development. In R. W. Woodman, & W. A. Passmore (Eds.), *Research in Organizational Change and Development.* Greenwich, CT: JAI Press.

Bass, B. M., & Avolio, B. J. (1990b). *Manual for the Multifactor Leadership Questionnaire.* Palo Alto, CA: Consulting Psychologists Press.

Bass, B. M., & Avolio, B. J. (1993). Transformational leadership: A response to critiques. In M. M. Chemers, & R. Ayman (Eds.), *Leadership theory and research: Perspectives and directions.* San Diego, Ca, Academic Press.

Bass, B. M., & Avolio, B. J. (1994). *Improving organizational effectiveness through transformational leadership.* Thousand Oaks, CA: Sage.

Bass, D., McClendon, M., Brennan, P., & McCarthy, C. (1998). The buffering effect of a computer support network on caregiver strain. *Journal of Aging and Health, 10*(1), 20–43.

Bauer, M. M., & McBride, L. (2003). *Structured group psychotherapy for bipolar disorder: The life goals program.* New York: Springer Publishing Company.

Baugh, S., & Graen, G. (1997). Effects of team gender and racial composition on perceptions of team performance in cross-functional teams. *Group & Organization Management, 22*(3), 366–383.

Bayless, O. (1967). An alternative pattern for problem solving discussion. *Journal of Communication, 17,* 188–197.

Beck, A., & Freeman, A. (1990). *Cognitive therapy of personality disorders.* New York: Guilford.

Beck, J. (1995). *Cognitive therapy: Basics and beyond.* New York: Guilford.

Becker, W. (1971). *Parents are teachers.* Champaign, IL: Research Press.

Bednar, K., & Kaul, T. (1994). Experimental group research: Can the cannon fire? In A. Bergen & S. Garfield (Eds.), *Handbook of psychotherapy and behavior change* (4th ed., pp. 631–663). New York: John Wiley & Sons.

Behroozi, C. S. (1992). A model for social work with involuntary applicants in groups. *Social Work with Groups, 15*(2/3), 223–238.

Bell, J. (1981). The small group perspective: Family group-therapy. In E. Tolson & W. Reid (Eds.), *Models of family treatment* (pp. 33–51). New York: Columbia University Press.

Benjamin, J. B., Bessant, J., & Watts, R. (1997). Working with groups in community work and social movements. In J. Benjamin, J. Bessant, & R. Watts, *Making groups work: Rethinking practice.* (pp. 165–188). Australia: Allen & Unwin Aust.

Benne, K., & Sheats, P. (1948). Functional roles of group members. *Journal of Social Issues, 4*(2), 41–49.

Berger, R. (1996). A comparative analysis of different methods of teaching group work. *Social Work with Groups, 19*(1), 79–89.

Bergeron, L. G., & Gray, B. (2003). Ethical dilemmas of reporting suspected elder abuse. *Social Work, 48*(1), 96–105.

Berne, E. (1961). *Transactional analysis in psychotherapy.* New York: Ballantine Books.

Bernstein, D., & Borkovec, T. (1973). *Progressive relaxation training: A manual for the helping professions.* Champaign, IL: Research Press.

Bernstein, D. B., Borkovek, T., & Hazlett-Stevens, H. (2000). *New directions in progressive relaxation training: A guidebook for helping professionals.* Westport, CT: Praeger.

Berry, J. (1997). Individual and group relations in plural societies. In C. Granose & S. Oskamp (Eds.), *Cross-cultural work groups: An overview* (pp. 17–35). Thousand Oaks, CA: Sage Publications.

Berry, T. (1991). *Managing the total transformation.* New York: McGraw-Hill.

Bertcher, H. (1990). *Tell-a-group: How to set up and operate group work by telephone.* Unpublished manuscript, University of Michigan, School of Social Work, Ann Arbor.

Bertcher, H., & Maple, F. (1977). *Creating groups.* Newbury Park, CA: Sage.

Bertcher, H., & Maple, F. (1985). Elements and issues in group composition. In M. Sundel, P. Glasser, R. Sarri, & R. Vinter (Eds.), *Individual change through small groups* (2nd ed., pp. 180–203). New York: The Free Press.

Biegel, D., Tracy, E., & Corvo, K. (1994). Strengthening social networks: Intervention strategies for mental health case managers. *Health and Social Work, 19*(3), 206–216.

Bion, W. (1991). *Experiences in groups and other papers.* London: Routledge.

Birnbaum, M. C., & Cicchetti, A. (2000). The power of purposeful sessional endings in each group encounter. *Social Work With Groups 23*(3), 37–52.

Birnbaum, M. M., Mason, S., & Cicchetti, A. (2002). Impact of purposeful sessional endings on both the group and the practitioner. *Social Work with Groups 25*(4), 3–19.

Blackmon, M., & Holland, T. (2000). *Measuring board effectiveness.* Washington, DC: BoardSource.

Blatner, H. (1996). *Acting-in: Practical applications of psychodramatic methods* (3rd ed.). New York: Springer.

Blau, P. (1964). *Exchange and power in social life.* New York: John Wiley & Sons.

Blay, S., Vel-Fucks, J., Barruzi, M., Di-Piertro, M., Gastal, F., Neto, A., DeSouza, M., Glausiusz, L., & Dewey, M. (2002). Effectiveness of time-limited psychotherapy for minor psychiatric disorders. *British-Journal of Psychiatry, 180*(5).

Blazer, D. (1978). Techniques for communicating with your elderly patient. *Geriatrics, 33*(11), 79–84.

Bloom, B., & Broder, L. (1950). *Problem-solving processes of college students.* Chicago: University of Chicago Press.

Bloom, M., Fisher, J., & Orme, J. (2003). *Evaluating practice: Guidelines for the accountable professional* (4th ed.). Boston: Allyn and Bacon.

Blouin, J., Schnarre, K., Carter, J., Blouin, A., Tener, L., Zuro, C., & Barlow, J. (1995). Factors affecting dropout rate from cognitive-behavioral group treatment for bulimia nervosa. *International Journal of Eating Disorders, 17,* 323–329.

Boatman, F. (1975). *Caseworkers' judgments of clients' hope: Some correlates among client-situation characteristics and among workers' communication patterns.* Unpublished doctoral dissertation, Columbia University, New York.

Bonito, J. (2002). The analysis of participation in small groups: Methodological and conceptual issues related to interdependence. *Small Group Research, 33*(4), 412–438.

Borkovec, T. D., Hazlett-Stevens, H., & Diaz, M. L. (1999). The role of positive beliefs about worry in generalized anxiety disorder and its treatment. *Clinical Psychology & Psychotherapy, 6*(2), 126–139.

Bouchard, T. (1972a). A comparison of two group brainstorming procedures. *Journal of Applied Psychology, 56,* 418–421.

Bouchard, T. (1972b). Training, motivation and personality as determinants of the effectiveness of brainstorming groups and individuals. *Journal of Applied Psychology, 56,* 324–331.

Bowman, L. (1935). Dictatorship, democracy, and group work in America. In *Proceedings of the National Conference of Social Work* (p. 382). Chicago: University of Chicago Press.

Bowman, R., & Bowman, V. (1998). Life on the electronic frontier: The application of technology to group work. *Journal for Specialists in Group Work, 23*(4), 428–445.

Boyd, N. (1935). Group work experiments in state institutions in Illinois. In *Proceedings of the National Conference of Social Work* (p. 344). Chicago: University of Chicago Press.

Boyd, N. (1938). Play as a means of social adjustment. In J. Lieberman (Ed.), *New trends in group work* (pp. 210–220). New York: Association Press.

Brabender, V., & Fallon, A. (1996). Termination in inpatient groups. *International Journal of Group Psychotherapy, 46*(1), 81–99.

Brackett, J. (1895). The charity organization movement: Its tendency and its duty. In *Proceedings of the 22nd National Conference of Charities and Corrections.* Boston: G. H. Ellis.

Bradford, L. (1976). *Making meetings work: A guide for leaders and group members.* La Jolla, CA: University Associates.

Bradford, L., & Corey, S. (1951). Improving large group meetings. *Adult Education, 1,* 122–137.

Brager, G., & Holloway, A. (1978). *Changing human service organizations: Politics and practice.* New York: The Free Press.

Brehmer, B., & Joyce, C. (1988). *Human judgment: The SJT view.* New York: North-Holland.

Brekke, J. (1989). The use of orientation groups to engage hard-to-reach clients: Model, method and evaluation. *Social Work with Groups, 12*(2), 75–88.

Brennan, J. W. (1995). A short term psychoeducational multiple family group for bipolar patients and their families. *Social Work, 40*(6), 737–743.

Breton, M. (1994). On the meaning of empowerment and empowerment-oriented social work practice. *Social Work with Groups, 17*(3), 23–37.

Breton, M. (1995). The potential for social action in groups. *Social Work with Groups, 18*(2/3), 5–13.

Breton, M. (1999). The relevance of the structural approach to group work with immigrant and refugee women. *Social Work With Groups, 22*(2–3), 11–29.

Brilhart, J. (1974). *Effective group discussion* (2nd ed.). Dubuque, IA: William C. Brown.

Brill, N. (1976). *Team-work: Working together in the human services.* Philadelphia: J. B. Lippincott.

Brill, N. (2001). *Working with people: The helping process* (7th ed.). Boston: Allyn and Bacon.

Brook, D., Gordon, C., & Meadow, H. (1998). Ethnicity, culture, and group psychotherapy. *Group, 22*(2), 53–80.

Brown, A., & Mistry, T. (1994). Group work with mixed membership groups: Issues of race and gender. *Social Work with Groups, 17*(3), 5–21.

Brown, B. M. (1995). A bill of rights for people with disabilities in group work. *Journal for Specialists in Group Work, 20,* 71–75.

Brown, L. (1991). *Groups for growth and change.* New York: Longman.

Browne, K., Saunders, D., & Staecker, K. (1997). Process-psychodynamic groups for men who batter. *Families in Society, 78,* 265–271.

Browning, L. (1977). Diagnosing teams in organizational settings. *Group and Organization Studies, 2*(2), 187–197.

Budman, S., Demby, A., Feldstein, M., Redondo, J., Scherz, B., Bennett, M., Koppenall, G., Daley, B., Hunter, M., & Ellis, J. (1987). Preliminary findings on a new instrument to measure cohesion in group psychotherapy. *International Journal of Group Psychotherapy, 37*(1), 75–94.

Budman, S., Simeone, P., Reilly, R., & Demby, A. (1994). Progress in short-term and time-limited group psychotherapy: Evidence and implications. In A. Fuhriman & G. M. Burlingame (Eds.), *Handbook of Group Psychotherapy* (pp. 319–339). New York: John Wiley & Sons.

Budman, S., Soldz, S., Demby, A., Davis, M., & Merry, J. (1993). What is cohesiveness? An empirical examination. *Small Group Research, 24*(2), 199–216.

Bufe, C., & DeNunzio, D. (1998). *Exercises for individual and group development.* Tucson, AZ: Sharp Press.

Burlingame, G., Kircher, J., & Honts, C. (1994). Analysis of variance versus bootstrap procedures for analyzing dependent observations in small group research. *Small Group Research, 25*(4), 486–501.

Burns, J. M. (1978). *Leadership.* New York: Harper & Row.

Burwell, N. (1998). Human diversity and empowerment. In H. W. Johnson et al. (Eds.), *The social services: An introduction* (5th ed., pp. 357–370). Itasca, IL: Peacock Press.

Butler, H., Davis, I., & Kukkonen, R. (1979). The logic of case comparison. *Social Work Research and Abstracts, 15*(3), 3–11.

Byers, P. Y., & Wilcox, J. R. (1991, Winter). Focus groups: A qualitative opportunity for researchers. *The Journal of Business Communication, 28*(1), 63–77.

Cambridge Educational. (2000). *Stress management.* Charleston, WV: Cambridge Research Group.

Carless, S. D., & De Paola, C. (2000). The measurement of cohesion in work teams. *Small Group Research, 31*(1), 71–88.

Carletta, J., Garrod, S., & Fraser-Krauss, H. (1998). Placement of authority and communication patterns in workplace groups. *Small Group Research, 29*(5), 531–559.

Carron, A., & Spink, K. (1995). The group size-cohesion relationship in minimal groups. *Small Group Research, 26*(1), 86–105.

Cartwright, D. (1951). Achieving change in people. *Human Relations, 4,* 381–392.

Cartwright, D. (1968). The nature of group cohesiveness. In D. Cartwright & A. Zander (Eds.), *Group dynamics: Research and theory* (3rd ed., pp. 91–109). New York: Harper & Row.

Cartwright, D., & Zander, A. (Eds.). (1968). *Group dynamics: Research and theory* (3rd ed.). New York: Harper & Row.

Chait, R., Holland, T. P., & Taylor, B. E. (1993). *The effective board of trustees.* Phoenix, AZ: Oryx Press.

Chau, K. (1992). Needs assessment for group work with people of color: A conceptual formulation. *Social Work with Groups, 15*(2/3), 53–66.

Chemers, M. M. (2000). Leadership research and theory: A functional integration. *Group Dynamics: Theory, Research. and Practice, 4*(1), 27–43.

Chiauzzi, E. J. (1991). *Preventing relapse in the addictions: A biopsychosocial approach.* New York: Pergamon Press.

Clark, A. (1998). Reframing: A therapeutic technique in group counseling. *Journal for Specialists in Group Work, 23*(1), 66–73.

Clark, C. H. (1958). *Brainstorming.* New York: Doubleday.

Clemen, R. T. (1996). *Making hard decisions: An introduction to decision analysis* (2nd ed.). Belmont, CA: Duxbury Press.

Clifford, M. W. (1998). A short-term model of social group work with adults: Theory, practice, teaching, and evaluation. *Psychotherapy in Private Practice, 17*(2), 11–27.

Cohen, M. B., & Mullender, A. (1999). The personal in the political: Exploring the group work continuum from individual to social change goals. *Social Work with Groups, 22,* 13–31.

Cohen, S. G., & Bailey, D. E. (1997). What makes teams work: Group effectiveness research from the shop floor to the executive suite. *Journal of Management, 23*(3), 239–290.

Cole, R., & Tachiki, D. (1983, June). A look at U.S. and Japanese quality circles: Preliminary comparisons. *Quality Circles Journal, 6,* 10–16.

Collaros, R., & Anderson, L. (1969). Effects of perceived expertness upon creativity of members of brainstorming groups. *Journal of Applied Psychology, 53*(2), 159–164.

Commission on Accreditation. (2001). *Handbook of accreditation standards and procedures* (5th ed.). New York, NY: Council on Social Work Education.

Cone, J., & Hawkins, R. (Eds.). (1977). *Behavioral assessment: New directions in clinical psychology.* New York: Brunner/Mazel.

Connelly, J. L., & Piper, W. (1984). *Pretraining behavior as a predictor of process and outcome in group psychotherapy.* Paper presented at the 15th Annual Meeting of the Society for Psychotherapy Research, Lake Louise, Alberta.

Connelly, J. L., Piper, W., DeCarufel, F., & Debbane, E. (1986). Premature termination in group psychotherapy: Pretherapy and early therapy predictors. *International Journal of Group Psychotherapy, 36*(1), 145–152.

Conrad, W., & Glenn, W. (1976). *The effective voluntary board of directors: What it is and how it works.* Chicago: Swallow Press.

Cooksey, R. W. (1996). *Judgment analysis: Theory methods and applications.* New York: Academic Press.

Cooley, D. (1909). *Social organization.* New York: Charles Scribner's Sons.

Cooper, C. (1977). Adverse and growthful effects of experimental learning groups: The role of the trainer, participant, and group characteristics. *Human Relations, 30,* 1103–1129.

Cooper, L. (1976). Co-therapy relationships in groups. *Small Group Behavior, 7*(4), 473–498.

Corey, M., & Corey, G. (2002). *Groups: Process and practice* (6th ed.). Pacific Grove, CA: Brooks/Cole.

Costin, H. (1999). *Strategies for quality improvement: TQM, reengineering, and ISO 9000.* Forth Worth, TX: Dryden Press.

Counselman, E. F. (1991). Leadership in a long-term leaderless women's group. *Small Group Research, 22,* 240–257.

Cox, E. (1988). Empowerment of the low income elderly through group work. *Social Work with Groups, 11*(4), 111–119.

Cox, E., & Parsons, R. (1994). *Empowerment-oriented social work practice with the elderly.* Pacific Grove, CA: Brooks/Cole.

Cox, M. (1973). The group therapy interaction chronogram. *British Journal of Social Work, 3,* 243–256.

Coyle, G. (1930). *Social process in organized groups.* New York: Richard Smith.

Coyle, G. (1935). Group work and social change. In *Proceedings of the National Conference of Social Work* (p. 393). Chicago: University of Chicago Press.

Coyle, G. (1937). *Studies in group behavior.* New York: Harper & Row.

Coyle, G. (1938). Education for social action. In J. Lieberman (Ed.), *New Trends in Group Work* (pp. 1–14). New York: Association Press.

Craig, T., Huffine, C., & Brooks, M. (1974). Completion of referral to psychiatric services by inner-city residents. *Archives of General Psychiatry, 31*(3), 353–357.

Crano, W., & Brewer, M. (1973). *Principles of research in social psychology.* New York: McGraw-Hill.

Croxton, T. (1985). The therapeutic contract in social treatment. In M. Sundel, P. Glasser, R. Sarri, & R. Vinter (Eds.), *Individual change through small groups* (2nd ed., pp. 159–179). New York: The Free Press.

Dalgleish, L. I. (1988). Decision making in child abuse cases: Applications of social judgment theory and signal detection theory. In B. Brehmer & C. R. B. Joyce (Eds.), *Human judgment: The SJT view.* New York: North-Holland.

Davis, F., & Lohr, N. (1971). Special problems with the use of co-therapists in group psychotherapy. *International Journal of Group Psychotherapy, 21,* 143–158.

Davis, G., Manske, M., & Train, A. (1966). An instructional method of increasing originality. *Psychonomic Science, 6,* 73–74.

Davis, I. (1975). Advice-giving in parent counseling. *Social Casework, 56,* 343–347.

Davis, L., Galinsky, M., & Schopler, J. (1995). RAP: A framework for leadership of multiracial groups. *Social Work, 40*(2), 155–165.

Davis, L., & Proctor, E. (1989). *Race, gender and class: Guidelines for practice with individuals, families and groups.* Englewood Cliffs, NJ: Prentice-Hall.

Davis, L., Strube, M., & Cheng, L. (1995). Too many blacks, too many whites: Is there a racial balance? *Basic and Applied Social Psychology, 17*(1/2), 119–135.

Davis, L., & Toseland, R. (1987). Group versus individual decision making. *Social Work with Groups, 10*(2), 95–105.

Davis, M., Eshelman, E., & McKay, M. (2000). *The relaxation and stress reduction workbook* (5th ed.). Oakland, CA: New Harbinger.

De Bono, E. (1968). *New think: The use of lateral thinking in generation of new ideas.* New York: Basic Books.

De Bono, E. (1971). *Lateral thinking for management.* New York: American Management Associations.

De Bono, E. (1972). *Lateral thinking: Productivity step by step.* New York: Harper & Row.

Delbecq, A., Van de Ven, A., & Gustafson, D. (1986). *Group techniques for program planning: A guide to nominal group and delphi processes.* Middleton, WI: Green Briar Press.

Delgado, M. (1983). Activities and Hispanic groups. *Social Work with Groups, 6,* 85–96.

Delucia-Waack, J. (1997). Measuring the effectiveness of group work: A review and analysis of process and outcome measures. *Journal for Specialists in Group Work, 22,* 277–292.

Denhardt, R., Pyle, J., & Bluedorn, A. (1987). Implementing quality circles in state government. *Public Administrative Review, 47*(4), 304–309.

Devore, W., & Schlesinger, E. (1999). *Ethnic-sensitive social work practice* (5th ed.). Boston: Allyn and Bacon.

Diaz, T. (2002). Group work from an Asian Pacific Island perspective: Making connections between group worker ethnicity and practice. *Social Work With Groups, 25*(3), 43–60.

Dienesch, R. M., & Liden, R. C. (1986). Leader-member exchange model of leadership: A critique and further development. *Academy of Management Review, 11,* 618–634.

Dies, R. (1994). Therapist variables in group psychotherapy research. In A. Fuhriman & G. M. Burlingame (Eds.), *Handbook of Group Psychotherapy* (pp. 114–154), New York: John Wiley & Sons.

Diller, J. (1999). *Cultural diversity: A primer for the human services.* Belmont, CA: Wadsworth.

Dillon, W., Madden, T., & Firtle, N. (1994). *Marketing research in a marketing environment* (3rd ed.). Burr Ridge, IL: Irwin.

Dinges, N., & Cherry, D. (1995). Symptom expression and use of mental health services among ethnic minorities. In J. Aponte, R. Rivers, & J. Wohl (Eds.), *Psychological interventions and cultural diversity* (pp. 40–56). Boston: Allyn and Bacon.

Dinkmeyer, D., & McKay, G. (1990). *Systematic training for effective parenting* (Rev. ed.). New York: Random House.

Dion, K. L. (2000). Group cohesion: From "Field of forces" to multidimensional construct. *Group Dynamics: Theory, Research, and Practice, 4*(1), 7–26.

Dion, K., Miller, N., & Magnan, M. (1970). Cohesiveness and social responsibility as determinants of risk taking. *Proceedings of the American Psychological Association, 5*(1), 335–336.

Dluhy, M. (1990). *Building coalitions in the human services.* Newbury Park, CA: Sage.

Dobson, K. (2001). *Handbook of cognitive-behavioral therapies.* New York, Guildford Press.

Dodge, K., Gilroy, F., & Fenzel, L. (1995). Requisite management characteristics revisited: Two decades later. *Journal of Social Behavior and Personality, 10,* 253–264.

Dolgoff, R., & Skolnik, L. (1992). Ethical decision making, the NASW code of ethics and group work practice: Beginning explorations. *Social Work with Groups, 15*(4), 99–112.

Douglas, T. (1979). *Group process in social work: A theoretical synthesis.* New York: John Wiley & Sons.

Drum, D., & Knott, J. (1977). *Structured groups for facilitating development: Acquiring life skills, resolving life themes and making life transitions.* New York: Human Science Press.

Drummond, M., Stoddart, G., & Torrance, G. (1987). *Methods for the economic evaluation of health care programmes.* Oxford, UK: Oxford University Press.

Drysdale, J. P., & Purcell, R. (1999). Breaking the culture of silence: Groupwork and community development. *Groupwork, 11*(3), 71–87.

Dunnette, M., Campbell, J., & Joastad, K. (1963). The effect of group participation on brainstorming effectiveness for two industrial samples. *Journal of Applied Psychology, 47,* 30–37.

Dutton, D., & Sonkin, D. (Eds.). (2003). *Intimate violence: Contemporary treatment innovations.* Binghamton, NY: Haworth Press.

D'Zurilla, T., & Goldfried, M. (1971). Problem solving and behavior modification. *Journal of Abnormal Psychology, 78,* 107–126.

Earley, P. R., & Randel, A. (1997). Self and other: "Face" and work group dynamics. In C. Granrose & S. Oskamp (Eds.), *Cross-Cultural Work Groups: An Overview* (pp. 113–133). Thousand Oaks, CA: Sage Publications.

Early, B. (1992). Social work consultation with the work group of the school. *Social Work In Education, 14*(4), 207–214.

Ebbesen, E., & Bowers, R. (1974). Proportion of risky to conservative arguments in a group discussion and choice shift. *Journal of Personality and Social Psychology, 29,* 316–327.

Edelwich, J., & Brodsky, A. (1992). *Group counseling for the resistent client: A practical guide to group process.* New York: Lexington Books.

Edleson, J., & Syers, M. (1990). The relative effectiveness of group treatments for men who batter. *Social Work Research and Abstracts, 26,* 10–17.

Edleson, J., & Tolman, R. (1992). *Intervention for men who batter.* Newbury Park, CA: Sage.

Edmunds, H. (1999). *The focus group research handbook.* Chicago: NTC Business Books.

Edson, J. (1977). How to survive on a committee. *Social Work, 22,* 224–226.

Edwards, W. (1977). How to use multiattribute utility measurement for social decision making. *IEEE Transactions on Systems, Man and Cybernetics, 7,* 326–340.

Egan, G. (2002). *The skilled helper* (7th ed.). Pacific Grove, CA: Brooks/Cole.

Eisenhart, C. (1972). The assumptions underlying the analysis of variance. In R. Kirk (Ed.), *Statistical issues* (pp. 226–240). Pacific Grove, CA: Brooks/Cole.

Elliott, H. (1928). *Process of group thinking.* New York: Association Press.

Ellis, A. (1962). *Reason and emotion in psychotherapy.* Secaucus, NJ: Lyle Stuart.

Ellis, A. (1992). Group rational-emotive and cognitive-behavior therapy. *International Journal of Group Psychotherapy, 42*(1), 63–82.

Empey, L., & Erikson, M. (1972). *The Provo experiment: Impact and death of an innovation.* Lexington, MA: Lexington Books.

Emrick, C. D., Lassen, C. L., & Edwards, M. T. (1977). Nonprofessional peers as therapeutic agents. In A. Gurman & A. Razin (Eds.), *Effective psychotherapy: A handbook of research* (pp. 120–161). New York: Pergamon Press.

Ephross, P. H., & Vassil, T. (in press). *Groups that work* (2nd ed.). New York: Columbia University Press.

Etcheverry, R., Siporin, M., & Toseland, R. (1987). The uses and abuses of role playing. In P. Glasser and N. Mayadas (Eds.), *Group workers at work: Theory and practice in the 1980s* (pp. 116–130). Lanham, MD: Littlefield, Adams & Company.

Etzioni, A. (1961). *A comparative analysis of complex organizations on power, involvement and their correlates.* New York: The Free Press.

Etzioni, A. (1968). *The active society: A theory of societal and political processes.* New York: The Free Press.

Evans, C., & Dion, K. (1991). Group cohesion and performance. *Small Group Research, 22*(2), 175–186.

Everly, G. S. (1989). *A clinical guide to the treatment of the human stress response.* New York: Plenum.

Ewalt, P., & Kutz, J. (1976). An examination of advice giving as a therapeutic intervention. *Smith College Studies in Social Work, 47,* 3–19.

Falck, H. (1988). *Social work: The membership perspective.* New York: Springer.

Fall, K., Howard, S., & Ford, J. (1999). *Alternatives to domestic violence: A homework manual for battering intervention groups.* Philadelphia: Taylor & Francis.

Fatout, M., & Rose, S. (1995). *Task groups in the social services.* Thousand Oaks, CA: Sage.

Feldman, R. (1986). Group work knowledge and research: A two-decade comparison. *Social Work with Groups, 9*(3), 7–14.

Feldman, R., Caplinger, T., & Wodarski, J. (1983). *The St. Louis conundrum: The effective treatment of antisocial youth.* Englewood Cliffs, NJ: Prentice-Hall.

Feldman, R., & Wodarski, J. (1975). *Contemporary approaches to group treatment: Traditional, behavior modification and group-centered.* San Francisco: Jossey-Bass.

Fern, E. (1982). The use of focus groups for idea generation: The effects of group size, acquaintanceship, and moderator on response quantity and quality. *Journal of Marketing Research, 19,* 1–13.

Festinger, L. (1950). Informal social communication. *Psychological Review, 57,* 271–282.

Fiedler, R. (1967). *A theory of leadership effectiveness.* New York: McGraw-Hill.

Fieldsteel, N. D. (1996). The process of termination in long-term psychoanalytic group therapy. *International Journal of Group Psychotherapy, 46*(1), 25–39.

Finn, J. (1995). Computer-based self-help groups: A new resource to supplement support groups. In M. Galinsky & J. Schopler (Eds.), *Support groups: Current perspectives in theory and practice* (pp. 109–117). New York: Haworth.

Finn, J., & Lavitt, M. (1994). Computer-based self help groups for sexual abuse survivors. *Social Work with Groups, 17*(1/2), 21–46.

Fisher, J. (1978). *Effective casework practice: An eclectic approach.* New York: McGraw-Hill.

Fisher, J., & Corcoran, K. (1994). *Measures for clinical practice: A sourcebook* (2nd ed.). (Vol. 1, Couples, Families, and Children & Vol. 2, Adults). New York: The Free Press.

Fisher, R., Ury, W., & Patton, B. (1997). *Getting to yes: Negotiating agreement without giving in* (2nd ed.). London: Arrow Business Books.

Flippen, A. (1999). Understanding group think from a self-regulatory perspective. *Small Group Research, 30*(2), 139–166.

Flores, M. (2000). *La familia Latina.* In M. flores (Ed.), *Family therapy with Hispanics: Toward appreciating diversity.* Boston: Allyn and Bacon.

Flowers, J. (1979). Behavior analysis of group therapy and a model for behavioral group therapy. In D. Upper & S. Ross (Eds.), *Behavioral group therapy, 1979: An annual review* (pp. 5–37). Champaign, IL: Research Press.

Follett, M. P. (1926). *The new state: Group organization, the solution of popular government.* New York: Longmans, Green.

Forester, J. (1981). Questioning and organizing attention: Toward a critical theory of planning and administrative practice. *Administration and Society, 13*(2), 181–205.

Forse, M. D., & Degenne, A. (1999). *Introducing social networks.* London: Sage.

Forsyth, D. (1999). *Group dynamics* (3rd ed.). Belmont, CA: Wadsworth.

Forsyth, D. (2000). One hundred years of groups research: Introduction to the special issue. *Group Dynamics Theory, Research, and Practice, 4*(1), 3–6.

Forsyth, D., & Corazzini, J. (2000). Groups as change agents. In C. Snyder & R. Ingram (Eds.), *Handbook of psychological change: Psychotherapy processes & practices for the 21st century* (pp. 309–366). New York, NY: John Wiley & Sons, Inc.

Fortune, A. (1979). Communication in task-centered treatment. *Social Work, 24,* 390–397.

Fortune, A. (1985, December). Planning duration and termination of treatment. In A. Fortune (Ed.), *Social Service Review* (pp. 648–661). Chicago: University of Chicago Press.

Fortune, A. (1987). Grief only? Client and social worker reactions to termination. *Clinical Social Work Journal, 15*(2), 159–171.

Fortune, A., Pearlingi, B., & Rochelle, C. (1991, June). Criteria for terminating treatment. *Families in Society: The Journal of Contemporary Human Services, 72*(6), 366–370.

Fortune, A., Pearlingi, B., & Rochelle, C. (1992). Reactions to termination of individual treatment. *Social Work, 37*(2), 171–178.

Fortune, A., & Reid, W. J. (1998). *Research in social work* (3rd ed.). New York: Columbia University Press.

Frances, A., Clarkin, J., & Perry, S. (1984). *Differential therapeutics in psychiatry: The art and science of treatment selection.* New York: Brunner/Mazel.

Frank, J. (1961). *Persuasion and healing: A comparative study of psychotherapy.* New York: Schocken Books.

Freeman, A., Pretzer, J., Fleming, J., & Simons, K. (1990). *Clinical applications of cognitive therapy.* New York: Plenum.

French, J., & Raven, B. (1959). The bases of social power. In D. Cartwright (Ed.), *Studies in social power.* Ann Arbor: Institute for Research, University of Michigan.

Freud, S. (1922). *Group psychology and the analysis of the ego.* London: International Psychoanalytic Press.

Fuhriman, A., & Barlow, S. (1994). Interaction analysis: Instrumentation and issues. In A. Fuhriman and G. M. Burlingame (Eds.), *Handbook of Group Psychotherapy* (pp. 191–222). New York: John Wiley & Sons.

Fuhriman, A., & Burlingame, G. (1994). Group psychotherapy: Research and Practice. In A. Fuhriman and G. M. Burlingame (Eds.), *Handbook of Group Psychotherapy* (pp. 3–40). New York: John Wiley & Sons.

Fuhriman, A., & Packard, T. (1986). Group process instruments: Therapeutic themes and issues. *International Journal of Group Psychotherapy, 36*(3), 399–525.

Furman, R. (2005). *An introduction to group work practice. Student workbook for Toseland and Rivas.* Boston: Allyn and Bacon.

Galinsky, M., Rounds, K., Montague, A., & Butowsky, A. (1993). *Leading a telephone support group for persons with HIV disease.* Chapel Hill: University of North Carolina Press.

Galinsky, M., & Schopler, J. (1977). Warning: Groups may be dangerous. *Social Work, 22*(2), 89–94.

Galinsky, M., & Schopler, J. (1980). Structuring co-leadership in social work training. *Social Work with Groups, 3*(4), 51–63.

Galinsky, M., & Schopler, J. (1989). Developmental patterns in open-ended groups. *Social Work with Groups, 12*(2), 99–114.

Garland, J., Jones, H., & Kolodny, R. (1976). A model of stages of group development in social work groups. In S. Bernstein (Ed.), *Explorations in Group Work* (pp. 17–71). Boston: Charles River Books.

Garland, J., & Kolodny, R. (1967). Characteristics and resolution of scapegoating. In National Conference of Social Welfare, *Social Work Practice* (pp. 198–219). New York: Columbia University Press.

Garvin, C. (1997). *Contemporary group work* (3rd ed.). Boston: Allyn and Bacon.

Garvin, C. (1998, October). *Potential impact of small group research on social group work practice.* Paper presented at the 20th Annual Symposium of the Association for the Advancement of Social Work with Groups, Miami, FL.

Garvin, C., Reid, W., & Epstein, L. (1976). A task-centered approach. In R. Roberts & H. Northen (Eds.), *Theories of social work with groups* (pp. 238–267). New York: Columbia University Press.

Garwick, G. (1974). *Guideline for goal attainment scaling.* Minneapolis: Program Evaluation Project.

Gazda, G., & Mobley, J. (1981). INDS-CAL multidimensional scaling. *Journal of Group Psychotherapy, Psychodrama and Sociometry, 34,* 54–72.

Gebhardt, L., & Meyers, R. (1995). Subgroup influence in decision-making groups: Examining consistency from a communication perspective. *Small Group Research, 26*(2), 147–168.

Gelles, R. (2002). Standards for programs for men who batter? Not yet. *Journal of Aggression, Maltreatment and Trauma, 5*(2), 11–20.

Gentry, M. (1987). Coalition formation and processes. *Social Work with Groups, 10*(3), 39–54.

Germain, C., & Gitterman, A. (1996). *The life model of social work practice* (2nd ed.). New York: Columbia University Press.

Getzel, G. (1998). Group work practice with gay men and lesbians. In G. P. Mallon (Ed.), *Foundations of social work practice with lesbian and gay persons.* (pp. 131–144). New York: Harrington Park Press.

Gibb, C. (1969). Leadership. In G. Lindzey & E. Aronson (Eds.), *The handbook of social psychology* (2nd ed., pp. 205–273). Reading, MA: Addison-Wesley.

Gibb, J. (1961). Defensive communication. *The Journal of Communication, 11,* 11–148.

Gibbs, L., & Gambrill, E. (1998). *Critical thinking for social workers.* Thousand Oaks, CA: Pine Forge Press.

Gibson, A. (1999). *Project-based group work facilitator's manual: Young people, youth workers, & projects.* Bristol, PA: Jessica Kingsley Publications.

Gill, S. (1991). *Learning nominal group technique a leader's guide.* Brighton, CO: Brighton Books.

Giordano, J. (1973). *Ethnicity and mental health.* New York: Institute of Human Relations.

Gitterman, A., & Shulman, L. (Eds.). (1994). *Mutual aid groups, vulnerable populations, and the life cycle* (2nd ed.). New York: Columbia University Press.

Glassman, U., & Kates, L. (1990). *Group work: A humanistic approach.* Newbury Park, CA: Sage.

Glassop, L. (2002). The organizational benefit of teams. *Human Relations, 55*(2), 225.

Glisson, C. (1986). The group versus the individual as the unit of analysis in small group research. *Social Work with Groups, 9*(3), 15–30.

Goebert, B., & Rosenthal, H. (2001). *Beyond listening: Learning the language of focus groups.* New York: J. Wiley.

Gold, M., Siegel, J., Russell, L., & Weinstein, M. (1996). *Cost-effectiveness in health and medicine.* New York: Oxford University Press.

Goldfried, M., & D'Zurilla, T. (1969). A behavioral-analytic model for assessing competence. In C. D. Spielberger (Ed.), *Current topics in clinical and community psychology* (Vol. 1, pp. 151–196). New York: Academic Press.

Goldstein, A., Keller, K., & Sechrest, L. (1966). *Psychotherapy and the psychology of behavior change.* New York: John Wiley & Sons.

Goldstein, H. (1983). Starting where the client is. *Social Casework, 64,* 267–275.

Goldstein, H. (1988). A cognitive-humanistic/social learning perspective on social group work practice. *Social Work with Groups, 11,* 9–32.

Goldstein, S. (1985). Organizational quality and quality circles. *Academy of Management Review, 10*(3), 504–517.

Gondolf, E. (1997). Batterer programs: What we know and need to know. *Journal of Interpersonal Violence, 12,* 83–98.

Gondolf, E. (2002). *Batterer intervention systems: Issues, outcomes, and recommendations.* Thousand Oaks, CA: Sage.

Goodman, P. (1986). *Designing effective work groups.* San Francisco: Jossey-Bass.

Good Tracks, J. (1973). Native-American noninterference. *Social Work, 18,* 30–34.

Gordon, T. (1975). *P.E.T.* New York: Plume Books.

Gordon, W. (1961). *Synectics: The development of creative capacity.* New York: Harper & Row.

Goto, S. (1997). Majority and minority perspectives on cross-cultural interactions. In C. Granrose & S. Oskamp (Eds.), *Cross-cultural work groups: An overview* (pp. 90–112). Thousand Oaks, CA: Sage Publications.

Gouran, D. (1982). *Making decisions in groups: Consequences and choices.* Glenview, IL: Scott Foresman.

Graen, G., & Schiemann, W. (1978). Leader-member agreement: A vertical dyad linkage approach. *Journal of Applied Psychology, 63,* 206–212.

Granrose, C. O., & Oskamp, S. (1997). *Cross-cultural work groups.* Thousand Oaks, CA: Sage, Publications.

Gray, G. (1964). Points of emphasis in teaching parliamentary procedure. *The Speech Teacher, 13,* 10–15.

Gray-Little, B., & Kaplan, D. (2000). Race and ethnicity in psychotherapy research. In C. R. Snyder & R. Ingram (Eds.), *Handbook of Psychological Change* (pp. 591–613). New York, John Wiley & Sons.

Grayson, E. (1993). *Short-term group counseling* (3rd ed.). Washington, DC: American Corrections Association.

Green, J. (1999). *Cultural awareness in the human services: A multi-ethnic approach* (3rd ed.). Boston: Allyn and Bacon.

Greenbaum, T. (1998). *The handbook for focus group research* (2nd ed., Rev.). Thousand Oaks, CA: Sage.

Gruenfeld, D. (Ed.). (1998). *Research on managing groups and teams, Vol. 1.* Stamford, CT: JAI Press.

Guetzkow, H., & Gyr, J. (1954). An analysis of conflict in decision-making groups. *Human Relations, 7,* 368–381.

Gulley, H. (1968). *Discussion, conference and group process* (2nd ed.). New York: Holt, Rinehart & Winston.

Gully, S., Devine, D., & Whitney, D. (1995). A meta-analysis of cohesion and performance: Effects of level of analysis and task interdependence. *Small Group Research, 26*(4), 497–520.

Gummer, B. (1987). Groups as substance and symbol: Group processes and organizational politics. *Social Work with Groups, 10*(2), 25–39.

Gummer, B. (1988). Post-industrial management: Teams, self-management, and the new interdependence. *Administration in Social Work, 12*(3), 117–132.

Gummer, B. (1991). A new managerial era: From hierarchical control to "collaborative individualism." *Administration in Social Work, 15*(3), 121–137.

Gummer, B. (1995). Go team go! The growing importance of teamwork in organizational life. *Administration in Social Work, 19*(4), 85–100.

Gummer, B., & McCallion, P. (Eds.). (1995). *Total quality management in the social services: Theory and practice.* Albany: State University of NY, University at Albany, School of Social Welfare, Professional Development Program of Rockefeller College.

Gutierrez, L., & Ortega, R. (1991). Developing methods to empower Latinos: The importance of groups. *Social Work with Groups, 14*(2), 23–43.

Hackman, J. (Ed.). (1990). *Groups that work (and those that don't).* San Francisco: Jossey-Bass.

Halpin, A. (1961). *Theory and research in administration.* New York: Macmillan.

Halstead, L. (1976). Team care in chronic illness: A critical review of the literature of the past 25 years. *Archives of Physical Medicine and Rehabilitation, 57,* 507–511.

Hammond, L., & Goldman, M. (1961). Competition and non-competition and its relationship to individuals' non-productivity. *Sociometry, 24,* 46–60.

Hanson, B. (2002). Interventions for batterers: Program approaches, program tensions. In A. Roberts (Ed.), *Handbook of domestic violence intervention strategies* (pp. 419–450). New York: Oxford.

Hare, A. P. (1976). *Handbook of small group research* (2nd ed.). New York: The Free Press.

Hare, A. P., Blumberg, H. H., Davies, M. F., & Kent, M. V. (1995). *Small group research: A handbook.* Norwood, NJ: Ablex.

Harmon, J., & Rohrbaugh, J. (1990). Social judgement analysis and small group decision making: Cognitive feedback effects on individual and collective performance. *Organizational Behavior and Human Decision Processes, 46,* 35–54.

Harnack, R., & Fest, T. (1964). *Group discussion: Theory and technique.* New York: Appleton-Century-Crofts.

Harrison, M. W., & Ward, D. (1999). Values as context: Groupwork and social action. *Groupwork, 11*(3), 89–103.

Hartford, M. (Ed.). (1964). *Papers toward a frame of reference for social group work.* New York: National Association of Social Workers.

Hartford, M. (1971). *Groups in social work.* New York: Columbia University Press.

Hasenfeld, Y. (1985). The organizational context of group work. In M. Sundel, P. Glasser, R. Sarri, & R. Vinter (Eds.), *Individual change through small groups* (2nd ed., pp. 294–309). New York: The Free Press.

Health Services Research Group. (1975). Development of an index of medical underservedness. Health Service Research, 10, 168–180.

Heap, K. (1979). *Process and action in work with groups.* Elmsford, NY: Pergamon Press.

Heimberg, R. B., & Becker, R. (2002). *Cognitive-behavioral group therapy for social phobia.* New York: Guilford Press.

Heinemann, G. Z., & Zeiss, A. (2002). *Team performance in health care: Assessment and development.* New York: Kluwer Academic/Plenum Publishers.

Hemphill, J. (1956). *Group dimensions: A manual for their measurement.* Columbus: Monographs of the Bureau of Business Research, Ohio State University.

Henry, S. (1992). *Group skills in social work: A four-dimensional approach* (2nd ed.). Itasca, IL: F. E. Peacock.

Hersey, R., & Blanchard, K. (1977). *Management of organizational behavior: Utilizing human resources* (3rd ed.). Englewood Cliffs, NJ: Prentice-Hall.

Hersey, R., Blanchard, K., & Natemeyer, W. (1979). Situational leadership, perception and the impact of power. *Group and Organization Studies, 4*(4), 418–428.

Herzog, J. (1980). Communication between co-leaders: Fact or myth. *Social Work with Groups, 3*(4), 19–29.

Hill, F. (1965). *Hill interaction matrix* (Rev. ed.). Los Angeles: Youth Studies Center, University of Southern California.

Hill, W. (1977). Hill interaction matrix (HIM): The conceptual framework, derived rating scales, and an updated bibliography. *Small Group Behavior, 8*(3), 251–268.

Ho, S. (1999). *TQM, an integrated approach: Implementing total quality through Japanese 5-S and ISO 9000.* Hong Kong: Hong Kong Baptist University.

Hogan-Garcia, M. (1999). *The four skills of cultural diversity competence: A process for understanding and practice.* Belmont, CA: Wadsworth.

Homans, G. (1950). *The human group.* New York: Harcourt Brace Jovanovich.

Homans, G. (1961). *Social behavior: Its elementary forms.* New York: Harcourt Brace Jovanovich.

Hopkins, K. (1998). *Educational and psychological measurement and evaluation* (8th ed.). Boston: Allyn and Bacon.

Hopps, J., & Pinderhughes, E. (1999). *Group work with overwhelmed clients.* New York: The Free Press.

Horne, A., & Rosenthal, R. (1997). Research in group work: How did we get where we are? *Journal for Specialists in Group Work, 22*(4), 228–240.

Howard, M., & Jenson, J. (2003). Clinical guidelines and evidence-based practice in medicine, psychology and allied professions. In A. Rosen & K. Proctor (Eds.), *Developing practice guidelines for social work intervention: Issues, methods, and research agenda* (pp. 83–107). New York: Columbia University Press.

Howe, F. (2002). *Fund-raising and the nonprofit board member* (3rd ed.). Washington, DC: National Center for Nonprofit Boards.

Hoyle, R., & Crawford, A. (1994). *Use of individual-level data to investigate group phenomena: Issues and strategies, 25*(4), 464–485.

Huber, G. (1980). *Managerial decision making.* Glenview, IL: Scott Foresman.

Hudson, W. (1982). *The clinical measurement package.* Homewood, CA: Dorsey Press.

Hudson, W. (1994). *MPSI: The MPSI technical manual.* Tempe, AZ: Walmyr.

Hugen, B. (1993). The effectiveness of a psychoeducational support service to families of persons with a chronic mental illness. *Research on Social Work Practice, 3*(2), 137–154.

Hughes, S., Lakey, B., & Bobowick, M. (2000). *The board building cycle: Nine steps of finding, recruiting, and engaging nonprofit board members.* National Center for NonProfit Boards.

Hula, K. (1999). *Lobbying together: Interest group coalitions in legislative politics.* Washington, DC: Georgetown University Press.

Jacobsen, B., & Jacobsen, M. (1996). The young bears. In R. Rivas & G. Hull (Eds.), *Case studies in generalist practice* (pp. 14–21). Pacific Grove, CA: Brooks/Cole.

Jacobson, E. (1978). *You must relax.* New York: McGraw-Hill.

Janis, I. (1972). *Victims of group think.* Boston: Houghton Mifflin.

Janis, I. (1982). *Groupthink* (2nd ed.). Boston: Houghton Mifflin.

Janis, I., & Mann, L. (1977). *Decision making: A psychological analysis of conflict, choice and commitment.* New York: The Free Press.

Janssen, P. (1994). *Psychoanalytic therapy in the hospital setting.* London: Routledge.

Jay, A. (1977). How to run a meeting. In F. Cox, J. Erlich, J. Rothman, & J. Tropman (Eds.), *Tactics and techniques of community practice* (pp. 255–269). Itasca, IL: F. E. Peacock.

Jehn, K. C., & Chatman, J. (2000). The influence of proportional and perceptual conflict composition on team performance. *The International Journal of Conflict Management, 11*(1), 56–73.

Jennings, H. (1947). Leadership and sociometric choice. *Sociometry* (10), 32–49.

Jennings, H. (1950). *Leadership and isolation* (2nd ed.). New York: Longman.

Jessup, L., & Valacich, J. (1993). Support group systems. [Special issue]. *Small Group Research, 24,* 427–592.

Jette, A. (2001). Disability trends and transitions. In R. Binstock & L. George (Eds.), *Handbook of aging and the social sciences* (5th ed., pp. 94–116). San Diego, CA: Academic Press.

Johnson, D. W. (2003). *Reaching out: Interpersonal effectiveness and self-actualization* (8th ed.). Boston: Allyn and Bacon.

Johnson, J. (1975). *Doing field research.* New York: The Free Press.

Johnson, J., & Raab, M. (2003). Take the first: Option-generation and resulting choices. *Organizational Behavior and Human Decision Processes, 91,* 215–229.

Johnson, L. (2004). *Social work practice: A generalist approach* (8th ed.). Boston: Allyn and Bacon.

Johnson, S., & Bechler, C. (1998). Examining the relationship between listening effectiveness and leadership emergence: Perceptions, behaviors, and recall. *Small Group Research, 29*(4), 452–471.

Kadushin, A., & Kadushin, G. (1997). *The social work interview: A guide for human service professionals* (4th ed.). New York: Columbia University Press.

Kaduson, H. G., & Schaefer, C. E. (Eds.). (2000). *Short term play therapy with children.* New York: Guilford Press.

Kahn, S. (1991). *Organizing: A guide for grassroots leaders.* Silver Spring, MD: NASW.

Kane, R. (1974). Look to the record. *Social Work, 19,* 412–419.

Kane, R. (1975a). The interprofessional team as a small group. *Social Work in Health Care, 1*(1), 19–32.

Kane, R. (1975b). *Interprofessional teamwork.* Syracuse, NY: Syracuse University School of Social Work.

Kane, R., & Kane, P. (1981). *Assessing the elderly: A practical guide to measurement.* Lexington, MA: Lexington Books.

Karakowsky, L., & McBey, K. (2001). Do my contributions matter? The influence of imputed expertise of member involvement and self-evaluations in the work group. *Group Organization & Management, 26*(1), 70–92.

Kart, G., Metress, E., & Metress, J. (1978). *Aging and health.* Reading, MA: Addison-Wesley.

Kaslyn, M. (1999). Telephone group work: Challenges for practice. *Social Work with Groups, 22,* 63–77.

Katten, S., & Janis, I. (2000). *Victims of groupthink.* CRM Productions.

Katz, A. H., & Bender, E. I. (1987). *The strength in us: Self-help groups in the modern world.* Oakland, CA: Third Party Associates.

Katz, A. H., Hedrick, H., Isenberg, D., Thompson, L., Goodrich, T., & Kutscher, A. (Eds.). (1992). *Self-help: Concepts and applications.* Philadelphia: Charles Press.

Katzenbach, J., & Smith, D. (1993). *The wisdom of teams.* Boston: Harvard Business School Press.

Kaul, T., & Bednar, R. (1994). Pretraining and structure: Parallel lines yet to meet. In A. Fuhriman and G. M. Burlingame (Eds.), *Handbook of Group Psychotherapy* (pp. 155–188). New York: John Wiley & Sons.

Keith, R. (1991). The comprehensive treatment team in rehabilitation. *Archives of Physical Medicine and Rehabilitation, 72,* 269–274.

Kelleher, K., & Cross, T. (1990). *Teleconferencing: Linking people together electronically.* Norman: University of Oklahoma Press.

Keller, T., & Dansereau, F. (1995). Leadership and empowerment: A social exchange perspective. *Human Relations, 48*(2), 127–146.

Kelley, H., & Thibaut, J. (1969). Group problem solving. In G. Lindzey & E. Aronim (Eds.), *Handbook of social psychology* (2nd ed., pp. 1–101). Reading, MA: Addison-Wesley.

Kellner, M. H. (2001). *In control, a skill-building program for teaching young adolescents to manage anger.* Champaign, IL: Research Press.

Kephart, M. (1951). A quantitative analysis of intragroup relationships. *American Journal of Sociology, 60,* 544–549.

Keyton, J. (1993). Group termination: Completing the study of group development. *Small Group Research, 24*(1), 84–100.

Kiesler, S. (1978). *Interpersonal processes in groups and organizations.* Arlington Heights, VA: AHM.

Kim, B., Omizo, M., & D'Andrea, M. (1998). The effects of culturally consonant group counseling on the self-esteem and internal locus of control orientation among Native American adolescents. *Journal for Specialists in Group Work, 23*(2), 143–163.

Kinlaw, C. D. (1992). *Continuous improvement and measurement for total quality: A team-based approach.* San Diego, CA: Pfeiffer & Co.; Homewood, IL: Business One Irwin.

Kinnear, T., & Taylor, J. (1996). *Marketing research: An applied approach* (5th ed.). New York: McGraw-Hill.

Kiresuk, T., & Sherman, R. (1968). Goal attainment scaling: A general method for evaluating comprehensive community mental health programs. *Community Mental Health Journal, 4*(6), 443–453.

Kirk, S. A., & Kutchins, H. (1999). Making us crazy. *DSM: The psychiatric bible and the creation of mental disorders* (2nd ed.). London: Constable.

Kirk, S. R., & Reid, W. (2002). *Science and social work: A critical appraisal.* New York: Columbia Press.

Kirst-Ashman, K., & Hull, G. (1999). *Understanding generalist practice* (2nd ed.). Chicago: Nelson Hall.

Kivlighan, D. M., & Tarrant, J. M. (2001). Does group climate mediate the group leadership-group member outcome relationship? A test of Yalom's hypotheses about leadership priorities. *Group Dynamics: Theory, Research, and Practice, 5*(3), 220–234.

Klein, A. (1953). *Society, democracy and the group.* New York: Whiteside.

Klein, A. (1956). *Role playing.* New York: Associated Press.

Klein, A. (1970). *Social work through group process.* Albany: School of Social Welfare, State University of New York at Albany.

Klein, A. (1972). *Effective group work.* New York: Associated Press.

Klein, M. (1997). *The American street gang* (2nd ed.). Oxford, UK: Oxford University Press.

Klein, R. H., Bernard, H. S., & Singer, D. L. (Eds.). (2000). *Handbook of contemporary group psychotherapy: Contributions from object relations, self psychology, and social systems theories.* Madison, CT: International Universities Press.

Kleindorfer, P. R., Kunreuther, H. C., & Schoemaker, P. J. H. (1993). *Decision sciences: An integrative perspective.* New York: Cambridge University Press.

Klosko, J., & Sanderson, W. (1998). *Cognitive behavioral treatment of depression.* Northvale, NJ: Jason Aronson.

Knottnerus, J. (1994). Social exchange theory and social structure: A critical comparison of two traditions of inquiry. *Current Perspectives in Social Theory* (Suppl. 1), 29–48.

Knox, G. (1999a). *Achieving moral health.* New York: Crossroad Publishing Co.

Knox, G. (1999b). A comparison of cults and gangs: Dimensions of coercive power and malevolent authority. *Journal of Gang Research, 6*(4), 1–39.

Kolb, J. (1997). Are we still stereotyping leadership? A look at gender and other predictors of leader emergence. *Small Group Research, 28*(3), 370–393.

Kolodny, R. (1980). The dilemma of co-leadership. *Social Work with Groups, 3*(4), 31–34.

Konig, K. (1994). *Psychoanalytic group therapy.* Northvale, NY: Jason Aronson.

Konopka, G. (1949). *Therapeutic group work with children.* Minneapolis: University of Minnesota Press.

Konopka, G. (1954). *Group work in the institution.* New York: Association Press.

Konopka, G. (1983). *Social group work: A helping process* (3rd ed.). Englewood Cliffs, NJ: Prentice-Hall.

Kopp, J. (1993). Self-observation: An empowering strategy in assessment. In J. Rauch (Ed.), *Assessment: A sourcebook for social work practice* (pp. 255–268). Milwaukee, WI: Families International.

Koss-Chioino, J. (1995). Traditional and folk approaches among ethnic minorities. In J. Aponte, R. Rivers, & J. Wohl (Eds.), *Psychological interventions and cultural diversity* (pp. 145–163). Boston: Allyn and Bacon.

Kottler, J. (1992). *Compassionate therapy: Working with difficult clients.* San Francisco: Jossey-Bass.

Kramer, J., & Conoley, J. (1992). *Eleventh mental measurement yearbook.* Lincoln, NE: Buros Institute of Mental Measurements.

Kramer, M., Kuo, C., & Dailey, J. (1997). The impact of brainstorming techniques on subsequent group processes. *Small Group Research, 28*(2), 218–242.

Krueger, R. (1998a). *Analyzing and reporting focus group results.* Thousand Oaks, CA: Sage.

Krueger, R. (1998b). *Developing questions for focus groups.* Thousand Oaks, CA: Sage.

Krueger, R., & Casey, M. (2000). *Focus groups: A practical guide for applied research* (3rd ed.). Thousand Oaks, CA: Sage.

Kurtz, L. (1997). *Self-help and support groups: A handbook for practitioners.* Thousand Oaks, CA: Sage.

Labrecque, M., Peak, T., & Toseland, R. (1992). Long-term effectiveness of a group program for caregivers of frail elderly veterans. *American Journal of Orthopsychiatry, 62*(4), 575–588.

Lakin, M. (1991). Some ethical issues in feminist-oriented therapeutic groups for women. *International Journal of Group Psychotherapy, 4,* 199–215.

Langelier, C. A. (2001). *Mood management: A cognitive-behavioral skills building program for adolescents: Leader's manual.* Thousand Oaks, CA: Sage Publications.

Lang, N. (1972). A broad range model of practice in the social work group. *Social Service Review, 46*(1), 76–84.

Lang, N. (1979a). A comparative examination of therapeutic uses of groups in social work and in adjacent human service professions: Part I—The literature from 1955–1968. *Social Work with Groups, 2*(2), 101–115.

Lang, N. (1979b). A comparative examination of the therapeutic uses of groups in social work and in adjacent human service professions: Part II—The literature from 1969–1978. *Social Work with Groups, 2*(3), 197–220.

Lauffer, A. (1978). *Social planning at the community level.* Englewood Cliffs, NJ: Prentice-Hall.

Lawler, E., III, & Mohrman, S. (1985, Spring). Quality circles after the fad: There are benefits for managers and employees—and there are limitations. *Public Welfare, 43*(2), 37–44.

Lawler, E., Mohrman, E., Albers, S., & Benson, G. (2001). *Organizing for high performance organizations: Employee involvement, TQM, reengineering. and knowledge management in the Fortune 1000: The CEO report.* San Francisco: Jossey-Bass.

Lawson, H., Bronstein, L., McCallion, P., Ryan, D., & Fish, F. (2003). Developing coalitions and collaborations: A resource guide for the 21st century. Albany, NY: New York State Office for the Aging.

Lazarus, J. (2000). *Stress relief & relaxation techniques.* Oakland, CA: New Harbinger Publications.

Lazarus, R. S., & Folkman, S. (1984). *Stress, appraisal, and coping.* New York: Springer.

Lazell, E. W. (1921). The group treatment of dementia praecox. *Psychoanalytical Review, 8,* 168–179.

Leahy, R. (1996). *Cognitive therapy: Basic principles and applications.* Northvale, NJ: Jason Aronson.

LeBon, G. (1910). *The crowd: A study of the popular mind.* London: George Allen & Unwin Ltd.

Lederman, L. C. (1989). *Assessing educational effectiveness: The focus group interview as a technique for data collection.* Paper presented at the meeting of the Speech Communication Association, San Francisco.

Lee, J. (2001). The empowerment group: The heart of the empowerment approach and an antidote to injustice. In J. Parry (Ed.), *From prevention to wellness through group work* (2nd ed., pp. 290–320). New York, NY: Columbia Univ. Press.

Lese, K., & MacNair-Semands, R. (2000). The therapeutic factors inventory: Development of a scale. *Eastern Group Psychotherapy Society, 24*(4), 303–317.

Leszcz, M. (1992). The interpersonal approach to group psychotherapy. *International Journal of Group Psychotherapy, 42*(1), 37–62.

Levi, D. (2001). *Group dynamics for teams.* Thousand Oaks, CA: Sage Publications.

Levin, H. M., & McEwan, P. (2001). *Cost-effectiveness analysis: Methods and applications.* Thousand Oaks, CA: Sage Publications, Inc.

Levine, B. (1979). *Group psychotherapy: Practice and development.* Englewood Cliffs, NJ: Prentice-Hall.

Levine, B. (1980). Co-leadership approach to learning group work. *Social Work with Groups, 3*(4), 35–38.

Levine, B., & Gallogly, V. (1985). *Group therapy with alcoholics: Outpatient and inpatient approaches.* Newbury Park, CA: Sage.

Levinson, D., & Klerman, G. (1973). The clinician-executive: Some problematic issues for the psychiatrist in mental health organizations. *Administration in Mental Health, 1*(1), 52–67.

Levinson, H. (1977). Termination of psychotherapy: Some salient issues. *Social Casework, 58*(8), 480–489.

Levitt, J., & Reid, W. (1981). Rapid assessment instruments for social work practice. *Social Work Research and Abstracts, 17*(1), 13–20.

Lewin, K. (1946). Behavior as a function of the total situation. In L. Carmichael (Ed.), *Manual of child psychology* (pp. 791–844). New York: John Wiley & Sons.

Lewin, K. (1947). Frontiers in group dynamics. *Human Relations, 1,* 2–38.

Lewin, K. (1948). *Resolving social conflict.* New York: Harper & Row.

Lewin, K. (1951). *Field theory in social science.* New York: Harper & Row.

Lewin, K., & Lippitt, R. (1938). An experimental approach to the study of autocracy and democracy: A preliminary note. *Sociometry, 1,* 292–300.

Lewin, K., Lippitt, R., & White, R. (1939). Patterns of aggressive behavior in experimentally created "social climates." *Journal of Social Psychology, 10,* 271–299.

Lewis, E., & Ford, B. (1990). The network utilization project: Incorporating traditional strengths of African-American families into group work practice. *Social Work with Groups, 13*(4), 7–22.

Lewis, H. (1982, October). Ethics in work with groups: The clients' interests. In N. Lang & C. Marshall (Chairs), *Patterns in the mosaic.* Symposium conducted at the Fourth Annual Meeting of Social Work with Groups, Toronto.

Lewis, R., & Ho, M. (1975). Social work with Native Americans. *Social Work, 20,* 379–382.

Lieberman, M. (1975). Groups for personal change: New and not-so-new forms. In D. Freedman & J. Dyrad (Eds.), *American handbook of psychiatry* (pp. 345–366). New York: Basic Books.

Lieberman, M., & Borman, L. (Eds.). (1979). *Self-help groups for coping with crisis.* San Francisco: Jossey-Bass.

Lieberman, M., Yalom, I., & Miles, M. (1973). *Encounter groups: First facts.* New York: Basic Books.

Lighthouse, Inc. (1995). *The Lighthouse National Survey on vision loss: The experience, attitudes and knowledge of middle-aged and older Americans.* New York: The Lighthouse.

Likert, R. (1961). *New patterns of management.* New York: McGraw-Hill.

Likert, R. (1967). *The human organization.* New York: McGraw-Hill.

Lippitt, R. (1957). Group dynamics and the individual. *International Journal of Group Psychotherapy, 7*(10), 86–102.

Loewenberg, F., & Dolgoff, R. (1996). *Ethical decisions for social work practice* (5th ed.). Itasca, IL: Peacock Press.

Lonergan, E. C. (1989). *Group intervention* (3rd ed.). Northvale, NJ: Jason Aronson.

Long, K., Pendleton, L., & Winter, B. (1988). Effects of therapist termination on group processes. *International Journal of Group Psychotherapy, 38*(2), 211–223.

Lopez, J. (1991). Group work as a protective factor for immigrant youth. *Social Work with Groups, 14*(1), 29–42.

Luft, J. (1984). *Group processes* (3rd ed.). Palo Alto, CA: Mayfield.

Lum, D. (2000). *Social work practice and people of color: A process-stage approach* (4th ed.). Pacific Grove, CA: Brooks/Cole.

Lum, D., Ed. (2003). *Culturally competent practice: A framework for understanding diverse groups and justice issues.* Sacramento, CA: Thomson, Brooks/Cole.

Macgowan, M. J., & Pennell, J. (2001). Building social responsibility through family group conferencing. *Social Work With Groups, 24*(3-4), 67–87.

MacKenzie, K. R. (1990). *Introduction to time-limited group psychotherapy.* Washington, DC: American Psychiatric Press.

MacKenzie, K. R. (1994). Group Development. In A. Fuhriman and G. M. Burlingame (Eds.), *Handbook of Group Psychotherapy* (pp. 223–268). New York: John Wiley & Sons.

MacKenzie, K. R. (Ed.). (1995). *Effective use of group therapy in managed care.* Washington, DC: American Psychiatric Press.

MacKenzie, K. R. (1996). Time-limited group psychotherapy. *International Journal of Group Psychotherapy, 46*(1), 41–60.

MacLennon, B. (1965). Co-therapy. *International Journal of Group Psychotherapy, 15,* 154–166.

Magen, R. (1999). *Recent Contributions to Empirical Group Work.* Thousand Oaks, CA: Sage Publications.

Maguire, L. (1991). *Social support systems in practice: A generalist approach.* Silver Spring, MD: National Association of Social Workers Press.

Mahoney, M. J. (1974). *Cognitive and behavior modification.* Cambridge, MA: Ballinger Books.

Mahoney, M. J. (Ed.). (1995a). *Cognitive and constructive psychotherapies: Theory, research and practice.* New York: Springer.

Mahoney, M. J. (Ed.). (1995b). *Constructive psychotherapy.* New York: Guilford.

Maier, N. (1963). *Problem-solving discussions and conferences: Leadership methods and skills.* New York: McGraw-Hill.

Maier, N., & Zerfoss, L. (1952). MRP: A technique for training large groups of supervisors and its potential use in social research. *Human Relations, 5,* 177–186.

Malekoff, A. (1997). *Group work with adolescents.* New York: Guilford Press.

Maloney, S. (1963). *Development of group work education in social work schools in U.S.* Unpublished doctoral dissertation, Case Western Reserve University, School of Applied Social Science, Cleveland.

Maltzman, I., Simon, S., Raskin, D., & Licht, L. (1960). Experimental studies in the training of originality. *Psychological Monographs, 7* (493).

Maluccio, A. (1979). *Learning from clients.* New York: The Free Press.

Maple, F. (1977). *Shared decision making.* Newbury Park, CA: Sage.

Marks, M., Mirvis, P., Hackett, E., & Grady, J. (1986). Employee participation in a quality circle program: Impact on quality of worklife, productivity, and absenteeism. *Journal of Applied Psychology, 71,* 61–69.

Marlatt, G. (1996). Taxonomy of high-risk situations for alcohol relapse: Evolution and development of a cognitive-behavioral model. *Addiction, 91* (supplement), S37–S49.

Marlatt, G., & Barrett, K. (1994). Relapse prevention. In M. Galanter & H. D. Kleber (Eds.), *The American Psychiatric Press textbook of substance abuse treatment* (pp. 285–299). Washington, DC: American Psychiatric Press.

Marsh, E., & Terdal, L. (Eds.). (1997). *Behavioral assessment of childhood disorders* (3rd ed.). New York: Guilford.

Marsh, L. C. (1931). Group treatment of the psychoses by the psychological equivalent of the revival. *Mental Hygiene, 15,* 328–349.

Marsh, L. C. (1933). An experiment in group treatment of patients at Worchester State hospital. *Mental Hygiene, 17,* 396–416.

Marsh, L. C. (1935). Group therapy and the psychiatric clinic. *Journal of Nervous & Mental Disorders, 82,* 381–393.

Marshall, C. R., & Rossman, G. (1999). *Designing qualitative research.* Thousand Oaks, CA: Sage Publications.

Marsiglia, F., Cross, S., & Mitchell-Enos, V. (1998). Culturally grounded group work with adolescent American Indian students. *Social Work with Groups, 21*(1), 89–102.

Masters, J., Burish, T., Hollon, S., & Rimm, D. (1987). *Behavior therapy: Techniques and empirical findings* (3rd ed.). San Diego, CA: Harcourt Brace Jovanovich.

Matsukawa, L. A. (2001). Group therapy with multiethnic minorities. In W. Tseng & J. Streltzer (Eds.), *Culture and Psychotherapy: A Guide to Clinical Practice.* Washington, DC: American Psychiatric Publishing Inc.

Mattessich, P., Murray-Close, M., & Monsey, B. (2001). *Collaboration: What makes it work?* Saint Paul, MN: Amherst H. Wilder Foundation.

Mayadas, N., & Glasser, P. (1981). Termination: A neglected aspect of social group work. *Social Work with Groups, 4*(2), 193–204.

Mayer, J., Soweid, R., Dabney, S., Brownson, C., Goodman, R., & Brownson, R. (1998). Practices of successful community coalitions: A multiple case study. *American Journal of Health Behavior, 22*(5), 368–369.

Mayer, J., & Timms, N. (1970). *The client speaks: Working class impressions of casework.* New York: Atherton Press.

Maznevski, M., & Peterson, M. (1997a). Societal values, social interpretation, and multinational teams. In C. Granrose & S. Oskemp (Eds.), *Cross-cultural work groups: An overview* (pp. 61–89). Thousand Oaks, CA: Sage Publications.

Maznevski, M., & Peterson, M. (1997b). Societal values, social interpretation and multi national executive realms. In C. Granrose & S. Oskamp (Eds.), *Cross Cultural Work Groups* (pp. 61–89). New York: Sage.

McCallion, P., Toseland, R., & Diehl, M. (1994). Social work practice with caregivers of frail older adults. *Research on Social Work Practice, 4,* 64–68.

McCaskill, J. (1930). *Theory and practice of group work.* New York: Association Press.

McClane, W. (1991). The interaction of leader and member characteristics in the leader-member exchange model of leadership. *Small Group Research, 22,* 283–300.

McCorkle, L., Elias, A., Bixby, F. (1958). *The highfields story: An experimental project for youthful offenders.* New York: Holt.

McDougall, W. (1920). *The group mind.* New York: G. P. Putnam's Sons.

McFarlane, W. (2002). *Multifamily groups in the treatment of severe psychiatric disorders.* New York, NY: Guilford Press.

McGee, T., & Schuman, B. (1970). The nature of the co-therapy relationship. *International Journal of Group Psychotherapy, 20,* 25–36.

McGrath, J. (1984). *Groups: Interaction and performance.* Englewood Cliffs, NJ: Prentice-Hall.

McGrath, J. (1992). Time, interaction, and performance (TIP): A theory of groups. *Small Group Research, 22,* 147–174.

McGrath, J., Arrow, H., & Berdahl, J. (2000). The study of groups: Past, present, and future. *Personality and Social Psychology Review, 4*(1), 95–105.

McGrath, P., & Axelson, J. (1999). *Accessing awareness & developing knowledge: Foundations for skill in a multicultural society* (3rd ed.). Pacific Grove, CA: Brooks/Cole.

McKay, M., & Paleg, K. (Eds.). (1992). *Focal group psychotherapy.* Oakland, CA: New Harbinger.

McKenna, K. Y. A., & Bargh, J. (1999). Causes and consequences of social interaction on the Internet: A conceptual framework. *Media Psychology, 1,* 249–269.

McKenna, K. Y. A., & Bargh, J. (2000). Plan 9 from cyberspace: The implications of the Internet for personality and social psychology. *Personality and Social Psychology Review, 4*(1), 57–75.

McKenna, K. Y. A., & Green, A. S. (2002). Virtual group dynamics. *Group Dynamics: Theory, Research, and Practice, 6*(1), 116–127.

McKenna, K. Y. A., Green, A. S., & Gleason, M. E. J. (2002). Relationship formation on the Internet: What's the big attraction? *Journal of Social Issues, 58*(1), 9–31.

McLeod, P., Lobel, S., & Cox, T. (1996). Ethnic diversity and creativity in small groups. *Small Group Research, 27*(2), 248–264.

McRoberts, C., Burlingame, G. M., & Hoag, M. J. (1998). Comparative efficacy of individual and group psychotherapy: A meta-analytic perspective. *Group Dynamics, 2*(2), 101–117.

McRoy, R. (2003). Cultural competence with African Americans. In D. Lum (Ed.), *Culturally Competent Practice: A Framework for Understanding Diverse Groups and Justice Issues.* Sacramento, CA: Thomson, Brooks, Cole.

Meichenbaum, D. (1977). *Cognitive-behavior modification: An integrative approach.* New York: Plenum.

Meichenbaum, D. (1985). *Stress inoculation training.* New York: Plenum.

Meichenbaum, D., & Cameron, R. (1983). Stress inoculation training: Toward a general paradigm for training coping skills. In D. Meichenbaum & M. E. Jaremko (Eds.), *Stress reduction and prevention* (pp. 115–154). Norwell, MA: Plenum.

Meichenbaum, D., & Fitzpatrick, D. (1993). A constructivist narrative perspective on stress and coping: Stress inoculation applications. In L. Goldberger & S. Breznitz (Eds.), *Handbook of stress: Theoretical and clinical aspects* (2nd ed., pp. 706–723). New York: Free Press.

Merenda, D. (1997). *A practical guide to creating and managing community coalitions for drug abuse prevention.* Alexandria, VA: National Association of Partners in Education.

Merton, R., & Kendall, P. (1946). The focused interview. *American Journal of Sociology, 51,* 541–557.

Meyer, C. (Ed.). (1983). *Social work in the eco-systems perspective.* New York: Columbia University Press.

Meyer, C. (1988). The ecosystems perspective. In R. A. Dorfman (Ed.), *Paradigms of clinical social work* (pp. 275–294). New York: Brunner/Mazel.

Middleman, R. (1978). Returning group process to group work. *Social Work with Groups, 1*(1), 15–26.

Middleman, R. (1980). The use of program: Review and update. *Social Work with Groups, 3*(3), 5–23.

Middleman, R. (1982). *The non-verbal method in working with groups: The use of activity in teaching, counseling, and therapy.* (Enlarged ed.). Hebron, CT: Practitioners Press.

Middleman, R., & Wood, G. (1990). Reviewing the past and present of group work and the challenge of the future. *Social Work with Groups, 13*(3), 3–20.

Milgram, D., & Rubin, J. (1992). Resisting resistance: Involuntary substance abuse group therapy. *Social Work with Groups, 15*(1), 95–110.

Milgram, S. (1974). *Obedience and authority.* New York: Harper and Row.

Miller, S., Nunnally, E., & Wackman, D. (1972). *The Minnesota couples communication program couples handbook.* Minneapolis: Minnesota Couples Communication Program.

Miller, W., & Rollnick, S. (Eds.). (2002). *Motivational interviewing: Preparing people for change.* New York: Guilford Press.

Mills, T. (1967). *The sociology of small groups.* Englewood Cliffs, NJ: Prentice-Hall.

Milter, R. G., & Rohrbaugh, J. (1988). Judgment analysis and decision conferencing for administrative review: A case study of innovative policy making in government. In R. L. Cardy, S. M. Puffer, & J. M. Newman (Eds.), *Advances in information processing in organizations* (pp. 245–262). Greenwich, CT: JAI Press.

Mistry, T., & Brown, A. (1997). *Race and groupwork.* London: Whiting & Birch.

Mizrahi, T., & Rosenthal, B. (1998, March). *Complexities of effective coalition-building: A study of leaders' strategies, struggles, and solutions.* Paper presented at the Annual Program Meeting of the Council on Social Work Education. Orlando, FL.

Mondros, J., & Wilson, S. (1994). *Organizing for power and empowerment.* New York: Columbia University Press.

Moore, C. (1994). *Group techniques for idea building.* Thousand Oaks, CA: Sage.

Moreno, J. (1934). *Who shall survive?* Washington, DC: Nervous and Mental Diseases.

Moreno, J. (1946). *Psychodrama* (Vol. 1). Boston: Beacon Press.

Morgan, D. (1997). *Focus groups as qualitative research* (2nd ed.). Thousand Oaks, CA: Sage.

Moscovici, S. (1994). Three concepts: Minority, conflict, and behavioral styles. In S. Moscovici, M. Faina, & A. Maass (Eds.), *Minority Influence* (pp. 235–251). Chicago: Nelson-Hall.

Moscovici, S. (1985). *The age of the crowd: A historical treatise on mass psychology.* Cambridge: Cambridge University Press.

Moscovici, S., & Lage, E. (1976). Studies in social influence: III. Majority versus minority influence in a group. *European Journal of Social Psychology, 6*(2), 149–174.

Moscovici, S., Lage, E., & Naffrechoux, M. (1969). Influence of a constant minority on the responses of a majority in a color perception task. *Sociometry, 32*(4), 365–380.

Mullen, B., & Cooper, C. (1994). The relationship between cohesiveness and performance: An integration. *Psychological Bulletin, 115*(2), 210–227.

Mullen, E. (1969). The relationship between diagnosis and treatment in casework. *Social Casework, 50,* 218–226.

Mullender, A., & Ward, D. (1991). *Self-directed groupwork: Users take action for empowerment.* London: Whitney & Birch.

Munzer, J., & Greenwald, H. (1957). Interaction process analysis of a therapy group. *International Journal of Group Psychotherapy, 7,* 175–190.

Murphy, M., DeBernardo, C., & Shoemaker, W. (1998). Impact of managed care on independent practice and professional ethics: A survey of independent practitioners. *Professional Psychology: Research and Practice, 29,* 43–51.

Myers, D., & Arenson, S. (1972). Enhancement of the dominant risk in group discussion. *Psychological Reports, 30,* 615–623.

Nadler, D. (1979). The effects of feedback on task group behavior: A review of the experimental research. *Organizational Behavior and Human Performance, 23,* 309–338.

Napier, H. (1967). Individual versus group learning: Note on task variable. *Psychological Reports, 23,* 757–758.

Napier, R., & Gershenfeld, M. (1993). *Groups: Theory and experience* (5th ed.). Boston: Houghton Mifflin.

Nas, T. (Ed.). (1996). *Cost-benefit analysis: Theory and application.* Thousand Oaks, CA: Sage Publications.

Newcomb, T. M. (1943). *Personality and social change.* New York: Dryden.

Newstetter, W. (1948). The social intergroup work process. In *Proceedings of the National Conference of Social Work* (pp. 205–217). New York: Columbia University Press.

Newstetter, W., Feldstein, M. J., & Newcomb, T. M. (1938). *Group adjustment: A study in experimental sociology.* Cleveland, OH: School of Applied Social Sciences, Western Reserve University.

Nixon, H. (1979). *The small group.* Englewood Cliffs, NJ: Prentice-Hall.

Northen, H. (1969). *Social work with groups.* New York: Columbia University Press.

Northen, H. (1995). *Clinical social work* (2nd ed.). New York: Columbia University Press.

Nosko, A., & Breton, M. (1997–98). Applying strengths, competence and empowerment model. *Groupwork, 10*(1), 55–69.

Nosko, A., & Wallace, R. (1997). Female/male co-leadership in group. *Social Work with Groups, 20*(2), 3–16.

Nunnally, J. C. (1994). *Psychometric theory* (3rd ed.). New York: McGraw-Hill.

Nye, J., & Forsyth, D. (1991). The effects of prototype-based biases on leadership appraisals: A test of leadership categorization theory. *Small Group Research, 22,* 360–379.

Oei, T. K., & Kazmierczak, T. (1997). Factors associated with dropout in a group cognitive behaviour therapy for mood disorders. *Behavior Research and Therapy, 35,* 1025–1030.

Ollendick, T., & Hersen, M. (Eds.). (1984). *Child behavioral assessment.* Elmsford, NY: Pergamon Press.

Olmsted, M. (1959). *The small group.* New York: Random House.

Olsen, M. (1968). *The process of social organization.* New York: Holt, Rinehart & Winston.

Orasanu, J., Fischer, U., & Davison, J. (1997). Cross-cultural barriers to effective communication in aviation. In C. Granrose & S. Oskamp (Eds.), *Cross-cultural work groups: An overview* (pp. 134–162). Thousand Oaks, CA: Sage Publications.

Oravec, J. (2000). Online counseling and the Internet: Perspectives for mental health care supervision and education. *Journal of Mental Health, 9*(2), 121–135.

Osborn, A. (1963). *Applied imagination: Principles and procedures of creative problem solving* (3rd ed.). New York: Charles Scribner's Sons.

Osgood, C., Suci, C., & Tannenbaum, P. (1957). *The measurement of meaning.* Urbana: University of Illinois Press.

Padgett, D. (1998). *Qualitative methods in social work research: Challenges and rewards.* New York: Sage Publications.

Papell, C. (1997). Thinking about thinking about group work: Thirty years later. *Social Work with Groups, 20*(4), 5–17.

Papell, C., & Rothman, B. (1962). Social group work models—possession and heritage. *Journal of Education for Social Work, 2,* 66–77.

Papell, C., & Rothman, B. (1980). Relating the mainstream model of social work with groups to group psychotherapy and the structured group approach. *Social Work with Groups, 3*(2), 5–23.

Parnes, S. (1967). *Creative behavior guidebook.* New York: Charles Scribner's Sons.

Parrillo, V. (2000). *Strangers to these shores: Race and ethnic relations in the United States.* Boston: Allyn and Bacon.

Parsons, R. (1991). Empowerment: Purpose and practice principle in social work. *Social Work with Groups, 14*(2), 7–21.

Parsons, T. (1951). *The social system.* New York: The Free Press.

Parsons, T., Bales, R., & Shils, E. (Eds.). (1953). *Working papers in the theory of action.* New York: The Free Press.

Passi, L. (1998). *A guide to creative group programming in the psychiatric day hospital.* New York: Haworth Press.

Patti, R. (1974). Organizational resistance and change: The view from below. *Social Service Review, 48*(3), 367–383.

Patton, M. (2000). Qualitative research and evaluation methods. Thousand Oaks, CA: Sage Publications.

Paulus, P., Larey, T., & Dzindolet, M. (2001). *Creativity in Groups and Teams.* NJ: Lawrence Erlbaum Associates, Inc.

Payne, M. (2000). *Teamwork in multiprofessional care.* Chicago: Lyceum.

Pearson, V. (1991). Western theory, Eastern practice: Social group work in Hong Kong. *Social Work with Groups, 14*(2), 45–58.

Pepitone, A., & Reichling, G. (1955). Group cohesiveness and the expression of hostility. *Human Relations, 8,* 327–337.

Perlman, H. (1970). The problem-solving method in social casework. In R. Roberts & R. Nee (Eds.), *Theories of social casework* (pp. 129–180). Chicago: University of Chicago Press.

Pernell, R. (1986). Empowerment and social group work. In M. Parnes (Ed.), *Innovations in social group work* (pp. 107–118). New York: Haworth Press.

Pescosolido, A. T. (2001). Informal leaders and the development of group efficacy. *Small Group Research, 32*(1), 74–93.

Pescosolido, A. T. (2003). Group efficacy and group effectiveness: The effects of group efficacy over time on group performance and development. *Small Group Research, 34*(1), 20–42.

Peters, A. (1997). Themes in group work with lesbian and gay adolescents. *Social Work with Groups, 20*(2), 51–69.

Pfeiffer, J., & Goodstein, L. (Eds.). (1984–1996). *The annual: Developing human resources.* San Diego, CA: University Associates.

Phillips, J. (1948). Report on discussion 66. *Adult Education Journal, 7,* 181–182.

Phillips, L. R., Torres de Aroon, E., Komnenich, P., Killeen, M., & Rusniak, R. (2000). The Mexican American caregiving experience. *Hispanic Journal of Behavioral Sciences, 22*(3), 296–313.

Pillari, V. (2002). *Social work practice: Theories and skills.* Boston: Allyn and Bacon.

Pincus, A., & Minahan, A. (1973). *Social work practice: Model and method.* Itasca, IL: F. E. Peacock.

Pinderhughes, E. B. (1979). Teaching empathy in cross-cultural social work. *Social Work, 2*(4), 312–316.

Pinderhughes, E. B. (1995). Empowering diverse populations: Family practice in the 21st century. *Families in Society, 76,* 131–140.

Pinkus, H. (1968). *Casework techniques related to selected characteristics of clients and workers.* Unpublished doctoral dissertation, Columbia University, New York.

Piper, W. (1992). *Adaptation to loss through short-term group psychotherapy.* New York: Guilford.

Piper, W. (1994). Client variables. In A. Fuhriman and G. M. Burlingame (Eds.), *Handbook of Group Psychotherapy* (pp. 83–113). New York: John Wiley & Sons.

Piper, W., Debbane, E., Bienvenu, J., & Garant, J. (1982). A study of group pretraining for group psychotherapy. *International Journal of Group Psychotherapy, 32,* 309–325.

Piper, W., & Joyce, A. (1996). A consideration of factors influencing the utilization of time-limited, short-term group therapy. *International Journal of Group Psychotherapy, 46*(3), 311–329.

Piper, W., Ogrodniczuk, J., & Duncan, S. (2002). Psychodynamically oriented group therapy. In F. W. Kaslow (Editor In Chief) & J. J. Magnavita (Vol. Ed.), *Comprehensive Handbook of Psychotherapy. Volume 1: Psychodynamic/Object Relations* (pp. 457–479). New York: Wiley & Sons.

Pomeroy, E. C., Rubin, A., & Walker, R. J. (1995). Effectiveness of a psychoeducational and task-centered group intervention for family members of people with AIDS. *Social Work Research, 19*(3), 142–152.

Postmes, T., Spears, R., & Lea, M. (1999). Social identity, normative content, and "deindividuation" in computer-mediated groups. In N. Ellemers, R. Spears, & B. Doosje (Eds.), *Social identity: Context, commitment, content* (pp. 164–183). Malden, MA: Blackwell Publishers.

Postmes, T., Spears, R., Sakhel, K., & de Groot, D. (2001). Social influence in computer-mediated communication: The effects of anonymity on group behavior. *Personality and Social Psychology Bulletin, 27*(10), 1243–1254.

Powell, T. (1987). *Self-help organizations and professional practice.* Silver Spring, MD: National Association of Social Workers Press.

Prapavessis, H., & Carron, A. (1997). Cohesion and work output. *Small Group Research, 28*(2), 294–301.

Prigmore, C. S. (1974). Use of the coalition in legislative action. *Social Work, 19*(1), 96–102.

Prince, G. (1970). *The practice of creativity.* New York: Harper & Row.

Prochaska, J., DiClimente, C., & Norcross, C. (1992). In Search of How People Change. *American Psychologist, 41*(4), 1102–1114.

Proctor, E., & Davis, L. (1994). The challenge of racial difference: Skills for clinical practice. *Social Work, 39,* 314–323.

Purdy, J. A., & Arguello, D. (1992). Hispanic familism in caretaking of older adults: Is it functional? *Journal of Gerontological Social Work, 19,* 29–43.

Putnam, R. D. (2000). *Bowling alone: The collapse and revival of American community.* New York: Simon & Schuster.

Putnam, R. D. (2001). *Bowling Alone.* New York: Touchstone.

Ramey, J. H. (Ed.). (1999). *Bibliography on group work.* Akron, OH: Association for Advancement of Social Work with Groups.

Ramos, B., Jones, L., & Toseland R. (in press). Culturally competent social work practice with elderly of color. In D. Lum (Ed.), *Social work practice and people of color: A process stage approach.* Belmont, CA: Brooks Cole.

Ramos, B., Toseland R., Smith. T., & McCallion, P. (In Press). Latino Family Caregivers of the Elderly: A Health Education Program. *Social Work.*

Rathus, J., & Sanderson, W. (1999). *Marital distress: Cognitive behavioral interventions for couples* (2nd ed.). Northvale, NJ: Jason Aronson.

Rauch, J. (Ed.). (1993). *Assessment: A sourcebook for social work practice.* Milwaukee, WI: Families International.

Reagan-Cirinicione, P. (1994). Improving the accuracy of group judgment: A process intervention combining group facilitation, social judgment analysis, and information technology. *Organizational Behavior and Human Decision Processes, 58,* 246–270.

Reamer, F. G. (1998). *Ethical standards in social work: A review of the NASW Code of Ethics.* Washington, DC: NASW Press.

Reamer, F. G. (2001). *The social work ethics audit: A risk-management tool.* Washington, DC: NASW Press.

Reder, P. (1978). An assessment of the group therapy interaction chronogram. *International Journal of Group Psychotherapy, 28,* 185–194.

Redl, F. (1942). Group emotion and leadership. *Psychiatry, 5,* 573–596.

Redl, F. (1944). Diagnostic group work. *American Journal of Orthopsychiatry, 14*(1), 53–67.

Reid, K. (1981). *From character building to social treatment: The history of the use of groups in social work.* Westport, CT: Greenwood Press.

Reid, K. (1997). *Social work practice with groups: A clinical perspective* (2nd ed.). Pacific Grove, CA: Brooks/Cole.

Reid, W. J. (1992). *Task strategies: An empirical approach to clinical social work.* New York: Columbia University Press.

Reid, W. J. (1997). Research on task-centered practice. *Social Work Research, 21*(3), 132–137.

Reid, W. J., & Shapiro, B. (1969). Client reactions to advice. *Social Service Review, 43,* 165–173.

Reinecke, M., Dattilio, M., & Freeman, A. (2003). *Cognitive therapy with children and adolescents.* New York: Guilford Press.

Rhode, R., & Stockton, R. (1992, Winter). The effect of structured feedback on goal attainment, attraction to the group, and satisfaction with the group in small group counseling. *Journal of Group Psychotherapy, Psychodrama, and Sociometry, 44*(4), 172–179.

Rice, C. (1987). *Inpatient group psychotherapy: A psychodynamic perspective.* New York: Macmillan.

Richards, T. (1974). *Problem solving through creative analysis.* New York: John Wiley & Sons.

Richmond, M. (1917). *Social diagnosis.* New York: Russell Sage Foundation.

Riess, H., & Dockray-Miller, M. (2002). *Integrative group treatment for bulimia nervosa.* New York: Columbia University Press.

Rittenhouse, J. (1997). Feminist principles in survivor's groups: Out-of-contact. *Journal for Specialists in Group Work, 22*(2), 111–119.

Rittner, B., & Nakanishi, M. (1993). Challenging stereotypes and cultural biases through small group process. *Social Work with Groups, 16*(4), 5–23.

Riva, M. T., Lippert, L., & Tackett, M. J. (2000). Selection practices of group leaders: A national survey. *Journal for Specialists in Group Work, 25*(2), 157–169.

Rivas, R., & Toseland, R. (1981). The student group leadership evaluation project: A study of group leadership skills. *Social Work with Groups, 4*(3/4), 159–175.

Roback, H., Moore, R., Bloch, F., & Shelton, M. (1996). Confidentiality in group psychotherapy: Empirical findings and the law. *International Journal of Group Psychotherapy, 46*(1), 117–135.

Roback, H., Ochoa, E., Bloch, F., & Purdon, S. (1992). Guarding confidentiality in clinical groups: The therapist's dilemma. *International Journal of Group Psychotherapy, 42*(1), 81–103.

Robert, H. (1983). *The new Robert's rules of order.* Glenview, IL: Scott Foresman.

Roberts, R., & Northen, H. (Eds.). (1976). *Theories of social work with groups.* New York: Columbia University Press.

Robinson, J., & Shaver, P. (Eds.). (1973). *Measures of social psychological attitude* (2nd ed.). Ann Arbor: University of Michigan Press.

Robson, M. (1988). *Quality circles: A practical guide* (2nd ed.). Aldershat, Hants, England: Gower.

Roethlisberger, F. (1941). *Management and morale.* Cambridge, MA: Harvard University Press.

Roethlisberger, F., & Dickson, W. (1939). *Management and the worker.* Cambridge, MA: Harvard University Press.

Roethlisberger, F., & Dickson, W. (1975). A fair day's work. In P. V. Crosbie (Ed.), *Interaction in small groups* (pp. 85–94). New York: Macmillan.

Rohrbaugh, J. (1979). Improving the quality of group judgment: Social judgment analysis and the delphi technique. *Organizational Behavior and Human Performance, 24,* 73–92.

Rohrbaugh, J. (1981). Improving the quality of group judgment: Social judgment analysis and the nominal group technique. *Organizational Behavior and Human Performance, 26,* 272–288.

Rohrbaugh, J. (1984). Making decisions about staffing standards: An analytical approach to human resource planning in health administration. In L. Nigro (Ed.), *Decision making in the public sector* (pp. 93–116). New York: Marcel Dekker.

Rokeach, M. (1968). *Beliefs, attitudes and values: A theory of organization and change.* San Francisco: Jossey-Bass.

Roller, B., & Nelson, V. (Eds.). (1991). The art of co-therapy: How therapists work together. London: Guilford.

Rooney, R. (1992). *Strategies for work with involuntary clients.* New York: Columbia University Press.

Rose, S. (1981). Assessment in groups. *Social Work Research and Abstracts, 17*(1), 29–37.

Rose, S. (1989). *Working with adults in groups: A multi-method approach.* San Francisco: Jossey-Bass.

Rose, S. (1991). The development and practice of group treatment. In M. Hersen, A. Kazdin, & A. Bellack (Eds.), *Handbook of Clinical Psychology* (pp. 627–642). New York: Pergamon Press.

Rose, S. (1998). *Group therapy with troubled youth.* Newbury Park, CA: Sage.

Rose, S., Cayner, J., & Edleson, J. (1977). Measuring interpersonal competence. *Social Work, 22*(2), 125–129.

Rose, S., & Edleson, J. (1987). *Working with children and adolescents in groups.* San Francisco: Jossey-Bass.

Rose, S., & Hanusa, D. (1980). *Parenting skill role play test.* Interpersonal skill training and research project, University of Wisconsin, Madison.

Rose, S., & LeCroy, C. (1991). Group treatment methods. In F. Kanfer & A. Goldstein (Eds.), *Helping people change* (4th ed., pp. 422–453). New York: Pergamon Press.

Rosen, A., & Proctor, K. (Eds.). (2003). *Developing practice guidelines for social work intervention: Issues, methods, and research agenda.* New York: Columbia University Press.

Rosenthal, L. (1978). *Behavioral analysis of social skills in adolescent girls.* Unpublished doctoral dissertation, University of Wisconsin, Madison.

Rossi, P., Freeman, H., & Lipsey, M. (1999). *Evaluation: A systematic approach.* Thousand Oaks, CA: Sage Publications.

Rossi, P., Freeman, H., & Wright, S. (1979). *Evaluation: A systematic approach.* Newbury Park, CA: Sage.

Rothman, J. (1974). *Planning and organizing for social change: Action principles for social science research.* New York: Columbia University Press.

Rothman, J., Erlich, J., & Tropman, J. (Eds.). (1995). *Strategies of community intervention* (5th ed.). Itasca, IL: F. E. Peacock.

Rothman, J., & Tumblin, A. (1994). Pilot testing and early development of a model of case management intervention. In J. Rothman & E. J. Thomas (Eds.), *Intervention research: Design and development for human service* (pp. 215–233). New York: Haworth Press.

Rounds, K., Galinsky, M., & Stevens, L. S. (1991, January). Linking people with AIDS in rural communities: The telephone group. *Social Work, 36,* 13–18.

Rubin, H., & Rubin, I. (2001). *Community organizing and development* (3rd ed.). New York: Macmillan.

Rutan, J. (1992). Psychodynamic group psychotherapy. *International Journal of Group Psychotherapy, 42*(1), 19–36.

Rutan, J., & Stone, W. (2001). *Psychodynamic group psychotherapy* (3rd ed.). New York: Guilford.

Salazar, A. (1996). An analysis of the development and evolution of roles in the small group. *Small Group Research, 27*(4), 475–503.

Sanchez-Ayende, M. (1998). Middle-aged Puerto Rican women as primary caregivers to the elderly: A qualitative analysis of everyday dynamics. *Journal of Gerontological Social Work, 30*(1/2), 75–97.

Santhiveeran, J. (1998, October). *Virtual group meetings on the net: Implications for social work practice.* Paper presented at the meeting of the Association for the Advancement of Social Work with Groups, Miami, FL.

Sarri, R., & Galinsky, M. (1985). A conceptual framework for group development. In M. Sundel, P. Glasser, R. Sarri, & R. Vinter (Eds.), *Individual change through small groups* (2nd ed., pp. 70–86). New York: The Free Press.

Sarri, R., Galinsky, M., Glasser, P., Siegel, S., & Vinter, R. (1967). Diagnosis in group work. In R. D. Vinter (Ed.), *Readings in group work practice* (pp. 39–71). Ann Arbor, MI: Campus Publishing.

Saunders, D. (1996). Feminist-cognitive-behavioral and process-psychodynamic treatments for men who batter: Interaction of abuser traits and treatment models. *Violence and Victims, 11,* 394–414.

Saunders, D. (2002). Developing guidelines for domestic violence offender programs: What can we learn from related fields and current research? *Journal of Aggression, Maltreatment and Trauma, 5*(2), 235–248.

Sax, G. (1996). *Principles of educational and psychological measurement* (4th ed.). Belmont, CA: Wadsworth.

Schachter, S. (1959). *The psychology of affiliation.* Stanford, CA: Stanford University Press.

Scheidel, T., & Crowell, L. (1979). *Discussing and deciding: A deskbook for group leaders and members.* New York: Macmillan.

Scheneul, J., Lecompte, M., Borgatti, S., & Nastasi, B. (1998). *Enhanced ethnographic methods: Audiovisual techniques, focused group interviews, and elicitation techniques.* Thousand Oaks, CA: Altamira Press.

Schilder, P. (1937). The analysis of ideologies as a psychotherapeutic method, especially in group treatment. *American Journal of Psychiatry, 93,* 601–615.

Schiller, L. (1995). Stages of development in women's groups: A relational model. In R. Kurland & R. Salmon (Eds.), *Group work practice in a troubled society* (pp. 117–138). New York: Haworth Press.

Schiller, L. (1997). Rethinking stages of development in women's groups: Implications for practice. *Social Work with Groups, 20*(3), 3–19.

Schinke, S. P., & Rose, S. (1976). Interpersonal skill training in groups. *Journal of Counseling Psychology, 23,* 442–448.

Schlenoff, M., & Busa, S. (1981). Student and field instructor as group co-therapists. Equalizing an unequal relationship. *Journal of Education for Social Work, 17,* 29–35.

Schmidt, W. H., & Finnigan, J. P. (1993). *TQ Manager: A practical guide for managing in a total quality organization.* San Francisco: Jossey-Bass.

Schmitt, M., Farrell, M., & Heinemann, G. (1988). Conceptual and methodological problems in studying the effects of interdisciplinary geriatric teams. *The Gerontologist, 28*(6), 753–763.

Scholtes, P., Joiner, B., & Streibel, B. (1996). *The Team Handbook.* Madison, WI: Oriel Incorporated.

Schopler, J. (1994). Interorganizational groups in human services: Environmental and interpersonal relationships. *Journal of Community Practice, 1*(3), 7–27.

Schopler, J., Abell, M., & Galinsky, M. (1998). Technology-based groups: A review and conceptual framework for practice. *Social Work, 43*(3), 254–267.

Schopler, J., & Galinsky, M. (1981). When groups go wrong. *Social Work, 26*(5), 424–429.

Schopler, J., & Galinsky, M. (1984). Meeting practice needs: Conceptualizing the open-ended group. *Social Work with Groups, 7*(2), 3–21.

Schopler, J., & Galinsky, M. (1990). Can open-ended groups move beyond beginnings? *Small Group Research, 21*(4), 435–449.

Schopler, J., Galinsky, M., & Abell, M. (1997). Creating community through telephone and computer groups: Theoretical and practice perspectives. *Social Work with Groups, 20*(4), 19–34.

Schreiber, B. (2002). Brief-term group psychotherapy with late adolescents. *Southern-African Journal of Child and Adolescent-Mental Health, 14*(1), 50–56.

Schriver, J. (1998). *Human behavior and the social environment* (2nd ed.). Boston: Allyn and Bacon.

Schuman, S., & Rohrbaugh, J. (1996, June). Meet me in cyberspace. *Government Technology, 9,* 32–34.

Schwartz, W. (1966). Discussion of three papers on the group method with clients, foster families, and adoptive families. *Child Welfare, 45*(10), 571–575.

Schwartz, W. (1971). On the use of groups in social work practice. In W. Schwartz & S. Zalba (Eds.), *The practice of group work* (pp. 3–24). New York: Columbia University Press.

Schwartz, W. (1976). Between client and system: The mediating function. In R. Roberts & H. Northen (Eds.), *Theories of social work with groups* (pp. 171–197). New York: Columbia University Press.

Schwartz, W. (1981, April). *The group work tradition and social work practice.* Paper presented at Rutgers University, School of Social Work, New Brunswick.

Seaberg, J., & Gillespie, D. (1977). Goal attainment scaling: A critique. *Social Work Research and Abstracts, 13*(2), 4–9.

Seashore, S. (1954). *Group cohesiveness in the industrial work group.* Ann Arbor: University of Michigan Press.

Seely, H., & Sween, J. (1983, March). Critical components of successful U.S. quality circles. *Quality Circles Journal, 6,* 14–17.

Segal, Z., Williams, M., & Teasdale, J. (2002). *Mindfulness-based cognitive therapy for depression.* New York: Guildford Press.

Seligman, L. (1998). *Selecting effective treatments* (2nd ed.). San Francisco: Jossey-Bass.

Seligman, M. (1975). *Helplessness: On depression, development, and death.* San Francisco: W. H. Freeman.

Selltiz, C., Wrightsman, L., & Cook, S. (1976). *Research methods in social relations* (3rd ed.). New York: Holt, Rinehart & Winston.

Sexton, T., & Whiston, S. (1994). The status of the counseling relationship: An empirical review, theoretical implications, and research directions. *Counseling Psychologist, 22*(1), 6–77.

Shapiro, J., Peltz, L., & Bernadett-Shapiro, S. (1998). *Brief group treatment for therapists and counselors.* Florence, KY: Wadsworth.

Shaw, C. (1930). *The jack roller.* Chicago: University of Chicago Press.

Shaw, M. (1964). Communication networks. In L. Berkowitz (Ed.), *Advances in experimental social psychology* (Vol. 1, pp. 111–149). New York: Academic Press.

Shaw, M. (1976). *Group dynamics: The psychology of small group behavior.* New York: McGraw-Hill.

Sheldon, B. (1995). *Cognitive-behavioural therapy: Research, practice and philosophy.* London: Routledge.

Shepard, C. (1964). *Small groups: Some sociological perspectives.* San Francisco: Chandler.

Sherif, M. (1936). *The psychology of social norms.* New York: Harper & Row.

Sherif, M. (1956). Experiments in group conflict. *Scientific American,* 195, 54–58.

Sherif, M., & Sherif, C. (1953). *Groups in harmony and tension: An introduction of studies in group relations.* New York: Harper & Row.

Sherif, M., White, J., & Harvey, O. (1955). Status in experimentally produced groups. *American Journal of Sociology, 60,* 370–379.

Shils, E. (1950). Primary groups in the American army. In R. Merton & P. Lazarsfeld (Eds.), *Continuities in social research* (pp. 16–39). New York: The Free Press.

Shimanoff, S., & Jenkins, M. (1991). Leadership and gender: Challenging assumptions and recognizing resources. In R. Cathcart and L. Samovar (Eds.), *Small group communication: A reader* (6th ed., pp. 504–522). Dubuque, IA: William C. Brown.

Shipley, R., & Boudewyns, P. (1980). Flooding and implosive therapy: Are they harmful? *Behavior Therapy, 11*(4), 503–508.

Shulman, L. (1978). A study of practice skills. *Social Work, 23*(4), 274–280.

Shulman, L. (1999). *The skills of helping individuals, families and groups* (4th ed.). Itasca, IL: F. E. Peacock.

Shuster, H. D. (1990). *Teaming for quality improvement: A process for innovation and consensus.* Englewood Cliffs, NJ: Prentice-Hall.

Siegel, J., Dubrovsky, V., Kiesler, S., & McGuire, T. (1986). Group processes in computer-mediated communication. *Organizational Behavior and Human Decision Processes, 37*(2), 157–187.

Silbergeld, S., Koenig, G., Manderscheid, R., Meeker, B., & Hornung, C. (1975). Assessment of environment-therapy systems: The group atmosphere scale. *Journal of Consulting and Clinical Psychology, 43*(4), 460–469.

Silver, W. B., & Bufiano, K. (1996). The impact of group efficacy and group goals on group task performance. *Small Group Research, 27*(3), 345–472.

Silverman, M. (1966). Knowledge in social group work: A review of the literature. *Social Work, 11*(3), 56–62.

Siporin, M. (1975). *Introduction to social work practice.* New York: Macmillan.

Siporin, M. (1980). Ecological system theory in social work. *Journal of Sociology and Social Work, 7,* 507–532.

Slavson, S. R. (1939). *Character education in a democracy.* New York: Association Press.

Slavson, S. R. (1939). Democratic leadership in education. *The Group, 2*(1–2).

Slavson, S. R. (1940). Group psychotherapy. *Mental Hygiene, 24,* 36–49.

Slavson, S. R. (1945). *Creative group education.* New York: Association Press.

Slavson, S. R. (1946). *Recreation and the total personality.* New York: Association Press.

Sluyter, G., & Mukherjee, A. (1993). *Total quality management for mental health and mental retardation.* Annandale, VA: National Association of Private Residential Resources.

Smith, A. (1935). Group play in a hospital environment. In *Proceedings of the National Conference of Social Work* (pp. 372–373). Chicago: University of Chicago Press.

Smith, G. (1998). Idea-generation techniques: A formulary of active ingredients. *Journal of Creative Behavior, 32*(2), 107–133.

Smith, H., & Doeing, C. (1985, Spring). Japanese management: A model for social work administration? *Administration in Social Work, 9*(1), 1–11.

Smith, K. K., & Berg, D. N. (1997). *Paradoxes of group life.* San Francisco: Jossey-Bass.

Smith, M. (1977). *Value clarification.* La Jolla, CA: University Associates.

Smith, M., Tobin, S., & Toseland, R. (1992). Therapeutic processes in professional and peer counseling of family caregivers of frail elderly. *Social Work, 37*(4), 345–351.

Smith, P. (1978). Group work as a process of social influence. In N. McCaughan (Ed.), *Group work: Learning and practice* (pp. 36–57). London: George Allen & Unwin.

Smokowski, P. R., Rose, S.D., Todar, K., & Reardon, K. (1999). Post-group casualty-status, group events and leader behavior: An early look into the dynamics of damaging group experiences. *Research on Social Work Practice, 9*(5), 555–574.

Smokowski, P. R., Galinsky, M., & Harlow, K. (2001). Using technologies in groupwork Part II: Technology-based groups. *Groupwork, 13*(1), 6–22.

Smokowski, P. R., Rose, S. D., & Bacallao, M. L. (2001). Damaging experiences in therapeutic groups: How vulnerable consumers become group casualties. *Small Group Research, 32*(2), 223–251.

Smucker, M., Dancu, C., & Foa, E. (1999). *Cognitive behavioral treatment for adult survivors of childhood trauma: Imagery rescripting and reprocessing.* Northvale, NJ: Jason Aronson.

Sosik, J., Avolio, B., & Kahai, S. (1998). Inspiring group creativity: Comparing anonymous and identified electronic brainstorming. *Small Group Research, 29*(1), 3–31.

Sosik, J., & Jung, D. (2002). Work group characteristics and performance in collectivistic and individualistic cultures. *Journal of Social Psychology, 142*(1), 5–23.

Spielberger, C., Gorsuch, R., Lushene, R., Vagg, P., & Jacobs, G. (1983). *Manual for the stait-trait anxiety inventory.* Palo Alto, CA: Consulting Psychologists Press.

Spink, K., & Carron, A. (1994). Group cohesion effects in exercise classes. *Small Group Research, 25*(1), 26–42.

Spitz, H. (1997). Brief group therapy. In S. Sauber (Ed.), *Managed mental health care: Major diagnostic and treatment approaches.* Philadelphia, PA: Brunner/Mazel.

Spitz, H. I., & Spitz, S. T. (1999). *Group psychotherapy.* Philadelphia, PA: Brunner/Mazel.

Starak, Y. (1981). Co-leadership: A new look at sharing group work. *Social Work with Groups, 4*(3/4), 145–157.

Stattler, W., & Miller, N. (1968). *Discussion and conference* (2nd ed.). Englewood Cliffs, NJ: Prentice-Hall.

Steckler, N., & Fondas, N. (1995). Building team leader effectiveness: A diagnostic tool. *Organizational Dynamics, 23*(3), 20–35.

Stein, L., Rothman, B., & Nakanishi, M. (1993). The telephone group: Accessing group service to the homebound. *Social Work with Groups, 16*(1/2), 203–215.

Steinberg, D. M. (1997). *The mutual-aid approach to working with groups: Helping people help each other.* Northvale, NJ: Jason Aronson.

Stern, R., & Drummond, L. (1991). *Practice of behavioural and cognitive psychotherapy.* New York: Cambridge University Press.

Stewart, D. W., & Shamdasani, P. N. (1990). *Focus groups: Theory and practice.* Newbury Park, CA: Sage.

Stewart, G., Manz, C., & Sims, H. (1999). *Team work and group dynamics.* New York: John Wiley & Sons.

Stockton, R., Rohde, R., & Haughey, J. (1992). The effects of structured group exercises on cohesion, engagement, avoidance, and conflict. *Small Group Research, 23*(2), 155–168.

Stogdill, R. (1974). *Handbook of leadership.* New York: The Free Press.

Stone, M., Lewis, C., & Beck, A. (1994). The structure of Yalom's Curative Factors Scale. *International Journal of Group Psychotherapy, 44*(2), 239–245.

Stoner, J. (1968). Risky and cautious shifts in group decisions: The influence of widely held values. *Journal of Experimental Social Psychology, 4,* 442–459.

Stouffer, S. (1949). *The American soldier, combat and its aftermath.* Princeton, NJ: Princeton University Press.

Stuart, R. (1970). *Trick or treatment: Who and when psychotherapy facts.* Champaign, IL: Research Press.

Stuart, R. (1977). *Behavioral self-management: Strategies, techniques, and outcomes.* New York: Brunner/Mazel.

Stuart, R., & Davis, B. (1972). *Slim chance in a fat world.* Champaign, IL: Research Press.

Sue, D. W., & Sue, D. (1999). *Counseling the culturally different: Theory and practice* (3rd ed.). New York: John Wiley & Sons.

Sue, S., Zane, N., & Young, K. (1994). Psychotherapy with culturally diverse populations. In A. Bergin & S. Garfield (Eds.), *Handbook of psychotherapy and behavior change* (4th ed., pp. 783–812). New York: John Wiley & Sons.

Sundel, M., Glasser, P., Sarri, R., & Vinter, R. (1985). *Individual change through small groups* (2nd ed.). New York: The Free Press.

Swenson, J., Griswold, W., & Kleiber, P. (1992, November). Focus groups method of inquiry/intervention. *Small Group Research, 23*(4), 459–474.

Syz, H. C. (1928). Remarks on group analysis. *American Journal of Psychiatry, 85,* 141–148.

Taylor, D., Berry, P., & Block, C. (1958). Does group participation when using brainstorming facilitate or inhibit creative thinking? *Administrative Science Quarterly, 3,* 23–47.

Taylor, N., & Burlingame, C. (2001). A survey of mental health care provider and managed care organization attitudes toward, familiarity with, and use of group psychotherapy. *International Journal of Group Psychotherapy, 51*(2), 243–263.

Taylor, R. (1903). Group management. *Transactions of the American Society of Mechanical Engineers, 24,* 1337–1480.

Teger, A., & Pruitt, D. (1967). Components of group risk-taking. *Journal of Experimental Psychology, 3,* 189–205.

Thelen, H. (1954). *Dynamics of groups at work.* Chicago: University of Chicago Press.

Thibaut, J., & Kelley, H. (1954). Experimental studies of group problem-solving process. In G. Kindzey (Ed.), *Handbook of social psychology* (Vol. 2, pp. 735–785). Reading, MA: Addison-Wesley.

Thibaut, J., & Kelley, H. (1959). *The social psychology of groups.* New York: John Wiley & Sons.

Thomas, E. (1978). Generating innovation in social work: The paradigm of developmental research. *Journal of Social Services Research, 2*(1), 95–115.

Thomas, E. (1990). Modes of practice in developmental research. In L. Videka-Sherman & W. Reid (Eds.), *Advances in clinical social work research* (pp. 202–217). Silver Spring, MD: National Association of Social Workers Press.

Thomas, E., & Rothman, J. (1994). An integrative perspective on intervention research. In J. Rothman & E. J. Thomas (Eds.), *Intervention research: Design and development for human service* (pp. 3–23). New York: Hawthorn Press.

Thoresen, C., & Mahoney, M. (1974). *Behavioral self-control.* New York: Holt, Rinehart & Winston.

Thorndike, R. (1938). On what type of task will a group do well? *Journal of Abnormal and Social Psychology, 33,* 409–413.

Thrasher, F. (1927). *The gang.* Chicago: University of Chicago Press.

Tolson, E., Reid, W., & Garvin, C. (1994). *Generalist practice: A task-centered approach.* New York: Columbia University Press.

Toseland, R. (1977). A problem-solving workshop for older persons. *Social Work, 22*(4), 325–327.

Toseland, R. (1981). Increasing access: Outreach methods in social work practice. *Social Casework, 62*(4), 227–234.

Toseland, R. (1990). Long-term effectiveness of peer-led and professionally led support groups for family caregivers. *Social Service Review, 64*(2), 308–327.

Toseland, R. (1995). *Group work with the elderly and family caregivers.* New York: Springer.

Toseland, R., & Coppola, M. (1985). A task-centered approach to group work with the elderly. In A. Fortune (Ed.), *Task-centered practice with families and groups* (pp. 101–114). New York: Springer.

Toseland, R., Decker, J., & Bliesner, J. (1979). A community program for socially isolated older persons. *Journal of Gerontological Social Work, 1*(3), 211–224.

Toseland, R., Diehl, M., Freeman, K., Manzanares, T., Naleppa, M., & McCallion, P. (1997). The impact of validation therapy on nursing home residents with dementia. *Journal of Applied Gerontology, 16*(1), 31–50.

Toseland, R., & Ephross, P. (1987). *Working effectively with administrative groups.* New York: Haworth.

Toseland, R., & Hacker, L. (1982). Self-help groups and professional involvement. *Social Work, 27*(4), 341–347.

Toseland, R., & Hacker, L. (1985). Social workers' use of groups as a resource for clients. *Social Work, 30*(3), 232–239.

Toseland, R., Ivanoff, A., & Rose, S. (1987). Treatment conferences: Task groups in action. *Social Work with Groups, 10*(2), 79–94.

Toseland, R., Kabat, D., & Kemp, K. (1983). An evaluation of a smoking cessation group program. *Social Work Research and Abstracts, 19*(1), 12–20.

Toseland, R., Krebs, A., & Vahsen, J. (1978). Changing group interaction patterns. *Social Service Research, 2*(2), 219–232.

Toseland, R., Labrecque, M., Goebel, S., & Whitney, M. (1992). An evaluation of a group program for spouses of frail, elderly veterans. *The Gerontologist, 32*(3), 382–390.

Toseland, R., McCallion, P., Smith, T., Huck, S., Bourgeois, P., & Garstka, T. (2001). Health education groups for caregivers in an HMO. *Journal of Clinical Psychology, 57*(4), 551–570.

Toseland, R., McCallion, P., Smith, T., Banks, S. (In press). *Journal of Ortho Psychology.*

Toseland, R., Palmer-Ganeles, J., & Chapman, D. (1986). Teamwork in psychiatric settings. *Social Work, 31*(1), 46–52.

Toseland, R., & Reid, W. (1985). Using rapid assessment instruments in a family service agency. *Social Casework, 66,* 547–555.

Toseland, R., & Rivas, R. (1984). Structured methods for working with task groups. *Administration in Social Work, 8*(2), 49–58.

Toseland, R., Rivas, R., & Chapman, D. (1984). An evaluation of decision making in task groups. *Social Work, 29*(4), 339–346.

Toseland, R., & Rizzo, V. (2003). Leading telephone caregiver support groups: A manual for a model psychoeducational program. (Unpublished Manuscript). Albany, NY.

Toseland, R., & Rose, S. (1978). Evaluating social skills training for older adults in groups. *Social Work Research and Abstracts, 14*(1), 25–33.

Toseland, R., & Rossiter, C. (1989). Group interventions to support family caregivers: A review and analysis. *The Gerontologist, 29*, 438–448.

Toseland, R., Rossiter, C., & Labrecque, M. (1989). The effectiveness of peer-led and professionally led groups to support family caregivers. *The Gerontologist, 29*(4), 465–471.

Toseland, R., Rossiter, C., Peak, T., & Hill, P. (1990). Therapeutic processes in support groups for caregivers. *International Journal of Group Psychotherapy, 40*(3), 279–303.

Toseland, R., Rossiter, C., Peak, T., & Smith, G. (1990). Comparative effectiveness of individual and group interventions to support family caregivers. *Social Work, 35*(3), 209–219.

Toseland, R., Sherman, E., & Bliven, S. (1981). The comparative effectiveness of two group work approaches for the evaluation of mutual support groups among the elderly. *Social Work with Groups, 4*(1/2), 137–153.

Toseland, R., & Siporin, M. (1986). When to recommend group treatment: A review of the clinical and research literature. *International Journal of Group Psychotherapy, 36*(2), 171–201.

Toseland, R., & Spielberg, G. (1982). The development of helping skills in undergraduate social work education: Model and evaluation. *Journal of Education for Social Work, 18*(1), 66–73.

Tracy, E., & Whittaker, J. (1990). The social network map: Assessing social support in clinical practice. *Families in Society, 71*(8), 461–470.

Trecker, H. (1956). *Group work in the psychiatric setting.* New York: William Morrow.

Trecker, H. (1972). *Social group work: Principles and practices.* New York: Association Press.

Trecker, H. (1980). Administration as a group process: Philosophy and concepts. In A. Alissi (Ed.), *Perspectives on social group work practice* (pp. 332–337). New York: The Free Press.

Triplett, N. (1898). The dynamogenic factors in pacemaking and competition. *American Journal of Psychology, 9*(4), 507–533.

Tropman, J. (1995). The role of the board in the planning process. In J. Tropman, J. Erlich, & J. Rothman (Eds.), *Tactics and techniques of community intervention* (3rd ed.) (pp. 157–170). Itasca, IL: F. E. Peacock.

Tropman, J. (1996). *Effective meetings: Improving group decision-making* (2nd ed.). Thousand Oaks, CA: Sage.

Tropp, E. (1968). The group in life and in social work. *Social Casework, 49*, 267–274.

Tropp, E. (1976). A developmental theory. In R. Roberts & H. Northen (Eds.), *Theories of social work with groups* (pp. 198–237). New York: Columbia University Press.

Trotter, C. (1999). *Working with involuntary clients.* London: Sage Publications.

Trotzer, J. (1999). *The counselor and the group: Integrating theory, training and practice* (3rd ed.). Pacific Grove, CA: Brooks/Cole.

Tuckman, B. (1963). Developmental sequence in small groups. *Psychological Bulletin, 63*, 384–399.

Turner, M. P., & Pratkanis, A. (1998). Twenty-five years of groupthink theory and research: Lessons from the evaluation of theory. *Organizational Behavior and Human Decision Processes, 73*(2–3), 105–115.

Tyson, T. (1998). *Working with groups* (2nd ed.). South Yarra, Australia: MacMillan Education.

Vaillant, G. (1995). *The natural history of alcoholism revisited.* Cambridge, MA: Harvard University Press.

Valacich, J. S., Dennis, A. R., & Connolly, T. (1994). Idea generation in computer-based groups: A new ending to an old story. *Organizational behavior and human decision processes, 57*(3), 448–467.

Van de Ven, A. (1974). *Group decision making and effectiveness: An experimental study.* Kent, OH: Kent State University Press.

Van de Ven, A., & Delbecq, A. (1971). Nominal versus interacting group processes for committee decision-making effectiveness. *Academy of Management Journal, 9*, 203–212.

VanGundy, A. B., Jr. (1988). *Techniques of structured problem solving* (2nd ed.). New York: Reinhold.

Vannicelli, M. (1992). *Removing the roadblocks: Group psychotherapy with substance abusers and family members.* New York: Guilford.

Vasquez, M., & Han, A. (1995). Group interventions in treatment with ethnic minorities. In J. Aponte & J. Wohl (Eds.), *Psychological inteventions and cultural diversity* (pp. 109–127). Boston: Allyn and Bacon.

Velasquez, M., Maurer, G., Crouch, C., & DiClemente, C. (2001). *Group treatment for substance abuse: A stages-of-change therapy manual.* New York: Guilford Press.

Verhofstadt-Deneve, L. (2000). The "Magic Shop" technique in psychodrama: An existential–dialectical view. *International Journal of Action Methods: Psychodrama, Skill Training, and Role Playing, 53*(3–13).

Vinokur-Kaplan, D. (1995). Enhancing the effectiveness of interdisciplinary mental health teams. *Administration and Policy in Mental Health, 22,* 521–529.

Vinter, R. (Ed.). (1967). *Readings in group work practice.* Ann Arbor, MI: Campus Publishing.

Vinter, R. (1985a). The essential components of social group work practice. In M. Sundel, P. Glasser, R. Sarri, & R. Vinter (Eds.), *Individual change through small groups* (2nd ed., pp. 11–34). New York: The Free Press.

Vinter, R. (1985b). Program activities: An analysis of their effects on participant behavior. In M. Sundel, P. Glasser, R. Sarri, & R. Vinter (Eds.), *Individual change through small groups* (2nd ed., pp. 226–236). New York: The Free Press.

Vorrath, H. H., & Brendtro, L. K. (1985). *Positive peer culture* (2nd ed.). Chicago: Aldine.

Vroom, V. H., Grant, L., & Cotton, T. (1969). The consequence of social interaction in group problem solving. *Journal of Organizational Behavior and Human Performance, 4,* 79–95.

Vroom, V. H., & Yetton, P. (1973). *Leadership and decision making.* Pittsburgh, PA: University of Pittsburgh Press.

Wakefield, J. C. (1996). Does social work need the eco-systems perspective? Part I. Is the perspective clinically useful? *Social Service Review, 70*(1), 1–32.

Waldo, C. (1986). *A working guide for directors of not-for-profit organizations.* New York: Quorum Books.

Wall, V. D., Jr., Galanes, G. J., & Love, S. B. (1987). Small task-oriented groups, conflict, conflict management, satisfaction, and decision quality. *Small Group Behavior, 18,* 31–55.

Wall, V. D., Jr., & Nolan, L. L. (1987). Small group conflict: A look at equity, satisfaction and styles of conflict management. *Small Group Behavior, 18,* 188–211.

Wallach, M., & Wing, C. (1968). Is risk a value? *Journal of Personality and Social Psychology, 9,* 101–106.

Walters, K., Longres, J., Han, C., & Icard, D. (2003). Cultural Competence with Gay and Lesbian Persons of Color. In D. Lum (Ed.), *Culturally competent practice: A framework understanding diverse groups and justice issues* (pp. 310–342). Sacramento, CA: Thomson, Brooks, Cole.

Walton, M. (1990). *Deming management at work.* New York: G. P. Putnam's Sons.

Wasserman, H., & Danforth, J. (1988). *The human bond: Support group and mutual aid.* New York: Springer.

Waterman, J., & Walker, E. (2001). *Helping at-risk students, A group counseling approach for grades 6–9.* New York and London: Guilford Press.

Watson, S. R., & Buede, D. M. (1987). *Decision synthesis: The principles and practice of decision analysis.* New York: Cambridge University Press.

Watson, W., Johnson, L., & Merritt, D. (1998). Team orientation, self-orientation, and diversity in task groups: Their connection to team performance over time. *Group & Organization Management, 23*(2), 161–188.

Watzlawick, P., Weakland, J., & Fisch, R. (1974). *Change: Principles of problem formation and problem resolution.* New York: W. W. Norton.

Wayne, J., & Avery, N. (1979). Activities for group termination. *Social Work, 24*(1), 58–62.

Weaver, H. (1999). Indigenous people and the social work profession: Defining culturally competent services. *Social Work, 44*(3), 217–225.

Weaver, H. W., & Wodarski, J. (1996). Social work practice with Latinos. In D. Harrison, B. Thyer, & J. Wodarski (Eds.), *Cultural Diversity and Social Practice* (pp. 52–86). Springfield: Charles C. Thomas.

Weber, A., & Freedman, G. (2000). *Managing stress.* Charleston, WV: Cambridge Research Group.

Wech, B., Mossholder, K., Steel, R., & Bennett, N. (1998). Does work group cohesiveness affect individuals' performance and organizational commitment? A cross-level examination. *Small Group Research, 29*(4), 472–494.

Weinberg, H. (2001). Group process and group phenomena on the Internet. *International Journal of Group Psychotherapy, 51*(3), 361–378.

Weinberg, N., Uken, J., Schmale, J., & Adamek, M. (1995). Therapeutic factors: Their presence in a computer-mediated support group. *Social Work with Groups, 18*(4), 57–69.

Weisner, S. (1983). Fighting back: A critical analysis of coalition building in the human services. *Social Service Review, 57*(2), 291–306.

Weissman, A. (1976). Industrial social services: Linkage technology. *Social Casework, 57*(1), 50–54.

Weissman, H. (Ed.). (1969). *Individual and group services in the mobilization for youth experiment.* New York: Association Press.

Wells, R. (1994). *Planned short-term treatment* (2nd ed.). New York: The Free Press.

Wender, L. (1936). The dynamics of group psychotherapy and its application. *Journal of Nervous & Mental Disorders, 84,* 54–60.

Wheelan, S. (1994). *Group processes: A developmental perspective.* Boston: Allyn and Bacon.

Whitaker, D. (1975). Some conditions for effective work with groups. *British Journal of Social Work, 5,* 423–439.

White, B., & Madara, E. (1998). *The self-help sourcebook: Your guide to community and online support groups* (6th ed.). Nutley, NJ: Hoffman La Roche.

Whittaker, J. (1985). Program activities: Their selection and use in a therapeutic milieu. In M. Sundel, P. Glasser, R. Sarri, & R. Vinter (Eds.), *Individual change through small groups* (2nd ed., pp. 237–250). New York: The Free Press.

Whyte, W. (1943). *Street corner society.* Chicago: University of Chicago Press.

Widmeyer, W., & Williams, J. (1991). Predicting cohesion in a coacting sport. *Small Group Research, 22*(4), 548–570.

Wiener, L. S., Spencer, E. D., Davidson, R., & Fair, C. (1993). Telephone support groups: A new avenue toward psychosocial support for HIV-infected children and their families. *Social Work with Groups, 16*(3), 55–71.

Williams, O. (1994). Group work with African-American men who batter: Toward more ethnically sensitive practice. *Journal of Comparative Family Studies, 25,* 91–103.

Wilson, G. (1976). From practice to theory: A personalized history. In R. W. Roberts & H. Northen (Eds.), *Theories of social work with groups* (pp. 1–44). New York: Columbia University Press.

Wilson, G., & Ryland, G. (1949). *Social group work practice.* Boston: Houghton Mifflin.

Wilson, G., & Ryland, G. (1980). The social group work method. In A. Alissi (Ed.), *Perspectives on social group work practice* (pp. 169–182). New York: The Free Press.

Wilson, S. (1980). *Recording: Working guidelines for social workers.* New York: The Free Press.

Winer, M., & Ray, K. (1996). *Collaboration handbook: Creating, sustaining, and enjoying the journey.* St. Paul, MN: Amherst Wilder Foundation.

Winterfeldt, D., & Edwards, W. (1986). *Decision analysis and behavioral research.* New York: Cambridge University Press.

Wittman, H. (1991). Group member satisfaction: A conflict-related account. *Small Group Research, 22*(1), 24–58.

Wolf, T. (1990). *Managing a nonprofit organization.* New York: Prentice-Hall.

Woods, M., & Hollis, F. (1990). *Casework: A psychosocial therapy* (4th ed.). New York: McGraw-Hill.

Worchell, S. (1994). You can go home again: Returning group research to the group context with an eye on developmental issues. *Small Group Research, 25*(2), 205–223.

Wright, J., Thase, M., Beck, A., & Ludgate, J. (Eds.). (1993). *Cognitive therapy with inpatients: Developing a cognitive milieu.* New York: Guilford.

Wright, M. (2002). Co-facilitation: Fashion or function? *Social Work With Groups, 25*(3), 77–92.

Wyss, D. (1973). *Psychoanalytic schools: From the beginning to the present.* New York: Jason Aronson.

Yalom, I. (1983). *Inpatient group psychotherapy.* New York: Basic Books.

Yalom, I. (1995). *The theory and practice of group psychotherapy* (4th ed.). New York: Basic Books.

Yan, M. C. (2001). Reclaiming the social in social group work: An experience of a community center in Hong Kong. *Social Work With Groups, 24*(3/4), 53–65.

Yee, R. (1999). *The art of breath and relaxation: Yoga exercises for a more balanced life.* Santa Monica, CA: Living Arts.

Yost, E., Beutler, L., Corbishley, M., & Allender, J. (1985). *Group cognitive therapy: A treatment approach for depressed older adults.* Elmsford, NY: Pergamon Press.

Zajonc, R., Wolosin, R., & Wolosin, W. (1972). Group risk-taking under various group decision schema. *Journal of Experimental and Social Psychology, 8,* 16–30.

Ziller, R. (1957). Four techniques of group decision making under uncertainty. *Journal of Applied Psychology, 41,* 384–388.

Name Index

Subject Index